50 Case Studies in Modern Palmistry

T Stokes

50 Case Studies in Modern Palmistry

T Stokes

Earth Star Publications
www.earthstarpublications.com
Cedaredge, Colorado

FIRST EDITION

March 2015
Second Printing March 2017

Copyright © 2015 by T Stokes
All Rights Reserved

Library of Congress Control Number: 2015932561

This book may not be reproduced in whole, or in part, by digital or mechanical, or by any other means, without the express written consent of the author. For information, address Earth Star Publications (www.earthstarpublications.com), e-mail: starbeacon@gmail.com.

ISBN 978-0-944851-40-1

Printed in the United States of America

Acknowledgments

With thanks to Sherry and John Henderson
at *Oracle 20/20 Magazine*.
and the old palmistry students who sorted through thousands of
hand prints going back many decades.
Also to Annie Miller at Earth Star
for putting this together.

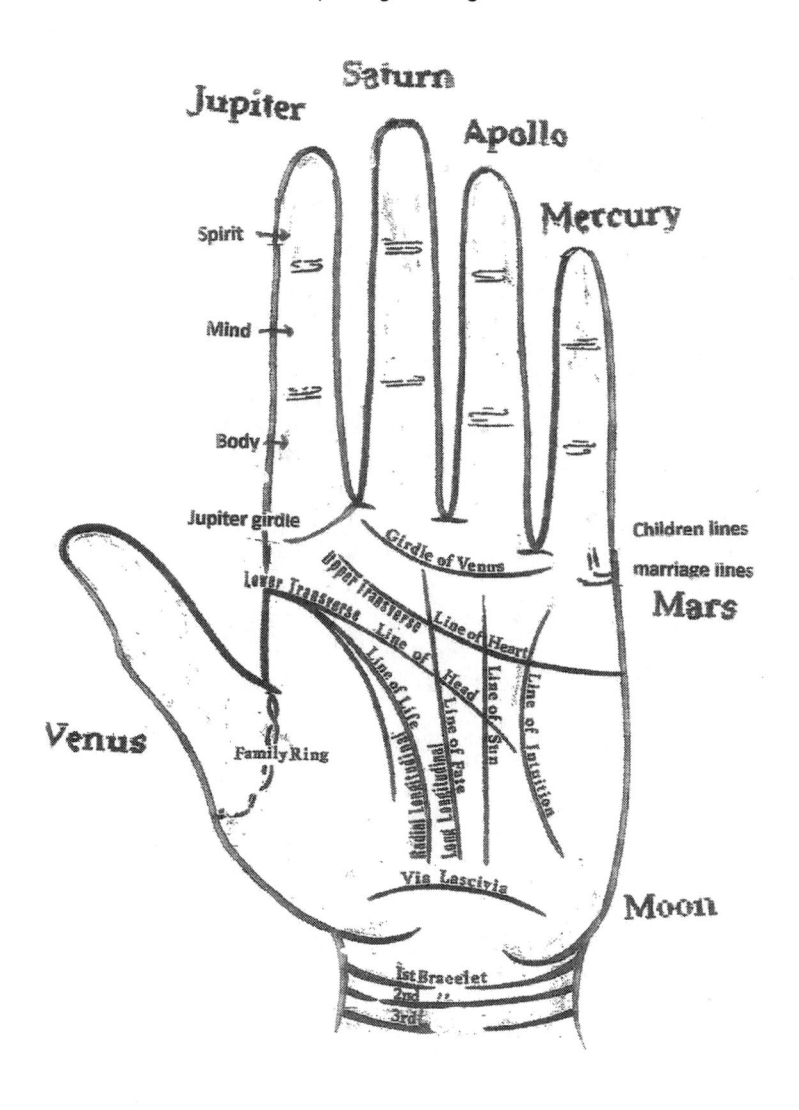

Contents

Introduction 1
Hand Shapes 3
Palmar Lines 13
Health Lines 28
The Bracelets 31
Relationship and Family Lines 32
The Thumb and Fingers 35
The Hawthorne Effect 42
Fingernails, A Neglected Area of Palmistry 45
Rings on the Fingers 48
Fortune Telling 51

Part I — Case Histories

Chapter 1 — Nicotine Poisoning 56
Chapter 2 — Destiny vs. Free Will 59
Chapter 3 — Christian Palmistry 62
Chapter 4 — Glastonbury Hand 67
Chapter 5 — Conquering Anxiety and Depression 69
Chapter 6 — How to Identify an Indigo Child 73
Chapter 7 — Eating Right for Your Type 77
Chapter 8 — A Boxer's Hand 80
Chapter 9 — Frozen Trauma 84
Chapter 10 — Misaligned Bite 88
Chapter 11 — Karma in the Hand Print 91
Chapter 12 — Chronic Obesity in the Palm 94
Chapter 13 — Taking Care of Your Heart 97
Chapter 14 — Tragedy in the Hands 101
Chapter 15 — The 9 Types of Love 105
Chapter 16 — Timing of Events: The Golfer—The Big Vee . . 109
Chapter 17 — The Fermoy Hand 112
Chapter 18 — Dealing With Child Trauma 115
Chapter 19 — Decisions in Love 118
Chapter 20 — Danger Averted 121

Case Histories, Continued

Chapter 21 — Are You Being Emotionally Abused? 125
Chapter 22 — Protection Against Vampires 129
Chapter 23 — Romance in the Palm 131
Chapter 24 — Awkward Client 134
Chapter 25 — The Hand and the Horoscope 138

Part II — Famous People's Hands

Chapter 26 — Lara Love 145
Chapter 27 — The Hand of Psychiatrist Henri Rey 148
Chapter 28 — Hugo Chavez 153
Chapter 29 — Princess Diana, Fated Destiny 157
Chapter 30 — Priyanka Chopra 161
Chapter 31 — Donald Trump 163
Chapter 32 — Imran Khan, 'The Shepherd' 165
Chapter 33 — Jimmy Saville, The Man Behind the Mask ..168
Chapter 34 — Show Biz Advice 172
Chapter 35 — Margaret Thatcher, the Iron Lady 175
Chapter 36 — Reincarnation As Seen in the Hand 178
Chapter 37 — Sonny Liston, World Boxing
              Champion 183
Chapter 38 — Peter O'Toole 185
Chapter 39 — Marlboro Man 188
Chapter 40 — Robin Williams,
              The Day the Laughing Stopped 191
Chapter 41 — The Palm of Michael Jackson 194
Chapter 42 — The Dalai Lama 197
Chapter 43 — Jawaharlal Nehru, A 'Voice of Prophecy'? ..200
Chapter 44 — Zulfikar Ali Bhutto,
              Prime Minister of Pakistan 203
Chapter 45 — Famous Footballer 205
Chapter 46 — Osteopath and Vegan Neil Fennel 209
Chapter 47 — Strange Death of Ehud Netzer 213
Chapter 48 — Matt Monro, Portrait of My Love 217
Chapter 49 — The Stolen Childhood 220
Chapter 50 — Spiritual Counselor Wendy Brindley 225

Introduction

Palmistry was not for me a chosen profession. It was something I found I could do quite by accident when I was around 7 years old, upon seeing a boy holding up his hand while queuing for school dinners. As I gazed at his hand, the lines turned to visions of his life, which then began to superimpose one on top of another. First, he was older and standing in a smart suit with a flower in his buttonhole alongside a girl in white ... then engrossed in a workplace setting ... then playing with children ... then at some awards ceremony ... then almost bald ... then much older again, with a very lined face, crying at a funeral.

I felt all these events in turn, as well as seeing them, and it was a ground-shaking experience for a young lad to see these layered visions, one on top of another, and to experience all the attendant emotions was a very upsetting and confusing experience.

I had no idea how it happened, but from that point on, I was able to read kids' hands in the playground, and then the teachers', and as news of my strange abilities grew, I would read for outsiders. Now, for a shy, awkward child, all this attention was something I did not like, and at various times in my life I promised myself not to read any more hands. But it would always catch up with me and I would be asked to begin again.

I did not discover Astrology until I was 10, and Psychology until my teen-age years. Then I really began to study books on palmistry, and related subjects in some depth, and read everything in the English language on the subject several times over. At one point I had over 300 books on the subject, which over the years I have whittled down to just 30, as most on the subject are rehashed copies of other books and often not very scholarly.

In my late teens, a friend and I went to the Spiritualist Church, where tests showed I had amazingly high psychic ability, and would then be a very popular draw at their fund-raising events, so much so that I had much jealousy from some other mediums, who had spent their lives developing various abilities. They were then very unhappy to find a shy, spotty little teenager who was streets ahead of them.

50 Case Studies in Modern Palmistry

I came from a family with developed intuitive abilities, and they saw nothing unusual in people traveling some distance to see me. It was many years before I charged a fee for this, and then only to deter time wasters, cranks and skeptics. Later, even when relying on my skill to feed my family, my fee has always been half, or even a third, of what others in the field—even those I had taught myself—charged.

One evening I was giving spiritual healing in a London Spiritualist Church, when I noticed a white-haired old man staring intently at me. I took no notice and, when he came over afterwards, I was very curious as to what he would say. He asked me if he could give me some healing tips and invited me to come to his home. This old chap talked me through some changes in healing technique, and I thoughtfully agreed to try them out.

Next week at the church, I was flabbergasted to learn this man was Harry Edwards, the greatest spiritual healer of his day, and I then studied at several of his groups for quite some time.

In the mid '70s, a long-running Competition in a psychic bookshop in East London meant I was the one chosen to read people's lives and give advice and sympathetic spiritual counseling, and it was here that I met several doctors from Wipps Cross Hospital and took part in an experimental study on patients' hand prints. This then led to a larger study at Bart's Hospital, and then with Professor Henri Rey at the famous Maudsley Psychiatric Hospital.

At my workshops in the early '70s, I taught my palmistry skills across London to various palmistry groups, and although today these same techniques are quite commonplace, I have great pride that many of today's practitioners are using those same skills, and for almost 55 years I was the world's only palmist to offer a money-back guarantee of satisfaction.

In 1970, while at my London consulting rooms, I published my first small book, on which this one is based, and these early copies now fetch big prices on Ebay. I have been asked many times to update the book, so here it is, the culmination of my life's work.

Introduction

The Hand Shapes

Any reading must begin with the hand shape, and there are many systems on the various shapes. There is the Oriental Astrological system of 10/12 hand categories, the Tibetan system based on animals, Benham and Chiero's spiritual system of seven hand types, Carus system of six palmar types. The elemental system of five hand types, the Gettings' Chinese based system of four types, another complicated Chinese system based on the I Ching, and my own developed style of three hand shapes, which is the easiest of them all.

But in a reading, I actually use all these systems, and filter them through the astrological sign and the psychological type, as well as the hand bone category for genetic inheritance. The most popular just now is the system of four, popularized in the West by Fred Gettings, who—along with Mir Bashir—formulated that the measurement from the top crease line at the wrist palm boundary to the crease at the base of the middle or Saturn finger, compared that to the length of the crease at the base of the Saturn finger to its tip, is what determines long and short fingers to palm ratio. The palm usually measures 4½ inches and the Saturn finger 3 inches. A finger length shorter will be considered short and longer counts as long fingers.

These four types are allied with the *Four Temperaments,* which is a proto-psychological interpretation of the ancient medical concept of humorism, and suggests that four bodily fluids affect human personality traits and behaviors, thus character and destinies, and these I check primarily with the fingernails.

The Greek physician Hippocrates (460-370 BC) incorporated the Four Temperaments into his medical theories. From then through modern times, they, or modifications of them, have been part of many theories of medicine, psychology, philosophy, physiology, spiritual anatomy and literature.

Carl Jung used a modern adaptation of this in his Sensation, Feeling, Thinking and Intuition categories of his work, which is the basis for a large part of my palmistry practice. All palmistry should be counseling-oriented, and CBT (or Cognitive Behavioral Therapy) lends itself readily for this, as real palmistry is actually a great healing modality, not a parlor game for old ladies and the credulous.

Tibetan palmistry is almost solely geared to medical problems. It incorporates seven types of pulse taking and uses herbs extensively, and the Buddhist philosophy of balance for human health. This Yin/Yang duality is plant-based and has proved better for treating cancers than allopathic medicine used in the West. But it has almost been stamped out since the Chinese invasion of 1950, and will not play a major part in this book, and neither will fingerprint analysis.

It should be said that there are two kinds of palmists. There are the scientific palmists, who say everything has its correct place in the hand, and any deviancy from this gives its own facts. And then you have the intuitive palmists, such as gypsies and spiritualists, who work by Dukkering and psychometry, or what they *feel* from the hand.

My method, and the one I taught across Britain in the '70s, was to use scientific analysis, then use the developed and trained intuition as a laser to focus in on and magnify what was seen. This I called "subconscious amplification."

PSYCHOLOGICAL TYPES

Type A

These are people always on the go, rushing from one job to the next. They are very time-conscious and often suffer from TAM (or Time Anxiety Disorder) and get stressed if the pizza they ordered is 15 minutes late. They never relax properly, and they cannot abide queuing in shops. They are the most prone to stress and often fly into immediate rages. For this reason they are called the "coronary type" as these blowups are not good for the heart.

Expect a gapped Life and Head, possible flexible thumb, often with short fingers, and often many lines.

Type B

A broad, strong hand with a stiff thumb and few lines and cross bars corresponds most to the Mesomorph body type and elementary hand.

These personality types have calm, unruffled natures and are the total opposite of Type A. They always seem self-absorbed, always relaxed and at ease, to the point of being really laid back. They never get wound up. They mind their own business and watch events unfolding around them with disinterest. Placid and calm describes them best—strong, silent types.

Expect joined life and head line, a broad strong hand with a stiff thumb and few lines.

Introduction — The Hand Shapes

Type C
Not really able to express emotion, these people bottle things in and, even when agitated, are never able to put into words what's wrong. This bottling up does mean occasional blowups and often at the wrong target. Anger does eat away at them, but you would never know as it's always internal. They naturally keep secrets and hold onto past hurts. A large part of what I do with this type is clearing painful and toxic memory patterns. Picture a lovely white swan gliding along calmly on the river, but under the surface the legs are paddling like mad; this sums them up well.

Expect a short Mercury finger, which means communications problems, either verbal or written; with this it's both, and implying difficult early bonding experiences, such as would be seen with bottle-fed babies, or absent fathers.

The psychiatrist Daniel Stern spent his career working with babies. Some knowledge of his work can be very helpful with communicating any problems from the Latency period with C.R.D. in personal readings. (C.R.D is Childhood Relating Difficulties.)

Types of Hands

The Earth Hand
This largely corresponds to Carl Jung's *Sensation* grouping. Expect a heavy, square hand with short, thick fingers, especially the first or Jupiter finger, and comprises a very practical, capable, unimaginative, active and physical person, ideal for anything physical from farming and

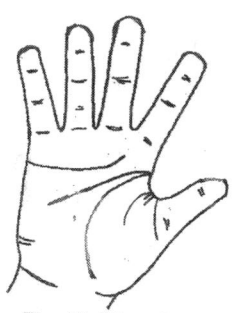

Earth Hand

soldiering to building and construction, to rough sports such as Rugby and boxing. This shows a reliable, practical and possessive plodder, but impatient of detail, suspicious, and working best outdoors. They are best being self-employed and are good with their hands and almost are always some sort of craftsman or fixer-upper in construction industries.

These hands are often hard with no flexibility, and this can show a single-minded plodder, who can suffer some anxiety, yet is a tireless worker. Most military types are Earth and many love four-wheel-drive vehicles and sporting guns, motorcycles, etc. These are usually Mesomorph body types, and better with machines than people. Dogs usually love this type, as dogs pick up on Earth energies.

This type is the most frequent to lack a fate line, and studies by Carl Jung and Charlotte Wolf both claimed this lack was frequently seen in criminal hands. Interestingly, a recent study (September 2013, Dr. Elaine Wong, California) said that men with wide faces statistically were more aggressive, less trustworthy and prone to deception; this is enhanced with no fate line. These Mesomorph types are usually nicotine addicts.

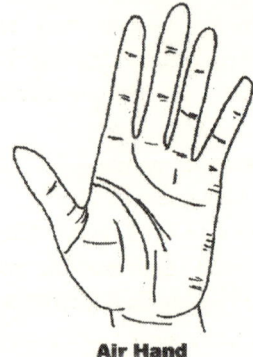

The Air Hand

This corresponds to Jung's *Thinking* category. This hand is again a square palm, but lighter in form with longer fingers, and these types look for intellectual pursuits, like chess, crosswords and Scrabble. They are communicators and can talk on any subject. They have enquiring minds and love intellectual challenge.

They ponder on life's questions and are curious and inquisitive, rationalizing everything. But although they can be humorous and inquisitive, they are very long-winded, and they are avid news watchers and like documentaries. They make good teachers, psychologists and analysts, bookkeepers and accountants.

They are very thorough and dot every "i" and cross every "t". They dislike sports and can talk on politics for ages. They have an almost inborn fear of anything emotional, and these tend toward being Ectomorph in build.

The Fire Hand

This mostly corresponds to Jung's *Feelings* category. The long, rectangular palm and short fingers show someone who is quick-acting and self-expressive. The fast actions often lead to risk taking. These are energetic people, who do things intuitively, on the spur of the moment.

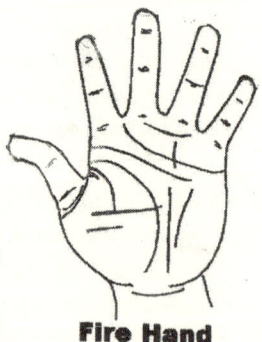

Sportsmen, such as rally drivers, motorcycle racers, badminton players or anyone who needs split-second reactions needs this combination, and often includes those who work closely with the public. They are the extrovert, intuitive, emotional exhibitionist type—who are often found in show biz—and are enthusiastic, changeable and exciting,

Introduction — The Hand Shapes

as well as good, overall organizers.

But they can't abide detail or small print, and have difficulty unwinding. These are usually Endomorphs.

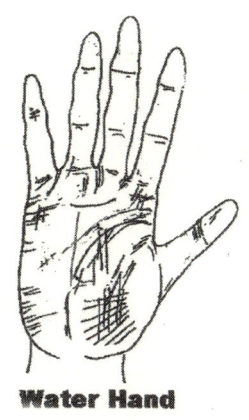

The Water Hand

These are in Jung's *Intuition* category. Long palm with long fingers, these people tend to be slightly unstable and sensitive emotionally, and when hurt, they withdraw into themselves and are statistically the most liable to have agoraphobic conditions, anxiety attacks and outdoor panic attacks, because they are uneasy in crowds.

They tend to be artistic and spiritual, but not practical or logical, and often suffer much hurt in their lives as they are often emotional loners. They are very artistic and feminine in their outlook, and can be quiet, withdrawn, secretive and over imaginative. They make good artists, poets, dancers, hairdressers, actors and beauticians. They will very often be Ectomorphs.

Water Hand

If seen with gaps at the finger bases and heavy knuckles, expect eating disorders and OCD (Obsessive-Compulsive Disorder) type anxieties.

Somatotopes

Constitutional psychology asserts that we think and act according to the three body sizes and shapes. Our size determines our reactions. This idea, popular in '30s Germany, was refined by Dr. William Sheldon, who also brought in psychological typing to the three basic body shapes. This particularly, using Carl Jung's introversion and extroversion categories, can give good back-grounding to any palmistry reading.

For instance, a subject who is powerfully built physically will act and live through his size being drawn to sport and heavy work, while a person small in build will be drawn to more head-centered work.

The Endomorph is a heavy build with wide hips, big bones and joints. These people will never be slim. Key words are: soft body, undeveloped muscles, roundish physique, gains muscle fairly easily and they are stomach centered, which is always visible.

The Mesomorph is an athletic shape with more muscle than fat, although piling on weight when older. Expect to see an athletic build, hard body, good natural posture, gains muscle easily, thick strong skin, and the females have—when young—an hourglass figure, and the males a strongly rectangular shape. They are muscle-centered.

Finally, the Ectomorph is a skinny, small frame with a narrow chest, with little muscle or fat. Key words are: delicate build, flat chest, fragile body, lean and thin, lightly muscled, small-shouldered. They are brain-centered, so pay special attention to the head and health lines.

ENDOTONIA—Love of relaxation and comfort, friendly, gregarious and food-minded, needs to experience different cuisines and share with friends.

MESOTONIA—Assertiveness, sporty and action-minded, military and needs physical stimulation and not brain-minded.

ECTOTONIA—Self-aware, quick thinking and thoughtful, needs mental stimulation, psychic abilities, and are often intellectuals.

Ayurvedic medicine consists of three *Doshas*. These are energy categories of *Vata, Pitta* and *Kapha,* and these roughly correspond to the Somatotopes of Dr. William Sheldon and are helpful in psychological and medical diagnosis, psychiatric problem analysis, and general palmistry work.

Hand Bones

The four strands of DNA link in with four bone types. Caucasoid is the bone type of the white race. Negroid is for black-skinned people. Mongoloid is for yellow people, and Mesoid is for brown people.

These bone types give distinguishing information to palmists about ancestral memories and heritage and correct diet for that type. In the past, you could tell a person's nationality by their hand, just as the face gives clues to ancestral heritage. But today, when the races are so mixed, it can be quite difficult. Ally this in with the four major blood types of positive or negative, and this will give clues to inherited strengths, weaknesses and illnesses, with good prognostic guides to their future.

Some doctors, especially in Japan, have been claiming for some years that you must eat right for your blood type, and people would often consult me about dietary advice from the hands.

The four Temperaments as described by Hippocrates (460 to 370 BC) is an interpretation of the ancient concept of Humorism, which infers that these four humors (or body-fluids) affect human behavior and personality traits.

Introduction — The Hand Shapes

These include *Sanguine* (or pleasure-seeking and sociable), *Choleric* (ambitious and leader-like), *Melancholic* (introverted and thoughtful) and *Phlegmatic* (which confers relaxed, introverted and quiet aspects). It is known that Hippocrates used palmistry and astrology in his medical work, and the saying, "A physician without a knowledge of Astrology has no right to call himself a physician" is from Hippocrates, who is known as the father of modern medicine. Doctors used to take the "Hippocratic Oath," which was based on Hippocrates' work from well before Christ.

The bone types give distinguishing information to palmists about ancestral memories and genetic heritage, correct eating patterns, and often the right career for that type. Ally this in with the four major blood types of positive or negative, and this will give clues to inherited strengths, weaknesses and inherited illnesses, which—if compared to the four ages described later—will give approximate dates.

Some doctors have aligned diet to blood type and are now saying your medication must align with your blood type. Type O thrives on physical activity. They were the early hunter-gatherers, who now have to watch for too much animal fat consumption, be sparing with dairy products, and avoid whole wheat, especially now when so much is genetically modified (GM). These people should eat fruit, nuts and vegetables, and drink herbal teas as they often have out-of-sync thyroids.

Neanderthals

Components of the Neanderthal type is very commonly found in the British Isles, and traces show 2 to 4 percent of bone structures, enhanced brow bones of the skull and heavy, basal palm bones. This shows largely in the Viking skeletons, who settled here and were of this same stock, as were the French Huguenots, who came later. These were physically very strong, with males about 1m 75cm, which is 5 feet 9 inches. Their bones and joints were larger, and much more heavily muscled.

In particular, they had huge, muscled chests, but with shorter, thick legs, and they lacked the chin, and their teeth were also different. They had a voice box which is almost identical to that seen today, and a brain that was 13 percent larger. Contrary to earlier suggestions, they walked upright and made many tools.

This body type is still seen in Norfolk, where centuries of inbreeding still show people with large chests and buttocks with short legs, and often with large eye sockets and large eyes. Expect the second toe to be as long as the first.

There is also a tendency to later life Dupuytrens contracture of the fingers.

Type A is for agrarian farmers. This blood type first appeared in Asia or the Middle East, possibly 25,000 years ago. The Cro-Magnons lived on agriculture, fruit and berries, animal husbandry and some hunting. This changed the digestive tracts and immune systems, and we can still track these changes through the hands. Even today they are more resistant to cholera, plagues and smallpox.

Blood Type B developed on the Indo/Pakistan continent, possibly 15,000 years back. As a mixture of Caucasian and Mongolian tribes, this blood type developed as they existed on a diet of herding domestic animals, with some meat and milk products being a large part. They usually lack magnesium. Type B blood is still the major type in Eastern Europeans. The two types of B blood groupings show most with the Asians, who use so little in the way of dairy.

Incidentally, Type B was prominent with German nationals in the 1930s and explains, in part, why they felt the Indo/Paks were kith and kin.

The four blood types, race and geography mix in together to form our initial identity, and developed from Type O over eons into who we are now. They are older than your race or ethnicity, and are the key to our entire immune system, because a chemical reaction occurs between the foods you eat and your blood type, and this gives you a predisposition to eat food that your ancestors ate and to which your blood is adapted. It is not as simple as the acid/alkali arguments.

The slim hand of the spirito/mental types are best suited to vegetarian diets. While the thick hands of the Mesomorphic Elementary and physical types may want to eat meat, many of the medical magazines are now decrying meat-eating on both nutritional and health grounds for all palmar types, as meat is linked to the two biggest killers, cancer and heart disease.

The palmar type must always be examined in with the eight wrist bones. The four closest to the hand are Trapezium, Trapezoid, Capitate and Hamate. The four closest to the arm are called Scaphoid, Lunate, Trioquetral and Pisiform. The wrist-to-hand sizing has given clues to several medical conditions, such as large wrist-to-hand ratios seen in cardiovascular anomalies. By bone structure analysis alone, you have a ready background handy for any forensic palmistry studies, as will be shown in the later case studies.

Soft Hands

Very soft hands are lovers of leisure. Press the Mount of Venus with

Introduction — The Hand Shapes

the thumb tip; this will give you an idea of stress and disease resistance and immune function. If seen with a thick, basal phalange to the Jupiter finger, this gives the gourmet or the guzzler.

Examine with other palmar signs to see if the person is a chocoholic or food faddist or drinks too much alcohol. A fat lower Jupiter phalange means they need dietary advice for the blood type and—if this phalange is fat, red and soft—these people will live for food and drink. This type is the category who watches sports from the comfort and safety of the settee.

Hard Hands

This is usually seen with the elementary or earth hand, and shows physical energy and how that energy is spent. The other lines will tell if that is mind, body or spirit, the three worlds of palmistry. They often have few lines, and statistically this is the most likely to have no fate or destiny line, showing a drifter, itinerant or casual worker. This can be a fairly common marking to those with no life plan.

Carl Jung, in his palmistry studies, made several mentions of this. Henri Rey, the great London psychiatrist, said he would always give these people jobs to keep them occupied as he saw them as worker drones.

They are the most likely to have an over-short index or Jupiter finger, giving the lack of self-confidence. These people are often craftsmen or manual workers, but not thinkers or planners. They would rather demolish a building than think through how to save it, and are the most likely of all the types to resort to alcohol or nicotine.

Make a mental note of the palmar muscle groupings, which are developed or undeveloped, as this will give info on their kind of manual work, or sport.

Thick Hands

The hand that is wide and thick in section usually has little more than the three main lines showing. It is primarily a common-sense, practical hand that loves nature, physical rhythms and the outdoors. Physical work appeals when young, and they have a feel for the changing seasons, the weather and the land. They are affable and easy going. They make good partners, but usually—being the Mesomorph body type—love their food and the energy of physical work and sport, and they tend to put on much weight in later life. They have energy, passion and drive for people and causes, such as public service, police work, the army, farming and construction work.

Thin Hands

Hands with thin, long palms, and with long, thin fingers are less robust than those with thick palms, and often have more illnesses—especially in childhood. They are often dreamy, visionary and distant emotionally, and so feel alone and misunderstood. They can be over-critical, obsessed with details, and when anxious, have emotional outbursts. They tend at times to be highly strung, unduly protective, and often are hypochondriacs. They do not respond well to Allopathic medication and get better personal results from Homeopathy, Ayurvedic medication and New German Medicine; in other words, "whole person" medicine rather than just acknowledging the symptoms.

They are fastidious with colour, shape and form. They are good at needlework, cooking and home skills. They are indoor people and good office workers. They love detail and can make a beautiful home anywhere, and be very feminine in their tastes. They make very good artists, psychics, decorators, actors and designers.

Jung's categories of *Feeling* and *Intuition* fit well here.

Palmar Lines

Although this has been covered so deeply and well in every book on the subject, I believe the hand should be read as a whole, not from singular signs. But lines will be covered in the main case files section, so this is just a very brief, short outline covering aspects not mentioned in any other books. See *front page illustration*.

The Line of Life

So called because it is the first to form on the foetus within the womb, showing the life itself. In fact, I used to read the ultrasound pictures of babies' hands in the womb some years back at London's famous Wipp's Cross Hospital, telling of events in the life-to-be. This is the most skilled but delicate aspect of palmistry and much misused.

The start to the life line does not show in a hand print, so I find it useful to ask the Date of Birth. At times, the star sign and numeral of the date can assist as a jump-off point, and in confirming other info. Extensive studies show that winter-born babies are very different to those born in summer, and are more prone to certain illnesses in later life.

Experts vary where they start their readings, but I start at the life line's edge at the side of the hand and progress through the hand from life in the womb, birth to the present, giving the times and dates of events as I see the times on the life line. This is the best method as it takes them through every year of their life, from birth, using every aspect and constantly cross-checking the other lines for more info. Included are details of career and attitude from the fate line, health from the health line, etc., but placing the most emphasis on the here and now, then using different techniques for the future, which must be handled with extreme care, with gentle advice and counseling. This is where many palmists go wrong. Remember the therapists' motto: "Do no harm," and if you are not sure of anything, say so.

Up to the life line's start, you will see a small line called the line of demarcation. This gives you info on the baby's start to life. A firm, strong, unbroken line is best, and the longer and stronger this is, the better. If it is weak or wavers, it shows the soul had second thoughts about being born, and if it starts above or below the life line it, will give additional info on the family events while in the womb.

50 Case Studies in Modern Palmistry

Some Indian schools read the Father in the line above and the Mother in that below. The father line must be compared to the Jupiter or first finger. Watch for a very thin, basal phalange to Jupiter, which will tell of unfinished paternal business going way back. Jupiter is the finger of both the father and the ego.

The mother line must relate to the Apollo, or third finger, and these tell of the early relationship struggles with mainly the mother, but occasionally both parents. The recent findings of Professor Manning's studies on digit comparisons have shown that testosterone is linked in the womb to the index or Jupiter finger, and estrogen is linked to the Apollo finger.

The Royal College of Psychiatry says that up until the age of 6 the quality of parental relationship is critical for later life stability. This can be told by comparing the start to the life line with its later thickness, colour, etc.

The Mercury, or little finger, tells how we cope with these relationships; however, these two small lines at the life line's start are what I call the demarcation lines and ideally should be balanced and even, and the same distance apart. Any closeness or bending from either line can be viewed as karmic indicators of parental anomalies, which can be read according to the rules of palmistry's long established line forms and shapes.

It often shocks people when I tell them their birth weight, but if you study the birth averages for the different body builds, you can get this down pretty close (e.g. Ectomorphs are light and Mesomorphs are heavy). Bear in mind, the Negroid bone structure tends to be denser and weighs more.

The life line itself can easily be divided, and for many years I used a transparent protractor to measure the life line's curve. But after a few years, it can be quickly assessed by eye, and in fact, while talking to clients, I would use my thumb tip placed on the life line. This gives four equal sections. The first is childhood; next youth; then adulthood, and old age. This corresponds to Spring, Summer, Autumn and Winter or Water, Fire, Air and Earth.

I call this the "rule of thumb": Spring is the early life and we are born in water. Summer is the first bloom of adulthood with the fires of love and passion and the joys of family, stability and children. Autumn is the late middle age, where wisdom and mental clarity corresponds to Air. Winter represents old age, where, of course, our bodies go back to the Earth.

I also divide the line into Decades, or spaces of 10 years each. Many palmistry books take you up to 90 or 100 years of age, but the life span of an average Englishman and American male is now down to 77 years of age and, in fact, insurance companies judge it to be 70 exactly as in biblical

Introduction — Palmar Lines

times. Incidentally, the miners who mine diamonds and gold in Africa live on average to 37 years of age. It is very rare indeed where you see people living to very old ages nowadays, so forget the newspaper theories of people living to advanced ages.

If you imagine the lines, particularly the life line, as a river cutting its course through the hand, notice if the line is thick and broad, showing a sluggish flow, or sharp and deep, showing fast-flowing energies and quick-healing properties. Notice if the life line has any blemishes, such as crossing lines, protective squares, islands or similar, and apply the standard rules of palmistry.

See if the hand has a hollow in any part under the life line, and note the colour or any fragmentation or crossings lines here. Hollow is most common, and at the start will tell if accompanied by a "barbed wire entanglement" of childhood difficulties. If so, look for a thin Apollo finger, which will infer maternal bonding difficulties, and the Jupiter finger will show early paternal or father problems. Either will show up later with CRD (Childhood Relating Difficulties) and often into adult life.

An examination of the Mercury finger will tell how much interrelating and sexuality are affected. (More info on this in the case studies.) If maternal deprivation does show in the vital early years, expect later a condition known as "affectionless psychopathy," which infers an inability to form deep, meaningful relationships, with no ability to accept or demonstrate affection to people or animals.

Any stress or trauma during the first six years usually results in nocturnal enuresis (or nighttime bed-wetting), the loss of father or mother, burns or fractures. Family discord, etc., will put back the child in its normal development; this enuresis is enhanced if seen with a short Jupiter finger and a bowed top bracelet.

If, when the fingers are closed together, gaps show at the bases, this shows someone who thinks too much, mulling over, and becomes brooding, over intellectualizing and over rationalizing with anything that troubles them. This over-thinking is one of the bases of anxiety. It is also one of the signs of chest problems in childhood, such as severe whooping cough or croup, especially with long fingers.

These gaps can also mean that money is hard to hold onto; it kind of falls through the gaps, especially with an open life and head junction. This is why a closed junction is called "the blessing of Shiva" as it gives caution, care and slowness. The longer this junction is closed, especially when it is flat under the line's start, the greater the shyness in youth, the more the fear of changes and the greater the reliance on family and friends for advice. This also shows in teen-age years a "need to belong."

These gaps also signify eating disorders, such as *Anorexia nervosa* symptoms. Especially look for lines down the side of the mouth from habitually being sick. Where the largest gap is found will also give you much info on that finger's contribution to the whole hand, so concentrate here. See the gap as leaking energy from the hand through that finger.

Jupiter gaps often show paternal problems, which often materialize as problems with authority, ego conflicts or self image. Saturn gaps often infer a tendency for brooding, anxious periods. Apollo gaps show emotional fear, which often relates to the mother and usually from early childhood, and can be from the five stages of pre-latency. Mercury gaps are unusual, and can infer sexual blockages, but always look for confirmation elsewhere in the hand, and check for timing to the life line.

The four types of Karma give us many clues which will show on the life line and the fate line in particular, but actually show in every palmar aspect. If the life line is separated from the head line, this shows someone with a fast karmic system, someone who heals quickly and who is adventurous, impatient and impulsive, as well as very independent. They mature early and tend to not look before they leap. In Tibetan palmistry it is known as the "sign of the tiger." Always refer to the hand shape and the thumb type before giving any summaries. But in general, my advice to people with the open lines of head and life is to "sleep on it" before making any major decisions.

Early illnesses are easy to spot on the life line with islands, gaps, thinning in the line and crossing bars. Many crossed lines across the palm centre in what is called a "full hand," showing nervous, irritable and gastric babyhood, especially if seen in the left hand; feeding and stomach colic tendencies, which should be looked at in combination with the health line and can be timed on the life line. When looking at every other line, compare to the life line, especially at that point in time.

Full hands make hypersensitive and highly strung children, who do not like change or upset in routine. These gaps at finger bases also go with a certain mental outlook, and you can tell what on by looking at the other palmar anomalies, such as a straight, strong head line. The thoughts will be on psychological aspects, economic and practical things; those with these gaps find holding onto cash difficult. I always imagine the coins falling through the gaps in the fingers.

Another aspect of gaps at the finger bases is that these are usually

Introduction — Palmar Lines

people with eating disorders, the mildest being Spasmodic eaters. These are the ones who eat well one day, but the next day are "too busy to eat" right through the spectrum of Bulimia and Anorexia.

A deeply sloping head line will be seen with imaginative, creative and artistic topics, and will look to discover their spiritual identity and destiny. This is their security, not money in the bank as with straight head lines. The straight head line type is more down-to-earth, rational and logical, and will be concerned with the laying down of secure material foundations, economic stability and general security issues. Note where the life line bulges widest into the hand; this shows the year of greatest effort, as after this, the decline gradually sets in.

The wider the curve covering the life lines, the better. Where the curve is non-existent, it infers in the straight life line poor resistance to illness, lacking immune function, and if the Venus mount is also soft to the touch, a couch-potato existence is suggested. Studies show these people do not burn with sexual desire, and if this flatness of Venus with a narrow life line is seen with a bowed top racette in a flat hand, these people are often childless. A flat Venus mount can also show a missing mother influence in childhood, and certainly a feeling of lack of maternal support and love during childhood.

A thumb's width is the ideal for this bulge. Note where the widest part touches the life line. If it's before the mid-line, these peak before 35-ish, which is the Summer period. Afterwards, like most people, they peak in later life, in the Autumn life period. Peaking is economic, relationship, career, etc. Gauge the age by this and for how long they touch. Much less and the person will be non-sporty and not strong in health.

Notice where the bulge occurs on the life line, and remember this is its widest reach from the thumb. This will tell of when the ambition must be reached, as after this comes the slow decline.

It should be said that although traditional palmistry is an intellectual study, the heart chakra should be activated and used alongside. Always use compassion, understanding and love for any fellow human being who consults you. Use reassurance and gentle advice as you take the subject through the major years and events of their life. See the lines as rivers which negotiate the Topography of the hand. See when the lines are smooth and fast flowing. If you see a line that is thick and wide or, as often seen, a heavily islanded heart or head line, know this is an area of difficulty.

Carl Jung's four categories of Thinking, Feeling, Intuition and Sensation, in general fit the four hand shapes in terms of the life lessons. The Earth hands lessons will be primarily Physical; the Air hand, Mental; the

Fire hand, emotional, and the Water hand spiritual. Use the rule of thumb along the life line, to assess important life changes, in health, relationships, family matters, etc.

Remember the four sectors of karma. Most important for Eastern peoples, the Vedic Scriptures speak of *Sanchita* karma. This represents the sum total of all past actions, payable at some point.

Parabadha karma, which is the sum total that lies in wait for you to experience.

Kryamana karma, which is the sum total of correct actions.

Agama karma is that which is created as a result of the actions you are now considering.

The famous seer Edgar Cayce, who would give his famous spirit readings, interpreted the four categories as *Assimilation, Elimination, Circulation* and *Relaxation*, which he felt were to do with North, South, East and West. Incidentally, the average human body contains enough iron to make a 6-inch nail, and the hand can be made to work as a compass, and will give the body's view on traveling to different directions. This can be helpful in decision-making.

The 19th Century society palmist Cheiro popularized the system of seven, and Shakespeare spoke of the seven ages of man at 10 years apiece. These are known as *Decamons*. This means up until the age of seven, we read of the instinctive developmental stages up to this age, with particular emphasis on the babyhood stages. The oral stage is when the baby experiences the sexio/social aspects of putting everything in its mouth, sucking, chewing and biting. The mouth is the libidinal focus of exploration. The knock-on effects through the life of whether a baby has been breastfed to term or bottle fed can easily be seen by the palmist in the Mercury finger and the effects are lifelong. More on this in the explanatory case histories section later in the book.

But remember, the Royal College of Psychiatrists say the personality is forming up to the age of 3, when it is then set. I don't totally agree with this, but it's a good guide for the budding palmist. The latency period starts from around age 7, and Freud agreed with the theory that there are five stages of babyhood, and each is clearly seen from the hand if later problems develop. The Oral phase, Anal phase, Phallic phase, Latency phase and the Genital phase.

Time Periods

Up to age 15, the difficult teenage years, are where we begin to find

Introductions — Palmar Lines

who we are and our path in various life arenas. Up to 21, discovery of love, growth, maturity and personal security. Up to 28-29, when we experience a Saturn return; this normally goes with a personal crash or time of crisis, and again just before age 60.

Age 35 is the life midpoint, and age 32 in marriage guidance shows peak marital problems, a time of maturity, family concerns and financial struggle. Up to age 42 is when the slowing-down process starts and all things begin to ease. Age 50 is the age of reflection, taking stock and looking back. Up to age 56, wisdom, unselfishness, pride in family and new delight in young people. Age 65 is autumn understanding, fitting past happenings into place. At age 70 memories of things long past take on a new sharpness, and yesterday's happenings seem less important. Taking stock of the life's lessons, humanity, understanding and kindness should then rule.

The system of Seven Years and Seven Hand Types also fits the seven chakras and the seven sacraments, the seven days of the week, and the seven major planets of ancient astrology. This system is in part used extensively in the East. For quicker, simpler readings, I go by every 10 years or decamons on the life line. Incidentally, the palmist/psychologist Julius Spier used Psycho-Chirology to gauge these personality difficulties from childhood, especially from the emotio/sexual arenas, and he would read the life line from the base upwards, claiming that the life current runs down toward the fingers. But for most palmists, we read from under the fingers down the life line to the wrist.

The strength of the life line is important. It must reach out wide into the hand and have no digs, cuts, islands or bars, and only be joined at its start by a thumb width. If it is joined for longer than this, it can mean the person is shy and not able to push forward. This reticence and slowness is why in Tibetan palmistry it is called the sign of the Tortoise. Over-cautiousness and sensitivity can hamper development, and the open lines of head and life show impatience, impulsiveness and impetuosity. Extremely wide is recklessness. In Tibetan palmistry this is the mark of the tiger, and tigers are very charismatic and usually so are people with this marking.

The ending to the life line at the hand base is very telling. If it splits into two large, equal forks, one going to Luna, this often means time spent overseas. This is often seen in Britain's Indo/Pak communities, and if this Luna branch is longer, they will long to go home. This is based on the fact that Luna rules the imagination and the life energies will follow. But if the inner life line branch tucks round the Venus base, this means they will die in their home country, and often near where they were born.

For those whose life lines split into several small branches, this can infer that as the line splits and frays, so do the life energies. At the time suggested, check the head line, to see if this also frays. Check the heart line and the health line and nails for more information.

Palmists generally use the intellect in analysis, but it could be said that truth is understood not by the ears but by the heart. So also learn to activate and use the heart chakra, so you are using both heart and head.

Other Lines in the Hand

The Heart Line

The line of heart shows the quality and quantity of the love and also the heart as an organ. Some palmists start from the edge and read to the Jupiter finger, while more modern palmists read from the fingers out to the thumb edge. I tend to let the rest of the hand determine where I start with both the cardiovascular system and the affections. But strictly speaking, the heart as a pump is seen primarily under the Apollo and Mercury fingers.

The development of the emotional aspects of the nature, and the way this develops and is expressed, is primarily (but not exclusively) under the Jupiter finger. *The Saunders Book of Palmistry* (1661) states that there were differences of opinion even then, but I read the general health on the line from under Mercury.

The main thrust of the romantic outlook and the main area for change occurs under the Jupiter finger, although both give fair results. The golden rule of palmistry is never to go by one sign alone. You have to weigh up the whole hand and this is the real skill, weighing up colour, temperature, hand type, bone category and body type. And, even during the reading, holding the wrist and checking the pulse Ayurvedic/Acupuncture style.

Remember to check the health line and press your thumb into the Venus mount to gauge firmness or softness, to show illness, resistance and immunity ratings.

Heart lines with the Jupiter ending show an idealist trait. Saturn endings, which curve up and end at the finger base, show a sensual, selfish, often bisexual slant, and a heart condition, which shows the more the person exerts, the slower the heart becomes—an unusual condition, which is often seen with this marking.

Apollo endings show a small heart and cardio weakness, seen at times with very premature babies. Remember, a straight heart line is very different to a curved one, in both emotional expression and also in physical health

Introduction — Palmar Lines

terms. In India this line is called the *Jivan Rekha* or life line, as they say that when the heart stops beating, death will come, so this is the true life line.

Aristotle claimed that in line with Tibetan palmistry, the heart should be read as man's most important organ, and it should be long and clear, with not too many splits or breaks. Many breaks are often seen in a full hand and go with Tachycardic conditions—fast or nervous heart. The Mesomorph body type, with the Elementary hand, is the one particularly pre-disposed to later life cardiovascular conditions, and with this, you will often see a strong, short, wide, red line of heart.

For each of the hand types there is a corresponding type of line. If a line is not the usual for that hand type, or is in the wrong place, it is what I call a "cuckoo line," and needs special attention. The Max Planck Institute carried out a huge study some years ago on illness and birth months. This pretty well backed up what Astrology has always said, and if you can get a copy, it has some good advice for the palmist.

Coronary Heart Disease (or C.H.D.) is the most common cause of death in the UK and America. Lifestyle choices, such as stress and diet, junk and processed foods, etc., all play a part, so if you can advise on diet and lifestyle from the hand, this is a bonus.

Long years of study have enabled me to show and diagnose sticky heart valves, impaired vascular and various cardiac anomalies, as well as predict strokes and much more, which will be seen in the case studies. In fact, there are almost 40 health conditions from comparing the heart line with other palmar areas.

The line should be clear, with not too many splits, islands or gaps. Many breaks are often seen in a full hand and go with Tachycardia, fast or nervous heart, the Mesomorph body type. Use the Max Planck and other studies to establish the overall risk.

C.H.D. is the most common cause of death among men in the UK. In C.H.D., the arteries that pump blood to the heart become narrow. This narrowing occurs when fatty material builds up within the artery walls. If the arteries become too narrow, the heart does not receive enough oxygen-rich blood, which causes chest pain known as angina. This narrowing can escalate to the point that the artery is blocked, which can then cause a heart attack, where the lack of oxygen-rich blood causes permanent damage to the heart.

A short meta-analysis of observational studies, published in medical papers in 2012, provided information on the association between baldness and C.H.D., and cannot say why they are associated or any associated causes.

Interestingly, the Tibetans, on seeing a newborn baby, would stroke the heart line with their fingers, so the baby would grow up caring and loving.

The Head Line

The head line is the lower of the two creases crossing the hand, and it is read from the thumb side out into the hand. When it is closely joined to the life line, it shows reticence, caution and shyness. The longer the join, the more this is so, and gaps between the two are seen as giving impatience, impulsiveness and independence. The bigger the gap, the more apparent this is. You can determine which areas the subject is—cautious or reckless—by the hand shape, structure lines and colour, etc., but more on this in the case studies later.

Head lines that go straight across the hand show practical, down-to-earth realists, economists, psychologists and people who are head-centered, while those head lines that drop to Luna show the artists, poets and spiritually creative types, those who live in the imagination. The first type value monetary security, whereas the second type see discovering their spiritual destiny as much more important.

A good head line is considered to be one that is free from breaks, cross bars and not too tightly joined at the start. Half an inch is about right and ends midway between the two types.

There is another kind of straight line, called a "Sydney line," and this is a powerful, straight line right across the hand. This is associated usually with allopathic medication toxicity in the womb, and often cardiovascular anomalies which the rest of the hand will determine how and when. Look also for bowel constipation with this marking.

Whether you use the 7 Hand category system or the Getting's 4 Hand type system, understand that each hand shape has its own head line. The heavy, short, thick hand of the Earth/Elementary type will have a short, straight, deep head line, tied at the start. The thin hand of the Ectomorph/Air category will have a many-lined hand with a sloping head line.

A wrong type of head line will tell you of someone who is not of his type; oddbods, misfits and geniuses are often of this category.

Forked Head Lines

Depending on where the forking begins ... if it starts under Saturn, it's too early and can show people of a divided mind, people who are always unsure of any decisions, and even dual personalities. If the break starts under Apollo, this is good and gives an ability to see others' points of view.

Introduction — Palmar Lines

Counselors, authors, actors, etc., often have this marking. Mercury gives the best ability for a flexible mental outlook.

The head line will tell of the kinds of things which occupy the thoughts. Confirmation will be given in the other hand areas. This is a good line to be able to predict from giving great accuracy. This forking looks like a fish's tail and was considered a lucky mark in ancient Christianity and in the old Hindu palmistry traditions, as it gave breadth of view and was called "the mark of the fish."

Keep in mind, the skin texture and colour. Fine texture sensitizes the subject, while coarse texture coarsens it. The thumb tip will give extra details. Red-colored hands give the subject fire to his views. White gives a coldness.

Using these facts together will enable you to categorize your subject and tell him the years when he will be at his absolute peak. For over 55 years I have been the only palmist to offer a full refund to anyone coming to me who was not fully satisfied. Apart from skeptics and cranks, no one was ever dissatisfied.

The Fate Line

Different schools refer to this as the destiny or luck line. Its journey usually starts from the wrist, palm base centre, or the life line. This varies usually, according to the hand type, but it almost always ends near the Saturn finger and is most often missing in the Mesomorph and Elementary types. When missing, it shows poor life plan and continuity.

Starting from the centre of the hand by the wrist, we see someone who wishes to be in charge to plan their own future. From the life line comes help from the family. This may be advice or monetary. Those who go into family businesses usually have this.

Originating from Luna shows imagination and help from the opposite sex. This is often seen in show biz people, entertainers and public favorites, and those like teachers, who have to stand up in front of an audience and rely on the public for their living.

Note whether life and head are open or closed. The start to the fate line should mirror the information at the start to the life line. Such things as a square to the start of the life line will often mirror that of the fate line. The centre of the hand as a starting point shows as a very good positive omen, and is seen often with those who are born with a silver spoon in the mouth.

Where the fate, destiny or luck line ends is of great importance. Toward Jupiter <u>shows ambition has paid off</u>. Management or people in authority often show this mark. Under Saturn shows success in worldly ventures, and under Apollo a career in show biz, art or design.

Mercury can mean communication or medicine, but check the four kinds of karma and the hand type for more information. Check the whole fate line for gaps, digs, breaks or minor signs. Any breaks usually coincide with career change or spinal injuries, and if it curves at the top, this can signify a whiplash injury. The spine from the palmar base, reading up toward the fingers, shows the sacral, lumbar, cervical and thoracic spinal sections.

Time this on any weak spots on the life line, and again on the health line, and always check the Mercury finger for communicative abilities, and the Venus mount for the firmness and energy to carry out projects and plans. The spine from the hand base up represents lumbar, thoracic and cervical. Many women have a short fate line as that part of the lumbar spine is damaged in childbirth.

The fate line is often seen attached to the life line, and as such it is more often seen in Indian families as it shows help from within the family. Look to other signs for more information, but always read the fate line with the Apollo line together, as this will show the degree of success. I should say here that many people come and ask, "Will I be successful?"

Success does not always mean money. I have read for some of the richest people on the planet, and they often are very unhappy and have become prisoners of their wealth, whereas the average Joe is happy to just survive. So a good, unbroken fate line will show good adjustment to one's sphere, and the Apollo line will add indications of success to the chosen way of life.

Incidentally, the Indian schools, especially the Kartikeyan, say that the lower the fate line starts, very near the wrist, that the karma will be in acting out things from previous lives, and those whom I have mentioned this to tend to agree. They felt they had been here before.

Always check this with the start to the life line and line of demarcation.

The Mars Line or Inner Life Line

The Mars line is often seen with a fragile life line, especially in the slim, full hand types. It should follow a similar curve, but inside the life line. If it is seen in an Elementary or Mesomorph hand, with just three or four lines, pay extra attention to it—where it starts and how it ends. Does it start from the Mars or Venus mount? This will tell you where it draws its power and of its nature and future development.

Is it stronger, deeper and redder than the life line? It's usually partial and moves away from the main life line around the hand centre. This line is considered a very good omen and a strengthener to the main line. If you see this, check the health line and nails, to see why this line occurs, and then the Venus mount at the base of the thumb, which will tell of resistance.

If you press your thumb tip into this mount and take it away quickly, the amount of time taken for the natural colour to resume will tell you of any underlying health condition, being acute or chronic. You want a quick return to the natural colour. Is the hand hard or soft? Take account of the age of the subject and remember palmistry's three worlds of Mind, Body and Spirit.

Just bear in mind that any line or marking partakes of the underlying planetary ruler, and this starting from Mars can make one defensive and at times aggressive. If the mount is full, expect this with martial artists, soldiers and those who love risky sports. Starting on Venus means it partakes of the love and care of the person and displays it through the other palmar markings.

In the East this is known as a defense line, as it gives just that. And, in the old days, it was seen as a parent line by many. But today it is often seen as a guardian angel line, because of its protective nature. Notice the strength of the life line after the Mars line ends, as this will give more information. Does the Mars line finish close or far from the life line?

I saw this mark once on a dare-devil racing driver's hand and I told him it ended at around age 35, so that was the time to stop racing. He told me racing was in his blood. In 1961 Wolfgang Von-Trips was tragically killed, aged just 33.

The Girdles
The Girdle of Venus

There are so many different interpretations of this in different books over the centuries. This line was first documented in 600 BC and, in fairness, all interpretations are true in some circumstances, but as in all you read here, this is based on long years of study and practice. Expect to see this mark with humanitarians, storytellers, sensitives, actors, artists and painters.

The hand shape will tell of the sphere in which these qualities will blossom. It can often be seen with temperamental dispositions and tachycardic anomalies, such as atrial fibrillation. I usually advise to not drink too much coffee, as caffeine is a heart stimulant and will make the heart race further.

Usually seen with the Ectomorph body type with slim, long, feminine hands and many lines, it gives a changeable, moody personality, which is related to the heart line, and gives a restless emotionality. Ectomorphs are emotionally very sensitive anyway, but notice if it starts from Jupiter, taking from it ambition, pride and individuality; from Saturn, a more selfish sexuality. But most times, this marking is seen just under the two middle fingers, with a ragged and broken heart line.

In brief, it tells of someone who seeks excitement and variety. In a strong hand, this can give empathy and emotional understanding. But if seen with a flexible thumb, open life and head, and gaps at the finger bases can be a sign of both the promiscuous and the sexual adventurer. I saw this line once on a famous homosexual pop musician, who bragged he had slept with over 1,000 fans.

The Girdle of Jupiter

The Girdle of Jupiter has been known since ancient times as Solomon's ring. Solomon was said to be wise and a perpetual student. This mark is a semi-circle under the base of the index or Jupiter finger. Carl Jung saw this as the mark of the psychologist, but it can also be seen in the hand of philosophers, mystics and students of humanity.

The rest of the hand will tell of the area studied, but in India it is seen as a very humanitarian marking. In a wide, hard Mesomorph hand, it could relate to the outdoors, a feel for trees and the ground, guns or the military. In a slim, multi-lined hand, look for some aspect of introversion, medicine, spirituality, parapsychology, etc. Always expect charisma and a magnetic personality.

The Archbishop of Canterbury showed me his Girdle with some pride some years back.

The Girdle of Saturn

This ring was generally not seen as a positive sign, as it shuts off the body's energy currents to this finger. The ancient Greek priests saw this as a warning omen of failure. Today we see this as a cautionary sign and, as it often connects with the fate line, in career matters.

But check first with the Apollo or sun line, which—if strong and positive—tempers the Saturn girdle. Make sure there are no sudden endings to the Apollo or sun line. If you see this, warn not to speculate on financial matters and keep your finances close. I have seen this on "show biz" personalities whose careers were wrecked by bad publicity.

Many times you will see this as an end marking to the fate line.

Introduction

Showing economic care must come before anything else. If seen with a short Jupiter finger, it will lend some aspects of self-sabotage, which we see in those who lack self-confidence and drive. As the fate or luck line represents the spine, one often sees the girdle atop a fate line, so dietary advice must be given as this can infer osteoporosis, teeth and calcium-based disorders, although the marking is more psychological than physical.

These people are often like a ship without an anchor, and always seem to be struggling against adversity, so in short, see it as a sign of restriction in some way.

The Girdle of Apollo

Usually this is seen with those who have difficult financial luck, such as compulsive gamblers, but it need not always refer to finances, but rather to a cutting off of the energies of emotional nutrition. It is often seen with a short sun or Apollo line and a malformed heart line. Warn to take extra care in making relationships and business partners.

The Girdle of Mercury

This is a rare marking and it occurs when the so-called marriage line curls around onto the Mercury mount, under the Mercury finger. This is really a deep relationship line that, in the old days, was called the widow's line. I have seen this a few times when indeed carried by a widow.

This Mercury mount in some Eastern schools is called the Domain of Buddha, and this line then tells of communicative roots in karmic love, something from long ago having its climax in this life, and not generally positive in nature. But in the West, when this is seen, it infers that the widow will close the door on possible relationships after this event.

Check the heart line for emotional upset and the health line for effects on health at that time. This marking is more common on the Ectomorph hand type and suggests an attitude of closing down of future close emotional relationships.

Health Lines

The Mystic Cross

The hand centers contain minor chakras, or power wheels, and these supply energy to the mounts underlying the lines and fingers. The lowest mount in terms of height will tell where the energy escapes.

Many hands show the point of insertion of the life line, showing the energy escape of childhood. Pay particular attention to this period on the upper part of the Venus mount. The famous psychologist, Henri Rey, himself a great intuitive, became quite adept at diagnosing the effect of childhood trauma from this, which can infer a troubled but intuitive childhood.

Pictures of Christ's crucifixion always show iron nails through this chakra to blank out his power, when in fact the nails were put through his wrist. The cross must always lay between the lines of Heart and Head, and symbolize both qualities of love and thought, or heart and head being subservient to the power of spirit.

These people give themselves for the benefit of others and are often very poor. Their wealth is the wealth of the spirit and can often seem distant and not of this earth. If seen with an intuition line and an Apollo line, see this as a very positive omen.

Rarely seen on empty hands with few lines, my own father had an empty hand with this marked very clearly and blood red in colour. He was consulted on many occasions by bigwigs on many matters for advice. If this cross is seen larger than a thumb nail, then it's important. The famous medium Doris Stokes had this, too, as did Edgar Cayce.

The Via Lasciva

Now mainly called the poison line, the Via Lasciva is a good barometer of allergies and sensitivities. This line is usually seen in a many-lined hand. Its significance is enhanced if seen with the Girdle of Venus, or if it joins or cuts the life line. If it does, note the age suggested and the quality of the life line afterwards, and check with the health line for its effects. Check the heart line for emotional and physical causes and after-effects, the head line for impaired thinking processes, etc., and the nails for health anomalies.

Introduction — Health Lines

The hand colour will tell of underlying dispositions and health proclivities. This line is mainly seen in two shapes, the short straight Hypothenar bar and the curved line, which usually touches the life line. Modern palmists tend to see this line as inferring a need for awareness to open skies and nature with a dislike for built-up city areas, and an avoidance for allopathic chemical medicine.

Expect to see this line with speed freaks, bungee jumpers and thrill seekers, but also it can be read as a poison line as it often means an allergy to processed foods and such things as seafood, peanuts, eggs, meat or cow's milk, caffeine or sugar.

Penicillin or anesthetic allergies are also quite common, and be aware that many who are addicted to drugs—both illegal and prescription, or alcohol—will show this marking, which can have a variety of places where it appears, but must always come from the side of Luna.

Check with the ending to the head line and the size of the Luna mount. People who have this should never ever play or experiment with drugs. How to define these sensitivities further with suggestions for remedies will be seen in the case studies.

Health Line

This is often confused with the Via Lasciva, but it must be read alongside it. As I said in my first book, published 40 odd years ago, health is not confined to this line. Be sure to check which end to the line is the thickest, as this will show the start to the line. Those that leave the life line to go up to Mercury's mount are seen less than those which come down and attack the life line. See the quality and colour of the life line after this, and make sure it does not look weaker after the join.

Note the age and the type of hand, which will give you the inherited health anomalies. Here the nails are vital to check for health weaknesses, hints on diet, and best remedies for any ills. German New Medicine, Ayurvedic or Homeopathy are the closest to palmistry's ancient philosophies.

In giving talks to doctors on palmistry and health over the years, Indian doctors seem more open-minded, but asked why is there such a preponderance of heart trouble in India, most of whom are vegetarian—so should not be so prone—Dalda ghee is a type of hydrogenated vegetable oil, which was originally meant for candles and soaps, which often contain lard or pork fat. This is not properly digestible and somewhat poisonous in effect, and it alters the configuration of the cell membrane, and increases the LDL-Cholesterol. It's hard to metabolize and its digestibility has been proved to be very low. With difference in metabolic rates, it weakens the heart and cardiovascular system.

Check the heart line and bones of the wrist, which will tell of weak areas, bone types and future problems. This line is best not seen at all, but if a straight, clear line is found, it's just a barometer of health. In ancient times, this line was called the hepatica or liver line, and it does give much info, particularly on the gastric system and general gut flora, etc.

The quality and health of the liver reflects the body's general health. Sailors were always checked for this, as it inferred seasickness or a weak stomach. A line with many breaks can tell of some aspect which can undermine the health. Read this in combination with the basal phalange of Jupiter finger, which will give pointers to acid/alkali balance and appetites, and will also tell of the chef or gourmet to the food guzzler.

I always recommend that they keep some real ginger or peppermint as good natural stomach settlers.

The Bracelets

Bracelets

These three lines are used to suggest wealth, health and happiness, and gave 30 years apiece. But this is not strictly true.

Clean, unbroken, even lines are good, and are now said to suggest 25 years each. But if the top one arches up, then this—since Roman times—has been seen as giving child-bearing difficulties in women and uro-genital niggles in men.

In fact, the late expert palmist David Brandon-Jones claimed that the ancient Greeks would put young women with this mark into the temples as temple virgins, because they should not have children.

If seen with a twisted, broken, islanded health line, with small crossing lines on Luna, investigate further. If also seen on a thin, white hand, this sign is enhanced. Girls who suffer from *Dysmenorrhea* (heavy or difficult periods) may also carry this marking. Check to see if the lines are very pale when the fingers are bent back, showing iron anemia, which is common during and just after a period, at pregnancy, and again at the menopause.

If seen with a Mercury finger with no nail moon, expect blockages, and if seen with an indented, central phalange, this infers ovaries, such as PCOS (Polycystic Ovary Syndrome). The hand with this marking will tell whether it is inherited or a developed condition. The left hand is inherited, but the right hand shows a developed condition.

If a square appears in the arch, safety is inferred, and there are many gynecological problems which show in the hand. A basic knowledge of counseling, medicine and anatomy is always helpful.

Many women have changes in their fingertip markings when pregnant. These are rather similar to having your hands in water for some time, and this is again similar to adrenal changes which can show in the fingers.

I always advise women who are trying to have a baby to keep off any allopathic medication for at least six months. No nicotine, and cut down on alcohol. Recent medical studies are now saying to cut down on coffee, as the caffeine can make your heart race.

Very cold hands, especially if the fingers change color, can be Raynaud's Syndrome. So, expect odd changes in skin texture. These sufferers should always carry gloves with them.

Relationship and Family Lines

Marriage Lines

Although all the books refer to these horizontal lines on the mount of Mercury on the side to the hand as marriage lines, they are really just relationship lines.

In Vedic palmistry, these are taken more seriously than in the West, and for arranged marriages these are still consulted. The left hand traditionally infers karmic loves, and the right those entered into from choice. One can tell a lot about relationships—where and when and who—but not much information from these alone. They are only of use when consulted as a back-up.

Lines ending with a downward slant are said to be pulled by Mars. They are Mangli lines, which show that, in our relationships, we express the aggressive and powerful energy indicated by the planet Mars. Ideally, if we have this line, we should find a partner with the same downward-turning union line, so that we don't overwhelm our partner with our possessive, forceful and demanding nature.

Downward lines must channel our intensity through physical work, intellectual pursuits or spiritual techniques, such as meditation. A forked ending is said to show separation.

Children Lines

These lines are traditionally read by the small standing lines which arise from the marriage lines. Not a week goes by without someone showing me the side of their hand and asking, "How many children will I have?" I always reply that they are the amount of children you "could" have had before contraception, and people should decide themselves how many and when and if at all.

Every palmistry book covers these lines, which most modern palmists see as suggestions. I should say, when I was 9 years old, a friend at school asked me about children and I said his hand showed seven children, and over the years he did indeed have seven children. But these lines are not at all to be taken as infallible.

Introduction — Relationship and Family Lines

Tradition has it that the strong lines are boys and the weaker lines girls, but what if it's a strong girl or a weak boy? Incidentally, the Hindus, who have a rich ancient tradition in palmistry, read children on the ball of the thumb, and the Kartikeyan system uses both.

Notice if the subject is psychological type A, B or C, as this will impact on the children, and you will be able to tell of the children's characters also.

Family Ring

This should be read alongside the relationship and children lines, but the whole hand must be taken into account. This family ring separates the Venus mount from the thumb's second phalange, and is the only time in the hand when a chained formation is considered normal.

The islands in the chain foretell periods of family tension and emotional difficulty. Splits in the chain show family splits, or family arguments, and when seeing this, check the early part of the life line for matching islands or problems.

The health line is for family health indicators. In other words, check to see why problems have manifested at the time shown. A good strong ring with even islands is said to show strong family commitments and a close family. Some palmists count the number of islands for the number of possible children. When this chain is poorly formed or gapped or broken, it usually implies no close family connections.

Apollo Line

The line of Apollo, or as I like to call it—the Sun line—shows the sunshine in a person's life. It is really a success line for people who are happy with who they are and their place on the ladder of life. It is usually seen rising from the heart line under the ring finger, as this shows success in the Winter period of the life.

Most people struggle in the early years, but mortgages are usually paid off and life is easier from the age of around 50. Ideally, the Sun line should begin at the wrist and travel straight up, in an unbroken line beside the fate line. I have only seen this a few times in all the years I have been reading.

If it does show in this way, in ancient Rome they would say, "Good fortune will follow you all your life." It is certainly an auspicious omen for success. If the line starts from the hand center, then judge it from the middle years.

It can begin at times from the outside of the hand on Mars, and this shows the Martian fight for that feeling of achievement. I saw this on two Archbishops over the years, so something in their psyche must have been responsible. Always use the thumb test first on the life line, each width of the thumb. Four to the average life line will tell you at a glance whether success comes in Spring, Summer, Autumn or the Winter periods, and the type of hand will determine the path, e.g. the wide, hard hand could be military, farming or sport.

The fingers will give the correct information here, or in a soft, thin hand, acting, maybe art, acting or fashion. Remember that when people ask you, the success line does not mean money. At times it will, and at times it won't, but it will tell you that the person has adapted and succeeded in their individual environmental milieu.

Cross lines, gaps and islands are negative in meaning and can show financial loss or loss of prestige and professional standing. Two Apollo lines show two sources of income. They may have a regular job and also rent a room, or maybe do something else in the evenings.

Three lines are meant to show you may at times be down at heel financially, but there will always be something in the kitty, no matter how small, because the line is protected by a line on either side. This was a popular mark among beggars in the Medieval times. A stranger seeing three lines would be reminded of the Trinity and would usually give a coin, hence the three lines' ancient name of the trinity mark.

At times you may see the Apollo line as it reaches the finger split into three, and this traditionally is known as a "money tree," as it shows an economically safe old age. Always check the life line's end, as when you see this mark, you see a protective square at the life line's end, showing an economically and emotionally safe old age.

Introduction — The Thumb and Fingers

The Thumb and Fingers

The Thumb

The tips to the fingers are very important, but the thumb tip in particular is vital. A square thumb tip infers a practical willpower and outlook, but also gives a love of order, time and routine. The person who can recite a railway timetable by heart, or the type of person found in the military that is more concerned with a soldier's uniform than in his wellbeing.

A round or conic thumb tip will give a person idealism and an artistic mind frame, and an appreciation of beauty.

Spatulate tips show an original thinker, a restless person of action, and a person who can see new ways of doing old things, and of cutting corners and shows the inventor.

A thick end to the thumb in both width and thickness, especially when stiff, will show an obstinate person who, when the thumb is very thick through, will steamroll his way across opposition. These people can be blunt and forceful and are often seen in the military. They can have blind rages.

But if the two phalanges to the thumb are unequal, and if the top is biggest, that shows the person will act first and think afterwards. If the second or lower phalange is much bigger, this shows that they plan and think things through, but do not carry the ideas out.

Long thumbs give a strong will. Make sure the head line backs it up and is a long, unblemished, unbroken head line ending high.

Low set thumbs into the hand often show an ability with D.I.Y. and construction type jobs. They often are instrumentalists and appreciate music, whereas the higher set thumbs are not so good at reasoning, but can do repetitive work on factory lines and similar.

The thumb which leans away from the hand when open shows someone who will never dodge paying their round of drinks. The tightly held thumb can show an anxious mental framework. Short thumbs show romance, especially if seen with drooping head lines.

Long thumbs give a feel for history and the past, whereas short thumbs show romantics. Thumbs that are stiff show tenacity, economy and stubbornness. They have a kind of practical willpower and believe strongly in justice.

In the palmistry of ancient Rome, this was considered a sign of reliability and political acumen, whereas as a thumb that bends back at the center joint is seen as someone who is mentally very flexible, adaptable and malleable, but who can change their mind at a moment's notice. These people will often leave a task half finished; the kind of task can be seen in the rest of the hand. They can often be extravagant with money, and they can seem to lack self control and discipline, but they take well to changes in country and working positions.

In certain Indian and Chinese systems, the thumb takes the most important place in the hand, and the Chinese say when the winds come, the corn that stands fast and will not bend breaks in the wind, but that which learns to bend will, after the winds have gone, straighten up again. The flexible-thumbed people are resilient if changeable.

The Fingers

The Semitic people—that is, Jews and Arabs—have their own prayers said on the fingers. The five books of the *Pentateuch* have their place on the fingers: Genesis, Exodus, Leviticus, Deuteronomy and Numbers. Similarly, the Muslims see the hand of Fatima as a sacred symbol, and the five fingers show their commandments. The thumb is a reminder to keep the feast of Ramadan.

Jupiter finger: Accomplish the pilgrimage to Mecca
Saturn finger: Give alms to the poor
Apollo finger: Perform all necessary ablutions
Mercury finger: Oppose the arguments of infidels.

The sikhs have five strict prayers which are said on the fingers. They also have the rule of the five K's:

KESH — uncut hair
KANGHA — a small hair comb
KIRPAN — a small sword
KARA — a silver bracelet
KACHURA or small shorts — to be worn instead of underwear

So remember this, if you are counseling any of these religious people: Relate it to the hand shape and the palmar type. The first, or Jupiter, finger is seen as the ego finger, the finger of the father, and in its three sections, or phalanges, they represent the world of Spirit at the top, mind in the center,

Introduction — The Thumb and Fingers

and body at its base. Please remember the theory of Mind, Body and Spirit permeate all aspects of all readings, and the medical motto to "do no harm."

The reason we have the measurements of an inch, of which there are 12 to the foot, comes from ancient times when each phalange on a finger represented an inch, and there were 12 to the fingers. The foot was an approximation of the length from toe to heel. The multiplication of the 12 phalanges by the five fingers gave us the number 60, which was the measure of minutes to the hour, and like the inch on the phalange, there were 12 hours to the day.

The Jupiter Finger

Jupiter, or the first or index finger, stands for ambition and ego. The whole of the finger is related to the lungs, breasts and the basal phalange to the stomach. It should be the same length as the Apollo finger in women and fractionally shorter in men.

A short Jupiter finger may reveal a sense of low self-worth and a lack of self-esteem, ambition or purpose, and a perception of personal inadequacy in social settings. This is why they are more rebellious at school, but are better at problem-solving and are more competitive and better at sports or music.

This often infers a more masculine nature than a longer Jupiter finger. While a very long one could infer a superiority complex (see hand of Margaret Thatcher in case studies), these people know all the answers and are very confident, and yet it is seen much more with allergies such as eczema.

Short Jupiter fingers in women show sports ability and aggression and often lesbianism. The Jupiter finger as a whole, and especially the shape of the tip, will tell of how the person sees themselves. The joints will tell of smooth intuition and mental quickness, especially with short fingers. Long fingers with prominent joints show deliberation and procrastination.

Remember the three phalanges from the tip down as mental, practical and physical worlds, or Spirit, Mind and Body.

A thin, central phalange across the fingers can show early abandonment anxiety, and in the Jupiter finger alone, bonding difficulties and abandonment issues with the father figure. The Jupiter finger as a whole tells of the early father experience. A thin, basal phalange with a large gap implies unfinished business with the father, usually from the Latency period as in an unavailable father, either emotionally or physically.

A finger leaning toward Saturn can suggest a damaged ego from an overly strict father in childhood, as can a short one. Note which phalange shows the bend, as this will give more information.

A finger twisted on its axis will infer a damaged outward view from the masculine self. Straight fingers show a "straight," honest personality, and a bent, or twisted one, shows some damage in the area represented by that finger.

Saturn fingers which lean to Apollo will show intestinal difficulties, and an attitude of not wanting to be too close to people. The left hand will show inherited malfunctions, and the right hand developed or learnt ones. Those who are left-handed may wish to reverse this.

The Saturn Finger

The middle finger represents our conscience and the arena in which it functions will show primarily in the hand shape. If large, it will also show someone serious, wise and introspective, and often with an interest in the supernatural. Palmists call this finger the medius, or balance wheel, as it stands between the thumb side or conscious mind or Sun side. The subconscious hand side is called Moon, and it partakes some of both sides.

A square tip on Saturn shows a bent for legal matters. Conic, or round, which is normal here, shows artistic and diplomatic interests, and especially an ability with numbers. A spatulate tip shows restlessness, originality and inventiveness.

The long Saturn finger is a trait of loners, who prefer their own company and being alone. Often bookworms, students of life and anoraks, they reject the trappings and interactions of the outside world and see no need to socialize, being quite introverted in nature.

Short Saturn fingers—that is, when the Saturn nail phalange if seen from the back—is less than half a nail above its neighbors, and can indicate someone materially unbalanced and somewhat frivolous. They can see the funny side in anything.

Saturn fingers which lean to Apollo will show intestinal difficulties. Long, heavy Saturn fingers, with a central apex to the mount, are known as Saturnians, and often have a yellowish skin and problems with teeth. The skeleton is often prone to problems in later life, after the middle years. Prominent Saturn fingers often relate to the land, especially in a Mesomorph or wide hand. Expect an interest in agriculture, mining, farming or similar. Strangely, I have often known these folks to have a feel for and even to inherit property.

Introduction — The Thumb and Fingers

On a prominent finger with two long, lower phalanges, especially with a long thumb, you will see a love of history and the past. A Mesomorph, Earth hand will show a love of old guns and weapons and military vehicles. A thin, Ectomorph hand will show a love of indoor antique furnishings and materials.

The Apollo Finger

The Apollo is the ring finger. This finger governs the emotions, arts, beauty, and shows talent for creativity, the arts (performing and aesthetics), and tells of the early mother experience. Apollo relates to the Sun, and a strong finger with an unbroken Apollo line underneath will show much sunshine in the life.

This finger is the most likely to be spatulate in shape, and—like the Jupiter finger—should reach to almost halfway up the Saturn nail phalange. A long ring finger signifies outstanding creativity, talents and usually excellent judgment and taste. But an emotional infrastructure out of balance. These people are usually also flashy and flamboyant and can be show-offs and lovers of fashionable clothes, as they are very concerned with "appearance."

This finger, long, will tell of the actor with an Air or Fire hand, or the sportsman in the more physical types such as Mesomorph. Very long Apollo fingers can be risk takers and gamblers, either on the race track, stock market or with life itself. These people believe in fate and the luck of the gods, and that they are favored people. This trait is increased if seen with a flexible thumb and open head and life lines.

It is very unusual to see a short Apollo finger, although they may appear short because of a tall Jupiter. Remember, the Jupiter should be the same height and width. The Apollo Finger, which really means Sun, rules the appendix, eyesight, blood and heart, so on seeing any anomalies in the three phalanges, check the whole hand for these health conditions.

The Mercury Finger

Just as Mercury is the smallest planet, so the Mercury finger is the smallest on the hand.

Mercury was the god of communication of healing and cleverness. It tells of tactfulness and power of expression. The ideal Mercury finger is a straight one that reaches at least to the top crease of the next or Apollo finger.

This gives a good communicative side to the nature. Teachers, doctors and managers are seen here.

If longer, it can be a sign of a salesman, verbalist or negotiator. Tricky lawyers, medics and politicians will carry this marking, and if Mercury is twisted, doubly so. If shorter than the crease, it will show people who hold back verbally, as these are good at keeping secrets. If very short, expect relationship problems. These people are often misunderstood and are often clumsy in company, as they are not quick with a reply.

The Mercury finger is often slightly low set into the hand, but when it's very low in the hand, this will alter somewhat the length of the finger, making it appear short. Remember the Golden Rule, never to go by one sign alone, but look at the whole hand.

Check that the three phalanges are the same thickness, length and size. Any differences must be related to the three worlds of palmistry—body near the hand, mind in the center, and spirit at the tip. The shape of the tips tell of the expression of the spirit. Square fingers will need a practical, everyday religion, and the spatulate a flexible dogma type religion. The pointed tips go for the spiritual, not religious, in their need for internal expression.

Fingers that twist on their axis show some dishonesty, first with themselves, secondly with others. This you see best from the hand backs. Compare the nails. The nail is the window into the finger, and that window should be a clear, pink, shiny, smooth nail with a regular-sized white moon or Lunalae on each finger base.

Fingers which lean toward Apollo show care for others, as if they have given over part of themselves to others. This is also seen with those whose entry to the world was difficult for the mother's health. In fact, this is often why the hand shows the desire to heal; it's from this same time.

Often you will see a Mercury leaning away from the other fingers. This shows a person needing their space and often not close at this point to the primary loved person in the life.

Each finger will have a line under it, which reaches up across the mount to the finger base. If the mount is large, with a centrally placed fingerprint apex, this will enhance the power to the finger. The exception is the Jupiter finger, which does not have a vertical line underneath, but often a horizontal crescent or straight line diagonally running down toward the thumb. Any large or odd knuckle will tell from that sector—be it spirit, mind or body—of a blockage. The 12 astrological signs which rule the fingers (phalanges) can give more information.

Introduction — The Thumb and Fingers

The Knuckles

Large knuckles are when you have difficulty getting finger rings down the finger. These are slow thinkers, philosophers, etc.—those who ponder the deeper aspects of life. Expect to see this with engineers in a Mesomorph hand and strategists and planners with an intellectual hand.

The knuckles as seen from the back should appear as knots in wood. If they appear as eyes on the finger, this is common among psychics and mystics, who usually have smooth fingers. An odd-shaped knuckle to the rest will mean a close examination of that finger, and will usually tell of some difference to the rest. Remember, the knots or knuckles are an impediment to the flow of energy to that finger.

The Hawthorne Effect

The Hawthorne effect is a term referring to the tendency of some people to work harder and perform better when they are participants in an experiment. Individuals may change their behavior, due to the attention they are receiving from researchers rather than because of any manipulation of independent variables.

This effect was first described in the 1950s by researcher Henry A. Landsberger, during his analysis of experiments conducted pre WWII at the Hawthorne Works electric company, which had commissioned research to determine the relationship between productivity and work environment. The focus of the original studies was to determine what increasing or decreasing the amounts of light would have on workers. This term was later extended by psychologists to cover occasions when the subject came up with the answers they thought the analyst required. Some recent psychologists dismiss palm reading, or Chirology, as part of the Hawthorne Effect.

But psychologists Carl Jung, Julius Spier, Charlotte Wolf, Hans Eysenck, Henri Rey and Aaron Beck have all expressed an interest in, or have studied, palmistry. No organ is as close to the human brain as the hand.

Handshakes

The International Institute for Applied Systems Analysis researched more than 50 other studies from around the world for their article in the journal *Plos One*. They claim a handshake can reveal a lot about a person. The research says the strength of someone's grip may reveal how fast they're aging, their education level, and even their future health. They found that people with more education at age 69 tended to grip just as strongly as less educated people at age 65, suggesting the latter were aging about four years faster. "According to handgrip strength, people with high education ... feel several years younger compared to people with lower education," says study co-author Sergei Scherbov.

Another study the authors reviewed was done on more than a million Swedish adolescent males, whose handgrip strength was measured as part of an exam for military service. The human body is increasingly recognized as

Introduction — The Hawthorne Effect

a biometric source of information for a wide spectrum of issues, including security, psychopathology, personality and health. Earlier, we reported that job interviews might be replaced by brain scans within five years, and denoted this news as a modern technological incarnation of occult palm reading.

Now it turns out that palm reading has been scientifically validated again, in a new incarnation—and it's in the ratio of your fingers.

John T. Manning, emeritus professor in psychology of the University of Central Lancashire and the University of Liverpool, has developed a new theory about how finger length relates to human biology and behavior. In the BBC series *Secret of The Sexes,* Manning successfully uses finger length ratio as a predictor for athletic ability; he does not go as far as established palmists' tradition, but says a significant part of his theory is focused on the so-called "digit ratio," which concerns the full length ratio of only two fingers: index finger (2D) vs. ring finger (4D), the Jupiter and the Apollo fingers. In women, the length of both fingers is usually about equal (2D:4D' digit ratio = 1.00), while in men the ring finger is usually slightly longer (digit ratio = 0.98): a tiny sex difference, and this is due to factors when the baby is in the womb, such as the estrogen/testosterone balance.

In boys, "during fetal development, there's a surge in testosterone in the middle of the second trimester that seems to influence future health and behavior," says Pete Hurd, a neuroscientist at the University of Alberta. One easy-to-spot result of this flood of testosterone is a ring finger that's significantly longer than the index finger.

Scientists are not at the point where they can factor in finger length to arrive at a diagnosis like palmists, but they've gathered evidence that shows how this prenatal hormone imbalance can affect a person for life, from increasing or decreasing your risk of certain diseases, to predicting how easily you get lost or lose your temper.

Finger Length and Sociability

The researchers on brain scans showed they can predict tendencies towards autism, which is thought to be related to "hypermasculinity" of the brains. The same is true for the "digit ratio." Multiple international studies have revealed that people with autism usually have typical male-like finger length ratios (2D:4D < 0). No mention is made here of the recognizable anomalies in the palmar lines or of Dysplastic hand shapes. Studies done at the Johns Hopkins University on successful prosthetic hand operations have inadvertently proved much of old palmistry teachings.

So why the reluctance from academics to recognize palmistry? The boffins themselves say fakes, cheats, cold readers and gypsies have long muddied the waters, and psychologists have never forgotten how they were all fooled with the Clever Hans hoax. Clever Hans was a German horse who could do arithmetic: addition, subtraction, multiplication, etc., and was a total sensation who threatened to re-write the whole of psychology from top to bottom. Hans would clop his foot on the ground to show the correct number of often complicated sums. Its owner admitted he would, while holding his hand around the horse's head, gently touch him for each clop on the ground to accomplish the sum.

Fingernails
A Neglected Area of Palmistry

There are 27 bones in the human hand, and the complex mechanical functions it performs cannot be bettered artificially. The amazing array of actions, from delicate embroidery to the smashing of blocks of concrete, demonstrate how wonderful is the human hand.

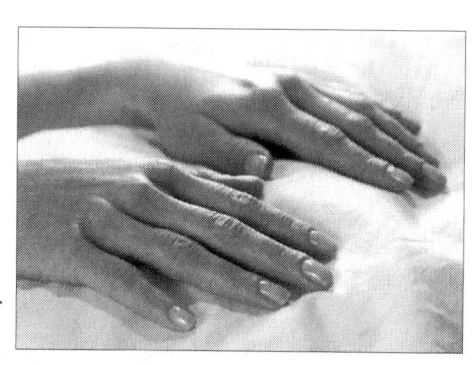

The 1883 International Frankfort Agreement divided man into a large array of skull types, which they said showed the racial ancestral type. Ethnologists are those who study racial characteristics and their bones, and have based other material on this information.

Palmists mostly use the four hand types with corresponding bone structure of the main root race system. These include Caucasian, Negroid, Mongolian and Australoids, and although the past 70 years have seen much mixing of racial types, these four broadly conform to the modern Earth, Air, Fire and Water system of palmistry.

Each type can be recognized by its shape and bone structural typology, and along with this, will always be seen as a certain shape of nail. For example, the Elementary palm, now called the Earth hand, will have thick, strong, short nails, while the slim, psychic, or Air hand, will have a graceful long nail.

The study of fingernails is a vital aspect of palmistry, and has three main sections: the nail shape, the fingertip size and shape, the fingerprint on the fingertip, and how they all relate to each other. The rounded tip relates to Air, the Square tip to Earth, the Spatulate tip to Fire, and the Pointed tip to Water.

The celebrated 19th century palmist Cheiro was one of the first to introduce in his books nail lore that is still valid today in terms of health and temperament diagnosis for the Western schools of palmistry. But the Chinese system goes much deeper and sections the nail into quadrants, the way Westerners do with the whole hand.

Both Tibetan and Chinese palmistry are difficult for Westerners, as they tie in with acupuncture and meridians, but are very harmonious with homeopathy, Hindu palmistry with Ayurvedic medicine, the Garuda Purana dealing with nails.

I studied Eastern palmistry for some years, and these ancient systems have much to teach us in the West.

Modern medicine recognizes some conditions by nail diagnosis, and the Hippocratic nail is one such condition. I have given talks to doctors some 35 years ago on health markers in the hands and nails, but progress with mainstream medicine is slow. Many hospitals will ask women to take off nail varnish before coming in for an operation, as an after examination can be enlightening as to recovery times. Color is an important factor. Blueish nails are usually cold to the touch and show circulatory, heart or lung conditions. Red can be cardiovascular, and a bright red can accompany a condition called "liver palms." White nails are often seen, and everything from alcoholism to severe anemia are indicated.

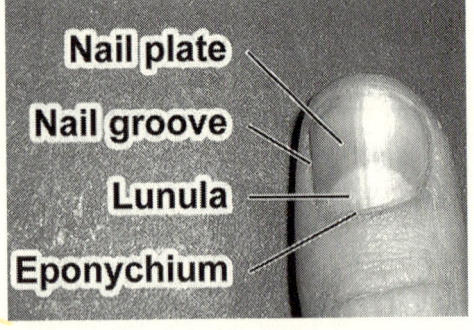

enwiki

Candida is very common, but will normally be accompanied by Paronychia, which is inflamed sides to the nail. There is also something called "yellow nail syndrome," which we see in lymphatic abnormalities, such as intestinal or thoracic lymphangiectasia, but this color is also seen with people who drink a lot of beta-carotene.

But always, confirmation in the other palmar sectors must be sought. It's possible to diplomatically venture possibilities in these areas, but please remember, a proper health diagnosis is the realm of the doctor. The fact that people come to alternative therapists is because allopathic doctors have lost their way and usually don't have this knowledge.

Nails with vertical lines will tell of the underlying strength of health being run down. Smokers always have these lines, and if the nails break easy as well, it can relate to osteoarthritic and similar ailments. It's often seen in

Introduction — Fingernails, A Neglected Area of Palmistry

elderly people, but it really means you have been burning the candle at both ends. The worst case I ever saw was on a chain-smoking, hard-drinking pop star aged just 28.

If you look at your own nails, they should be shiny and smooth with a good eponychium at the base. This cuticle should lay in front of a perfectly shaped white moon. Any nail without a nail moon, or an unusually shaped moon, will tell of the possibility of a health problem. Each nail and finger is represented by a planet and an organ, among much else.

Many nails have white flecks, and so-called experts have argued over these for years. Some old doctors' magazines said they are a calcium or magnesium deficiency, while some say iron, and yet others say they are knocks to the nails. The truth is probably all of the above and it's called *Leukonychia striata* in medicine.

There is a wonderful old rhyme from the palmistry of the Middle Ages, which I have used since a young boy. The rhyme runs: "a present, a friend, a foe, a beau, a journey to go," and this tells the meanings of white flecks from the thumb to the little fingernail.

In WWI, a doctor called Dr. Beau noticed that traumatized soldiers would have a deep diagonal line running across the nail, and he could date the trauma from the position it lay across the nail, as it takes five to six months to grow out. But this deep groove that crosses the nail can also be seen where an illness has left its mark, and even a severe period can be marked in this way.

One sometimes sees red streaks across the nail bed, and this shows heart valve infection. But this will always be confirmed in the heart line, and *Leukonychia striata*, or white streaks on the nails.

Mild arsenic poisoning is often recognized in the fingernail, and the reason is that so many people eat a lot of mass-farmed chicken, and because these chickens live their lives crammed against other chickens, if one gets a bug or parasite, they all get it, so they have arsenic added to the food in sufficient quantities, so that when a parasite bites the chicken, it dies off.

Now, arsenic is an accumulative poison, which means it builds up in the system, and one of the typical signs of arsenic poisoning is deeply striated nails the whole way down, and the nail colour is darker than it should be. This can be seen with other conditions, but not the darkness, so when I see nails like this, I usually ask, "How much factory farmed chicken do you eat?"

Rings on the Fingers

The subconscious drive to wear a ring on any finger is a neglected aspect of palmistry. This was a very popular way in the Middle Ages to make statements about your social standing, ambitions, and whether you were betrothed or not. This aspect in palmistry is known as "Sphragistics," a word of Greek origin which the dictionary tells us "is a method of studying seals, signs and signet rings, and their meanings."

The ancient Greeks, who gave the world philosophy—meaning a love of wisdom—also gave us psychology, or literally a study of the soul. A large part of palmar psychology is the study of gestures and finger rings applied to the individual's psychological framework.

Many people assume it's just about the palmar lines; *far from it*. Well, what do the finger rings mean? People, if asked, will rationalize and say, "It's the only finger the ring will fit," but then confess they have several rings at home that would fit other fingers.

The National Gallery is a great place to look for huge jewels on certain fingers. Britain's King Henry VIII is often pictured with a large precious stone on his thumb. A fashion for thumb rings is coming back.

Carl Jung based his theories on personality on his planetary studies. Hans Eysenck, the greatest psychologist of his generation, spoke out in favor on the theory of astrological influence. The book on his life, *Rebel With a Cause* (1990), is still a landmark book today. The planets play a big part in our lives and each finger is named after one or more planets by the ancients.

The Moon

Silver is the metal of the Moon. Silver's atomic number is 47, which is one of the Moon's numbers, as 47 added together in traditional

Introduction — Rings on the Fingers

numerology makes 11, which reduces to 2, the Moon's primary number. The Moon also represents the feminine aspect, and Moon worshippers try to connect with their femininity.

The thumb represents the phallus in some psychology schools. Some women will put the silver ring on the thumb to show they have feminized, subdued and transmuted the woman's need for phallus, and in some circles, women will wear a silver ring on the thumb to signal to other women of their sexual availability.

Jupiter

The first, or Jupiter finger represents the ego. A ring on this finger will tell of a need for the wearer to be in charge in some way. On the left or subjective hand, this need is at home or in some home project, but the right hand will always indicate the control issues are at work or exterior aspects of life. Medieval palmists would call this the finger of ambition, and there is much truth in this. Politicians and priests often wear a ring on this finger, as it is the finger we hold up to admonish or show our power and authority.

Traditionally, the yellow sapphire should be worn on the finger for those whose birthdays fall under the sign of Jupiter or Sagittarius.

Saturn

The second is the finger of Saturn, the second largest of our planets. The finger stands between the conscious and unconscious sides to the hand. This finger relates to discipline, money and detail.

At one time, this finger was related to the study of religion, but today it is connected with science, math, logic and the building skills. Both Carl Jung and Hans Eysenck held these Saturnine concepts to be true. Any ring on the Saturn finger should contain lead, Saturn's metal, and be bought or made on Saturn's day, *Saturday*, and a ring worn here can show some insecurity. The other signs will determine just what.

The Sun or Apollo

Apollo was originally a Sun god and the father of Aesculapius, the founder of modern medicine. The Apollo finger is the natural finger to place a wedding ring.

Medicine and healing are also associated with this finger. The ancient apothecaries would place a gold ring on this finger while stirring medicines.

Recent university studies by Professor John Manning have shown that this finger is influenced in the womb by estrogen. The ancients believed this finger to be directly allied to the heart and the affections, and it can show painful maternal rejection influences and early conflict with the mother, especially early in life.

Mercury

Rings worn on the Mercury finger tell of a primary need in the area of communication. Many people not in contact with their sexuality wear Mercury rings. Actors and sensitive individuals are particularly prone to wear rings here.

Business men whose sexual energy is directed towards money-making will often wear a ring here. Many Renaissance pictures show women as having Mercury fingers standing crookedly well away from the hand, since—in those days—the church ruled even in the bedroom. Many women of that era were desperately sexually undernourished.

If you look at your own hands, the gaps between the fingers and the three finger sections will all tell their unique story, which—added to the rings and the astrological sign and psychological type—can give much information into your psychological makeup.

Fortune Telling

Modern palmistry has almost lost the art of seeing ahead. Many of those who come to a palmist seek guidance on issues in the future. This usually may have to do with health, economics or romance. Sometimes we can see these aspects and sometimes not.

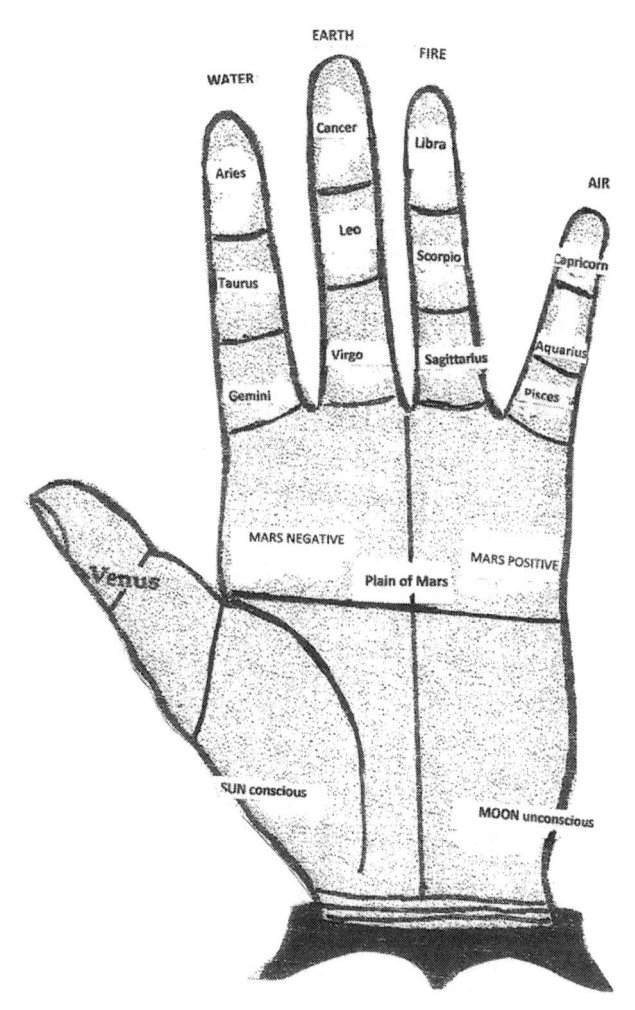

50 Case Studies in Modern Palmistry

Astrologers work a lot with futures, but palmists—including myself—only do it when pressed for answers.

The easiest ways, as I explained in detail in the first book written in the early '70s and on which this is based, is by gently squeezing the hand either side of each line to be examined. By using this method, you will see the route the line will take in the future. Good lighting is essential for this.

The second is shown in the graph on page 51. Each segment of the fingers is governed by a Zodiac sign. In India these signs are different, in their Vedic system, to ours here in the West. But we start with Aries, the Ram, at the tip of the Jupiter finger. This begins with the Spring Equinox. The Saturn finger shows the Summer Solstice, Apollo the Autumn Equinox, and the Mercury finger the Winter Solstice. So we have the four seasons shown in the fingers.

For anyone wishing to look deeper into this, the palmist Rodney Davies, in his excellent book *Fortune Telling by Palmistry,* has a whole chapter on this topic.

Remember, straight lines down each individual finger phalange goes with the energy flow, and cross bars impede it. So, by checking the small lines on the fingers, which come and go with some frequency during the year, you gain some insight into possible changes.

The shape of the fingertip can be important here. Pointed tips give psychic impulses and impressions. Conic, or round, shows artistic, friendly and emotional impulses. Square give practical, logical reactions that—like precision and order—and the splayed, or spatulate, gives a restless creativity, inventive and changeable.

The small mounds at the finger bases, called Mounts, are particularly important. If they are high and firm and with a central fingerprint apex, this is considered an auspicious omen.

The ancient wisdom is that the straight lines with a good mount mean the energy flow is positive and uplifting. Any fingers which are stunted, malformed, bent and especially twisted on its axis will negate from any positivity.

The best way to check the fingers—and remember, straight fingers show straight qualities in that finger and what it represents—is to look from the finger backs at the finger's faces. The face of the finger is the nail, and this should look straight forward. Any twisting on its axis should be looked at, whether the twist is in the spirit, mind or body sectors; this will tell of some event, aspect or opinion which is not what it should be.

If the lines separating the finger phalanges have islands, and on

Introduction — Fortune Telling

occasion these are seen in the lower joints, see these as blockages to the regular energy flow. An island in the central thumb joint is known in ancient Hindu texts as the mark of Ganesh, the Elephant god, and in the East is seen as a great marking, as this usually goes with an affinity to, or a spiritual love of, animals.

The large cross in the hand, in the illustration, separates the heavy mounts at the palmar base as being the instinctual impulses. Higher up we have the qualities of heart and head, with the thumb side showing the conscious impulses and the Mercury and heel of the hand showing the ancestral images and unconscious motivations.

50 Case Studies in Modern Palmistry

Part I

Case Histories

1

Nicotine Poisoning

The British government, in two world wars, gave the servicemen free cigarettes, the idea being that after the war, the men would continue with the habit. Because the taxation revenue from smokers was so vast, the government spokesmen would continually repeat the mantra, "There is no proven link between smoking and lung cancer."

The British Health Service believed that the revenue paid by a smoker during his lifetime would more than pay for any hospital stays at the end of their lives, but a change came in with the secret government paper, NHS E3105, revealing that mass immigration showed incoming smokers who had never paid the heavy British tobacco taxes were now availing themselves of all hospital facilities. So, a sharp about-turn by government spokesmen then insisted that all cigarette packs carry health warnings, and an admission was then made that cigarettes *do* cause severe health damage.

In the USA, Obama claimed the steep cigarette taxes would go toward sick children, including those with Fetal Nicotine Syndrome (FNS), but no proof of this help has ever been seen.

Tobacco companies jumped on the USA Women's Lib bandwagon and paid women celebrities to smoke on TV, and even paid women protest marchers to be seen with cigarettes, and so smoking took off with women as never before.

Nicotine is known to be absorbed by the mother and this then crosses the placenta into the baby's bloodstream. A 1985 study published in the journal *Developmental Pharmacology and Therapeutics* measured the levels of nicotine and its main metabolite, cotinine, in amniotic fluid and fetal plasma, and discovered that the fetus is actually exposed to higher nicotine concentrations than the smoking mother.

In the placenta and the fetus, nicotine damages placental tissues and reduces blood flow, which deprives the fetus of nutrients and oxygen. In more severe cases of deprivation, the fetus can die. Death rates are also higher after birth when the mother smokes.

A 2006 study published in *National Vital Statistics Reports* indicated

Nicotine Poisoning

that the mortality rate for infants of smokers was 71 percent higher than for infants of nonsmokers (11.25 percent versus 6.65 percent).

Tobacco smoke contains more than 4,000 different chemicals, and at least 50 are known to be carcinogens (causing cancer in humans) and many are poisonous.

Cigarettes are one of few products which can be sold legally which can harm and can even kill you.

There are ongoing lawsuits in the USA which aim to hold tobacco companies responsible for the effects of smoking on the health of long-term smokers and their offspring.

The palm print shown is perhaps the most extreme taken at a study of 250 babies born to women nicotine addicts at London's Whipps Cross Hospital in the early 1970s. The monitoring went on every five years subsequently to see what illnesses developed. SIDs, or Sudden Death

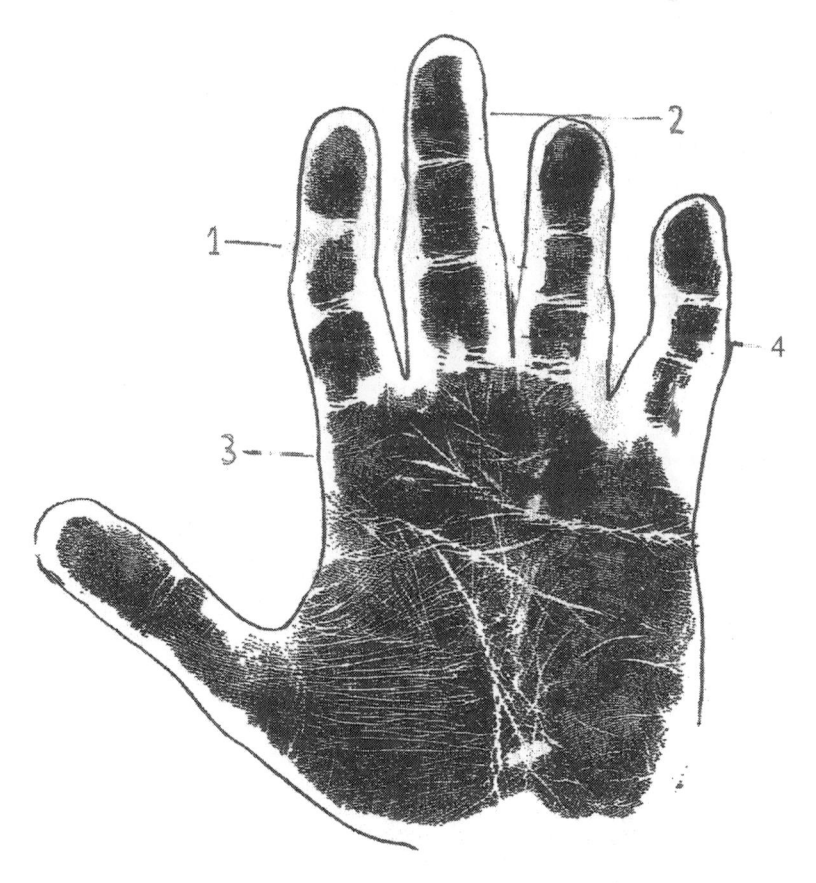

Syndrome, is the most dramatic result, but also heart and lung problems, miscarriage and much smaller babies with short fingers or *Brachydactyly* are more common. The hand print was from a woman much smaller than the norm.

(1) Bent in Index or Jupiter finger typical of FNS

(2) Very short Apollo or third finger also typical.

(3) Expect uneven ragged and interrupted heart line inferring an atrial septal defect (ASD) common in FNS cases.

(4) Bent in Mercury finger; also notice the ragged life line around the thumb with its many breaks, showing impaired immune function.

2 Destiny vs. Free Will

One of the most common emails I get is asking how to tell if an event was pre-determined to happen, or was just free will.

Firstly, although I want to cover the fate or destiny line, which in India is called the luck line, and in Tibetan palmistry the *Nang* or inner line, in reality, the whole hand will tell the destiny, not just the line of destiny, which runs from the hand base up towards the middle or Saturn finger, called the Finger of Fate.

The correct dating of events on the destiny line is complex. It runs from hand base toward the Saturn finger, opposite to the life line, which runs down the hand, and dating should be done together.

If you look at your own hands, the lines will have variations between the two, as indeed they are ruled by different sides to the brain, which crosses over and rules the other side of the body, including the hands.

Karma is a Sanskrit term meaning actions, works or deeds, and its causes and effects. Both Tibetan and Chinese palmistry put particular emphasis on aspects of karma in the hand and the horoscope. Incidentally, this is basically the same information being accessed from different sources.

The concept of rebirth is common in Eastern palmistry schools, and although in the West many followers of the Christian palmistry school do not accept the karma concept, we do have the word *fate*, which traditionally means a power or force which is unavoidable and inevitable. Islamic palmistry has the word "Gadar," which means the will of Allah, and suggests there is a fixed order of events in our lives.

My studies show that we all do have certain milestones to cover, and these can be told accurately from the hand, but how we deal with these milestones, and what we do between them, is largely free will, and on these decisions future karma is built.

The ancient Greeks gave us much of the learning, but sadly the destruction of the huge libraries at Alexandria was to hide this knowledge from the masses. We are still struggling to get back that knowledge on philosophy, palmistry, medicine and astrology.

50 Case Studies in Modern Palmistry

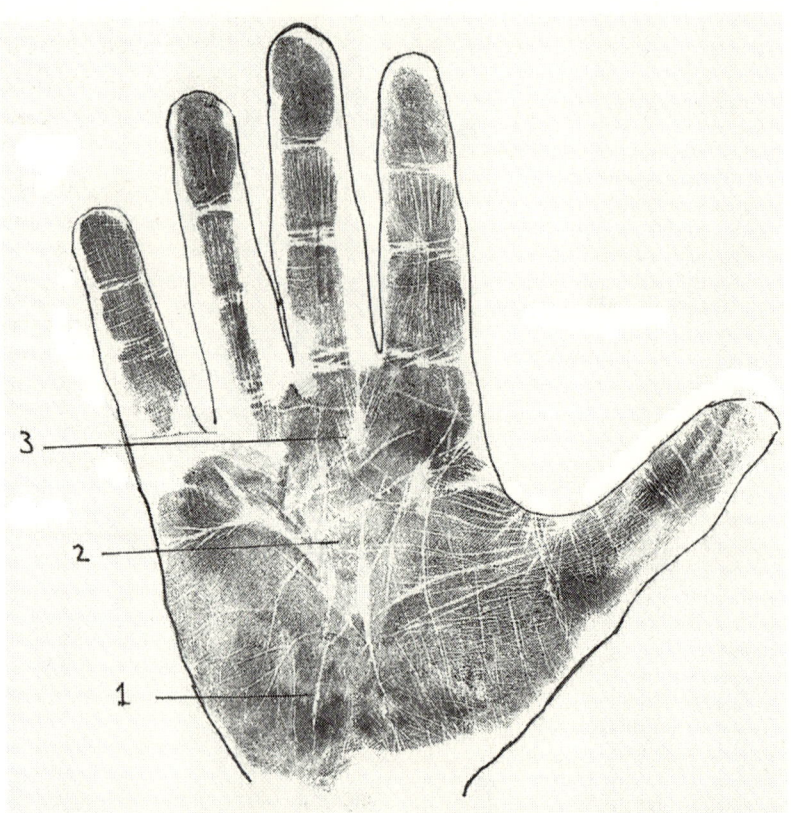

The word *Moirai* is the ancient Greek word for Fate, while Destiny is used with regard to the finality of events as they have worked themselves out, and to that same sense of "destination," projected into the future to become the flow of events as they will work themselves out.

I taught the complex methods for determining whether an event or person in someone's life is pre-destined or happenstance across London in palmistry talks in the 1970s. That is, to check closely the dates in the hand and ally them to the event.

Often when we meet someone, we feel we have connected at a deep level and feel we knew them before. The mechanics of palmistry often show the star signs of those who come into our lives. I would describe being with someone like this as feeling as comfortable as putting on an old pair of slippers.

The great Indian teacher, Jiddu Krishnamurti, said, *"In oneself lies the whole world, and if you know how to look and learn, the door is there and the key is in your hands."*

Destiny vs. Free Will

The hand print shown has at No. 1 an early start to the fate line, which in Indo/Pak palmistry infers past-life baggage. As this line starts from Luna, these people are often helped by the opposite sex, and you often see them as public favorites. This marking can suggest an ability with artistic or creative subjects.

(2) The fate line here is joined by a large protective square. This tells us at this time period the subject is kept safely within a box. This can mean emotionally, financially or similar. Other signs will give more detail.

(3) We have under the Saturn finger the part of the fate line which is common to most people, and that is the small line up the Saturn mount. Always check for an Apollo line at this same period as it enhances the feeling of success in the 60s age group. This is where most people have some degree of stability and security in their lives.

Golden rules are never go by one sign alone, and always use diplomacy and kindness if reading for others.

3 Christian Palmistry

The majority of questions that get sent to me usually run something like this ... "I have a line near my thumb that runs right across. What does it mean?"

Please understand, you cannot take any one line in isolation and read accurate data from it. You have to consider the whole hand category, psychological type and zodiac sign for total results, and although I do try to keep the articles simple, if you look at hands, bear in mind the old medical motto only to diagnose by "sign and symptom" and not just by one line alone.

The color, shape, density and depth will all play a part, and remember to read the line from the thickest end out, as the thickest part is always where the energy is concentrated to begin its travel.

I always promise to answer every email, including the ones that tell me that the devil will get me, and I am going to go to hell. How Christians and religionists arrive at this is beyond me, because in the Medieval monasteries, Astrology, Numerology and Palmistry were called the "three sisters" and were taught as learned sciences. Biblical numerology is still practiced by theologians, but since Nicolai Copernicus (1473-1543) said the sun was the centre of the solar system and not the earth, Astrology and Palmistry have been generally frowned upon. The theory of Heliocentrism, or that the sun was the center of the solar system, was not a popular one with the Vatican of the time.

The illustration is taken from the 12th century and shows the hand in its religious aspects.

Figure (1) shows the three sections to the thumb, and was applied as the trinity finger, the three persons in one God, from Matthew 28-16.

Figure (2) shows the 12 sections to the fingers, between what medical anatomists call the interphalangeal joints, which were said to represent the 12 apostles. Those monks, who spent many hours in prayer, would hold the thumb against the finger phalange as they prayed to each apostle in turn, for the sick, for a good harvest, or for good fortune, until all 12 prayers had been completed.

The illustration shows the 12 zodiac signs, as each apostle represented

Christian Palmistry

a sign, which were granted from God to be observed in the heavens, and no one today doubts that the three wise men who followed the star were actually astrologers; incidentally, astrologers claim that Christ was born in 6 BC and not on December 25.

Early Catholicism saw the thumb as representing the Godhead, the index (or Jupiter finger) the Holy Ghost, and the middle (or Saturn finger) the Christ, and a priest will still today bless with these three fingers uppermost.

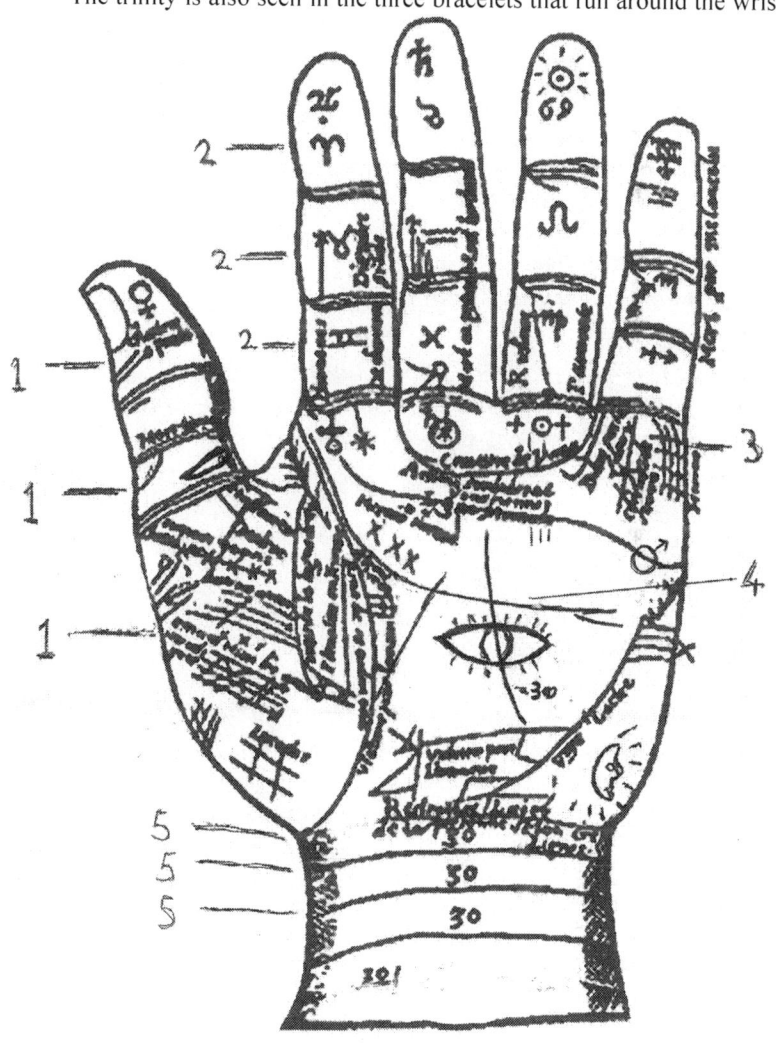

The trinity is also seen in the three bracelets that run around the wrist (seen at Figure 5). These were said to be health, wealth and happiness, and the three gifts from the blessed Trinity, which—if you were very lucky—would each confer a 30-year span. Today palmists generally work on 25 years.

Palmistry is one of those arts that is often condemned by those who know nothing about it. The patron saint of palmistry and astrology, St. Hugh, was above all else a healer and a caregiver for the sick.

Figure (3) is the main mark for healers, when seen under the Mercury finger, and is also a tri-gram CHI'EN, representing the creative power seen in the i Ching.

Remember, the international torch symbol for healers, the "Wand of Aesculapius," is the sign for Mercury, the messenger of the gods, and Mercury's star sign, Gemini, is the sign for palmists as Gemini covers the hands.

Hippocrates (born 460 BC) said, "*A physician without a knowledge of astrology has no right to call himself a physician,*" and palmistry is above all else a healing art.

Over many years, I used to read and study all the medical journals until eventually it dawned on me that these were sent for free to all the doctors, because they were advertising allopathic drug cartel pharma-chemicals, not real healing modalities. The pharmaceutical industry is worth billions, so much so that they dictate policy to governments, and they did not like the trend away from chemical tablets, so originated several studies which condemned herbal and natural products.

"He who pays the piper calls the tune" runs the saying and, of course, drug company-sponsored surveys are very damning, hence the movement to ban anything not produced by the big pharma cartels themselves.

Stage two is interesting as they have aligned with two big Christian churches to ban what are called in preliminary papers unwholesome and devilish psychic readings and healings. So, while I agree there are many scammers out there, to lump it all together and ban it seems very wrong and anti-democratic to me and eliminates free choice.

In fact, the words of the Master were quite clear in Luke 17-21: "*The kingdom of God is found within you,*" not in churches. Dogmatic, hellfire preachers who tell us you can only use "this" kind of medicine or "that," and you can't have any kind of reading or spiritual healing or counseling, just can't be right.

Gandhi said, "*God has no religion,*" so people who claim God says this or that, or wants this war or that, or tells other people what is a right or a wrong thing to believe are out of focus with the democratic spirituality we should all have. God has no favorites, there are no chosen people, no religious supremacists, because for someone to get preference, someone else would have to be penalized.

Do you think God would do this? Because I don't. Remember, there are no special "get out of jail free" cards, and you can't buy your way into the next life.

Palmistry was mentioned particularly by God's prophets Job and Isaiah, so it is the Lord's invention, not the devil's.

Strict Jews have what is called the Hand of Miriam, and the five fingers represent the five books of the Torah, and remind us to use all five senses when we pray to God. Similarly, we have the Hand of Fatima, Muhammad's daughter, and the five fingers are sacred to Muslims as they represent the five persons in the prophet's family. To them, this is a very holy sign, but of greater interest is the cross in the palm center (4), which covers the minor chakras in the palm centers.

This was supposed to represent the place where Christ was nailed to the cross, but later historians have said the nails went through the wrist. A cross seen in this part of the hand over the chakra is known as a psychic cross and suggests psychic ability or second sight. Old manuscripts often depict an eye in the hand center, on the chakra or plain of Mars.

The seven religious ceremonies from baptism to the last rites should have been more aligned to the seven chakras, rather than to dull them, but all religions function on control, and so much has been intentionally suppressed. The philosopher David Hume said, *"In all ages priests have been the enemies of liberty."*

Such stories as Adam and Eve are meant to be allegorical tales, but millions believe this literally, that Eve tempted Adam with an apple, and when Adam took a bite, it lodged in his throat and we all today have an Adam's apple, to remind us not to be tempted by women.

In the first translations, the word *apple* is interchangeable with *breast*, so we begin to see the sexual aspects. But if Eve was given to man as an equal and a companion, why has every religion put women into a poor second?

The *Bhagavad Gita*, the Hindu holy book, has many mentions of hands, but tells us the sign of the hand is protective in all its forms.

Buddhism contains a lot of palmistic lore, which I will cover when we look at the hand of the Dalai Lama in an upcoming chapter.

Remember, scripture tells us that the hand is God's gift to mankind, and it is with our hands that we create all things of value, from food for the family, to artworks for pleasure, and it is only when we injure a hand that we remember how reliant we are on this anatomical part.

The hand contains all the planets from when we were born, just as in the horoscope. In fact, I often read horoscopes from the hand. The Creator in his wisdom has left us many signs, and in the Chaldean version of the Bible, which many experts say is the oldest, we see it says at Job 37-7 that "God has placed signs and seals in the hands of men that all may know their works."

We may give thanks to our God in different ways, but never judge or look down on another man's faith, and if he wants to worship his God through the trees of the earth, the stars in the sky, or the signs in nature, so be it.

Remember the words of Krishnamurti: *"Truth is a pathless land, it cannot be approached by any path whatsoever, by any religion or by any sect."*

4

Glastonbury Hand

The Glastonbury Festival was a great success this year, and as the Festival palmist/counselor, I was struck by the similarity of the problems of many of those who consulted me.

The Festival is run for charities, and healers give their time for small donations. Many of those who attend save their money all year to experience the Festival and see the best pop groups around.

Among the attendees was a large contingent of American youngsters. With these very difficult times, the lack of opportunities and employment has particularly hit the young, and many are feeling disillusioned, fearful, hopeless and angry. An increasing amount of emotional burnout, stress, fatigue, weight issues, suicidal thoughts and substance dependence are now increasingly seen by counselors.

Aaron Beck, M.D., on a previous visit to Glastonbury, told me, "Anxiety may be distinguished from fear in that the former is an emotional process, while fear is a cognitive one. Fear involves the intellectual appraisal of a threatening stimulus. Anxiety involves the emotional response to that appraisal."

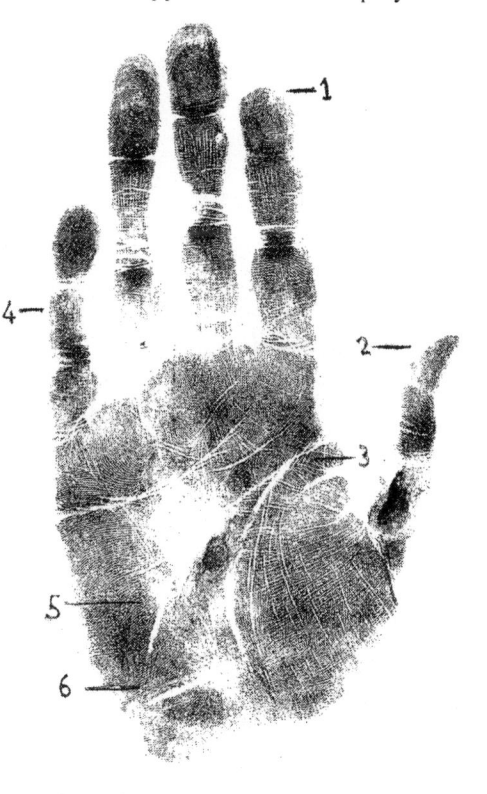

50 Case Studies in Modern Palmistry

This hand print exemplifies all that I saw in many hands in the one hand. Let's look closely and see what it can tell us.

(1) A short index or Jupiter finger always goes with low self-esteem. This person's confidence has been badly hit and his fear failure can paralyze him from continuing to try; the negativity becomes a personal issue and where self-blame becomes a habit, low self-confidence makes us vulnerable.

(2) The thin end to the thumb tip, known as a "nervous thumb" among experts, shows depleted energy levels we associate with junk food, and is usually seen with (3), which shows sensitivity and excess caution.

In his studies of palmistry, Carl Jung, the great psychologist, called this "The Jailer," as this mark is seen with those who are anxious, apprehensive and procrastinate far too much. They are the thinkers and planners who never carry out their plans. In Tibetan palmistry, it's called the sign of the Tortoise, as these people are slow and methodical. In India, it's known as "the blessing of Shiva," the caution of the Tortoise which prevents jumping in with instinctive and hasty actions.

(4) The short and curved finger of Mercury, the smallest finger, if not reaching the line marking the top phalange on the next or Apollo finger shows communication difficulties. A whole raft of things are revealed by this sign but it especially shows that when things get bottled up they often explode. This has its genesis in the early bonding process. If this finger is very small or low set, expect the loner, one who cannot confide or share with others.

(5) The head line drops down at the end, showing a predisposition to unworldly thoughts and depression. In the hand prints I took at the London Psychiatric Hospital for a study in the late '70s, this feature occurred frequently, as it does today with so many of our young students.

(6) This is an allergy line and has many names. When I see this, I warn of the dangers of drugs, both recreational and prescribed. The latest anti-depressant used by many of the young is Citalopram, which replaced Seroxat and Prozac. It has the danger of addiction and serious side effects. If you have a friend of family member who is in this age bracket, please talk with them and keep a watchful eye that they are OK; some of their stories I heard at Glastonbury worried me greatly.

Healthy food and the elimination of drugs, both prescription and street drugs, and junk foods could go a long way towards changing the outcome for today's youth.

5

Conquering Anxiety and Depression

Before we look at this palm print, let's answer a couple of questions which keep reoccurring in emails.

Now some people think, to have your palms read is just about telling someone about things in their future. This is both inaccurate and irresponsible. Seeing within the scope of someone's life, past and present, are simple things to deal with, but explaining what may lie ahead in someone's future needs the utmost tact.

Often it's best to remain silent. No one sees the whole future, just snatches of it, and to take something out of context for someone can be problematic for them.

The second point is that I get a lot of emails about people becoming upset after gypsies grabbed their hands and gabbled a couple of things, and then asked for money. You would not trust a dentist or doctor who stopped you in the street and asked to examine you, so please be careful here.

Look closely at this hand print. Can you see any anomalies?

The palm print shown is of a suicidal lady who first wanted her hands read some eight years back, to find out why she just could not get a boyfriend. Since the reading, she has halved her body weight and takes better care of herself. Doctors are now saying that obesity is as big a killer as tobacco, and the next decade will see many go well before their time.

This interesting lady's social life was non-existent. Her diet was awful and her self-esteem was negligible. I hypnotized her and suggested she had a gastric band fitted, and that she needed half what she was eating. Many women who emotionally eat are from single-parent families and will fill the void with junk food.

New studies from the huge recent Rohner Study show that children from one-parent families, or even from two of the same sex, suffer the pain of rejection. All children need a man *and* a woman, or a lopsided emotional infrastructure may later develop.

The palmistry studies I helped with at the London Psychiatric Hospital

50 Case Studies in Modern Palmistry

had many with this, and also showed the low set little (Mercury) finger as here.

On seeing her the second time recently, her heart line under Jupiter (1) had crashed down to collide with the head line. This means that at the time indicated on the life line and relationship lines, a traumatic event happened, which caused the subject to feel a deep sense of disappointment and disillusionment over romance, leading to the head taking more control of the heart. Carl Jung spoke of the battle between head and heart, or *thinking* versus *feeling*, and this mark always shows an emotional hurt which left a deep shadow over the life at the age indicated.

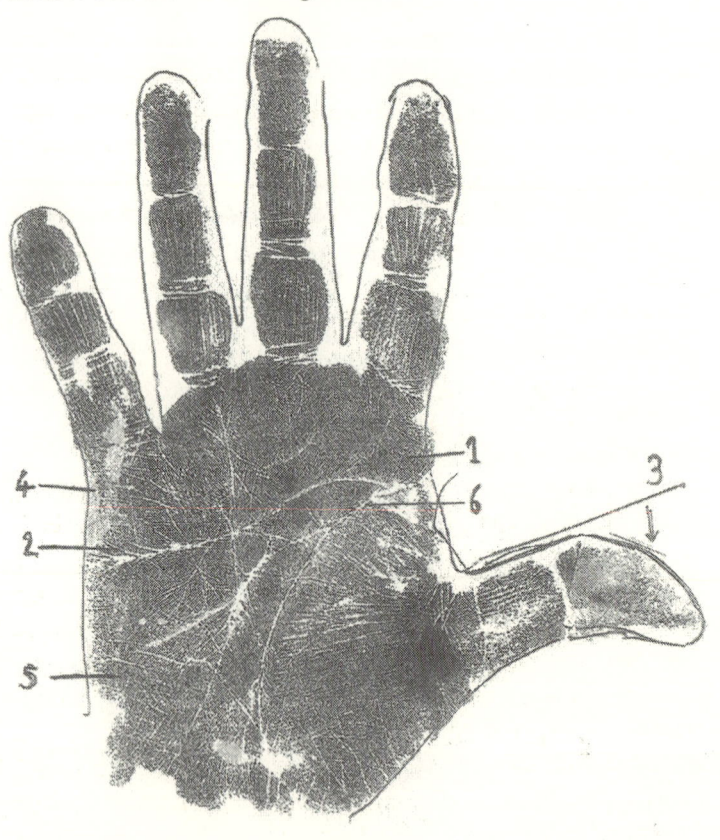

Conquering Anxiety and Depression

The heart line at (2) shows a doubling or trebling under the ring or Apollo finger. This, if eye shaped, refers to congenital eye problems, but this shape indicates metallic absorption. This is usually from drinking water from lead or copper pipes or eating from aluminum pans, but as she has many metal teeth fillings and facial piercings, I asked to see behind her earrings and—sure enough, green/blue marks show a nickel allergy.

I see a lot of problems from metals in the body, and many of the young do not realize how this puts you at risk. When I see a girl who is very overweight with tattoos and metal piercings, it screams of no confidence, anxiety and low self-esteem. Incidentally, this linear formation is predictive of later life Dupuytrens contracture.

The flexible thumb at (3) is interesting as a stiff thumb shows a stiff mind. People who stick to their guns are stubborn and tenacious, but very flexible-thumbed people can be the opposite—charming, capable and brilliant in short spurts, but swap about too much; they are malleable and changeable, and usually jacks of all trades—masters of none.

The three worlds of palmistry—Spirit, Mind and Body—show well in the thumbs, three phalanges. The tip is willpower, and this would be a flexible willpower. The middle shows logic; the larger phalange will tell you which one rules the subject, and the base is the love and sex potential of the Mount of Venus.

(4) shows the many relationship lines. These are women who change their partners often, and usually make do with DUFANS (*Do For Now* relationships).

(5) Shows a fate line, which leaves the life line showing family assistance to the career. This can be advice or financial, usually both, and the veering off at the top shows that just after the age of 50, a position in authority is given. As this line can represent the spine, this sign usually infers whiplash injury or stiffness across the shoulders. Basically, it's the thoracic area which will need attention.

(6) The wispy head line, which is vague in places, coincided with her general anxiety and worries over memory loss. Have you ever walked into a room and then forgotten why you went there in the first place? This is because your brain perceives the doorway as an "event boundary," and memories from the room you just left are "stored" there for when you need them, and this is why, when you go back through the doorway into the prior room, you can often remember what it is that you forgot. So nothing to worry about for some years yet.

So, to sum up:

50 Case Studies in Modern Palmistry

(1) In her effort to find someone special, she was contacted by a man online dating, who sent her pics with film-star looks, who claimed he was a well paid actor and was crazy about her. After three weeks of intense love letters, he told her he was in a crisis and needed a large monetary loan for one week. She borrowed money from her mum and, of course, the chap disappeared off the Net and his address proved false. This wrecked her life and left her very bitter.

(2) Make sure your drinking water is filtered and minimize your contact with all metals, including teeth fillings, aluminum-based underarm sprays, and carpet and furniture anti-inflammable chemicals.

(3) Very flexible thumbs are linked to joint and possible gynecological difficulties.

(4) "*Marry in haste, repent at leisure*" runs the old saying. This girl, since she lost weight, rushed headlong into several recent relationships which did not work out, a common phenomenon with women from one-parent families and flexible thumbs.

(5) Carrying that huge amount of weight for so many years gave her spinal trouble, which even a classical osteopath found hard to fix.

(6) Anxiety over a period can cause memory problems, junk diets, irregular hours, and particularly mercury and aluminum will cause this over a period.

Convincing her to strive for good health rather than be jealous of looks was the most important thing for relationships, and that some women are not beautiful, they only *look* as though they are.

If you think you suffer with weight issues, anxiety or depression, consult a proper, qualified hypnotherapist.

If you are meeting partners over the Net on Facebook, etc., you need to read *The Psychodynamics of Social Networking: Connected up instantaneous culture and the self,* by Aaron Balick, a master in the various anxieties.

6

How to Identify an Indigo Child

As we move through 2015 and further into the Age of Aquarius, many people have noticed that children of a new energy and soul color are being born. This phenomenon began slowly in the baby boom after World War II, and in the 1980s, '90s and later has multiplied into huge numbers. Although there is much disagreement amongst experts, certain aspects involving these children are universal.

There is a great trend which began with the baby boomers to question authority, and the rise of environmental issues has led substantial numbers to the new Green political movement, and the many spiritually gifted children to reject the external formal religions, in favor of a personal, often earth-based and internal spirituality, free from an outside manipulation.

Coupled to this, we have a significant rise in the rejection of mainstream or allopathic medication, in favor of alternative and complementary therapies. So we have a sudden groundswell of opinion away from the corruption of modern politics, religion and government, for we now have the New Age children with auras that range from lilac, to pale maroon and purple.

Children of the Bomb

Experts first recognized that these new children could not be forced to hate other children, and they banded together to form the hippies and beatniks of the "flower power movement." They claimed spiritual satisfaction was as much in loving our neighbors' differences as in loving the familiarity of our own. They were very opposed to both war and the short satisfactions of materialism.

The growth in New Age studies is in answer to the corruption in authority and materialism, under the shadow of the weapons industries in which we all lived during the Cold War. The findings suggest that many who died in World War II are back with us now, and with a firm mission of peace.

50 Case Studies in Modern Palmistry

How can we recognize these children in our midst? They have problems with authority, especially if it is mindless. They may not feel they belong in school, and the environment can be difficult for them, for they are often bullied. Strangely, they are born technology-literate, and can work computers from an early age. For many, their favorite pastime is to play Nintendo all day.

Many of these children are in the "special needs" categories, and sadly many are on drugs, such as Ritalin for hyperactive behavior. At very least, they are non-conformist, and it is possible that a sudden leap in evolution has brought in these children, to harness the vibrations of the new Aquarian Age. I am sometimes shocked at my talks and lectures, to have these spiritually conversant young children walk straight up to me to chat. They are so in tune with their inner world.

This is the hand of 10-year-old "Gemma."

Notice first the hand shape, which is square to oblong, with fairly long fingers. Most modern palmists use the fourfold "Gettings" system, and this hand shape is a "water hand." This always goes with a highly strung temperament, with low nervous tolerance and many lines.

The many-lined hand is called a "full hand," and with first or Jupiter finger shorter than Apollo, and with the head line sloping down, with the lines of head and life tightly joined. These four factors confirm the sensitive, unconfident, anxious and intuitive base to the personality, common to receptive, feminine, psychic and artistic types.

(2) The little finger does not reach the upper finger crease of Apollo, and the finger is low set into the hand, giving communication and relationship difficulties. This and the thin or wasted Apollo finger shows feelings of low emotional self-worth. Events in the latency period, 6 to 12 years of age, and highlighted in the island in the life line at age 6, show the father leaving home after a series of huge rows.

Children are always the main victims in any family breakup, and subconsciously this child typically suffers from self-blame. Incidentally, the shortness of Jupiter's finger, in comparison to Apollo's, is a sign of estrogen imbalance inherited from the mother's womb, and the fingernail shape (not shown) is symbolic of either insufficient pituitary or thyroid secretion, also from the womb.

The line across the palmar base (3) is now known as the poison line, as it shows an addictive personality. It is a common factor in both Indigo children and in A.D.H.D type disorders. This line is also statistically very common in alcoholics, food intolerances, and drug addicts, and remembers

How to Identify an Indigo Child

that *Doctor Magazine* says their doctor initially hooks most people.

Many Indigo children have food allergies, and palmistry is a valuable tool in this diagnosis. This finely tuned gastric system should experiment with avoiding wheat, citrus, nuts, salt, sugars and particularly dairy.

Some years ago, we found at the Graywood Natural Clinic that Aspartame, Cochineal and Sunshine Yellow, and particularly Tartrazine, could induce restlessness and erratic behavior. Studies show much help is gained from dietary change and spiritual healing.

Where this palmascope is typical is that, her teacher says, "She is away with the fairies." She has an amazing imagination. Her creativity, in terms of color and shape, make her a promising artist. The beautiful bow shape to the line of heart (4) gives her care for others and love for animals, especially birds.

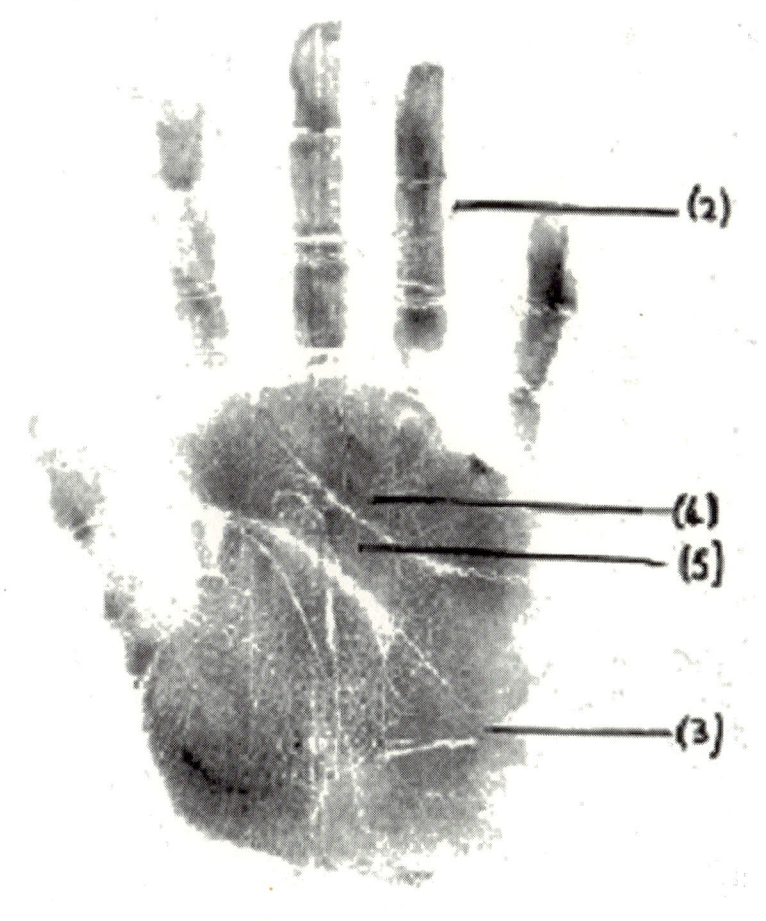

She is psychologically a "Type B," being gentle, kind and very laid back, yet still gets insomnia and restlessness. She has quiet powers of leadership and tells the other children delightful animal and fairy stories. In general, she is a lovely child, but not an easy one.

The line that runs up the hand center from the palmar base is the fate or destiny line (5), and this with a curved top, in this position, can show a spiritual leader, someone who will blaze a new trail. It is known as the "shepherd's crook."

Exodus 4-2: *"Then the Lord asked him, What do you have there in your hand? A shepherd's crook, Moses replied."*

"Just as a candle cannot burn without fire, men cannot live without a spiritual life." — Gautama Buddha

7

Eating Right for Your Type

This palm print epitomizes all that is wrong with the diet and eating habits of its owner.

So how can we arrive at a healthy diet for him?

Just as the facial features will tell of the ancestral heritage, so does the hand.

The little (or Mercury) finger has not come out in the palm print because the finger is curved. This is a medical condition called "Dupuytrens contracture" and is only seen in those who are descended from Neanderthals.

The hand shape with its particularly muscular thumb and strong fingers is typically Neanderthal as was the pale skin and red hair.

Experts say interbreeding came around 100,000 years back with the Europeans, and later the Anglo Saxons, who now have much that is Neanderthal in origin. The true Neanderthal type died out just 30,000 years ago, but throwbacks do occur, and this hand tells its own story.

Hand shape tells of the racial heritage, and from this we can ascertain the blood type, which is Type O. From this, we can gauge the diet that is correct for this type, and which illnesses and when they will occur, due to eating habits. We can also make a shrewd guess as to employment.

Contrary to popular belief, the Neanderthals had large skulls, showing they had larger brains than was previously thought. Not only were they much more clever than suspected, but they were stronger with very large chests and heavier bones. They were, by far, the strongest of the humans around at that time. No expert has come forward with any theory as to why they died out, but disease is the favorite theory. Incidentally, as more information becomes available, the less experts agree with Darwin's theory of evolution.

The Neanderthals were later the Vikings, who were then the Huguenots. The early name for Huguenots was "Ape" people or monkeys because of their appearance.

In what became known as the St. Bartholomew's Day Massacre of August 24 to October 3, 1572, Catholics killed thousands of Huguenots in

50 Case Studies in Modern Palmistry

Paris. Similar hunts and massacres took place in other towns in the weeks following. The main provincial towns and cities involved in the Massacre were Aix, Bordeaux, Bourges, Lyon, Meaux, Orleans, Rouen, Toulouse and Troyes. Nearly 3,000 Protestants were slaughtered in Toulouse alone. The exact number of fatalities throughout the country is not known. Many Huguenots then immigrated to England, where with their crooked Mercury fingers, which they used to hold the threads on their looms, became known as "weaver's fingers." British ex Prime Minister Margaret Thatcher told me she was quite proud of her weaver's fingers.

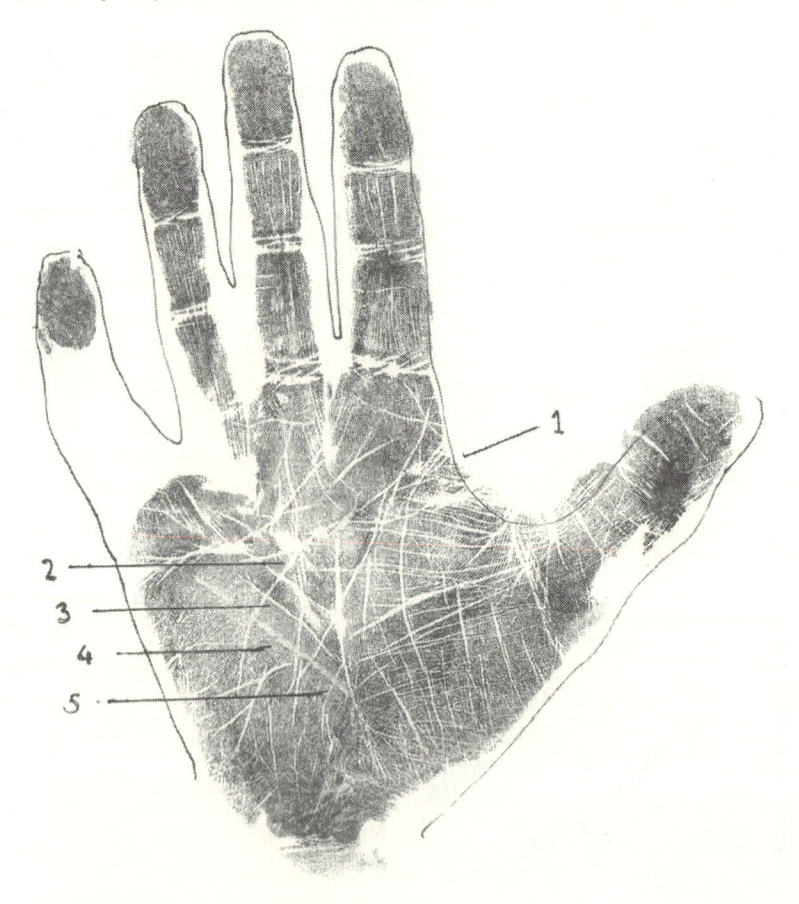

If you look at the tiny white blotches in this hand print, they show inherited trauma. It's now scientifically recognized that when someone goes through deep trauma, this is imprinted on their genes and their descendents will carry this trauma. Many people are carrying what happened to their

Eating Right for Your Type

grandfathers in WWI and later WWII. These trauma signs, which we first discovered with Professor Henri Rey at the famous London Maudsley Psychiatric Hospital, could well be from the mass murders during the French purges. Whatever the cause, the tightly wound life and head lines at the start of the life show a childhood which was ridden with young anxiety. (1)

Homeopathy has proved that water has its own memory. Eighty percent of the body is water and we exist for nine months in water inside the womb. So, being part of water, we carry our ancestors' lives and trauma within us.

In 1901, Dr. Karl Landsteiner discovered the four blood types and the correct diet for blood type O.

Here's what expert Dr. Peter D'Adamo recommends for this type: a high-protein diet heavy on lean meat, poultry, fish, nuts and vegetables, and light on grains, beans, and dairy. Dr Peter D'Adamo also recommends various supplements to help with tummy troubles and other issues he says people with Type O tend to have. Other experts say they should eat organic meat very sparingly, as the Neanderthal is the Mesomorph body type, which puts on weight easily after the age of 40, and meat now contains growth promoters and hormones which upset the Neanderthal digestive system. There are 100,000 nerve cells in the gut, and it is often called the second brain. This palm shows that its owner's stomach is rebelling against what it has to digest.

If we look at (2), (3) and (4), they are all in the gastric area and show that dairy should be avoided as the lactase could be harmful. Cow's milk is really liquid meat which clogs the arteries, giving the Mesomorph body type heart trouble. White bread should also be avoided as the gluten could be a problem. Nuts, fruit and vegetables are a must.

As these lines hit the life line, we can date the gastric problems, and at (4) this coincided with a growth in the intestines, which was causing a blockage. From this time at age 58-60, we see a thinning of the life line and life energies. Let's hope our clever Neanderthal heeds my words.

8

A Boxer's Hand

Forensic Palmistry — Case 2210

The hand represents the whole body in microcosm, and this hand print is that of a typical top sportsman inasmuch as the musculature at the palmar base is significant, being both red with activity, very firm and wide. This shows the considerable physical energy available, and is always the sign of a physical athlete.

The heel of the hand is known to medicine as the "hypothenar eminence," and is traditionally ruled by the Moon, so this being large means affinity with water. The huge volume of energy available to the subject in this area tells us in high probability that he was a successful swimmer, in his latency and teen-age years.

The few simple line formations, in what palmists call "an empty hand," tell that the subject is uncomplicated, and non-intellectual, as is typical with the Mesomorph body type. The relationship of the body type with the psychological landscape was initiated by William Sheldon, and this man's hand is an "elementary regressive."

The building blocks of his persona determine that he is a man who can only relate through his physique. We see every day in our newspapers the child-like antics of football stars, who although physically developed are just intellectually children.

Some years ago, I would have to write psychological assessments for young criminals, for the courts, often before a prison sentence.

These physical types would continually be in trouble, and regrettably, social workers would get them into boxing as a method of channeling their energy and aggression. These men would then be trained aggressives, and would, as a rule, end up as builders, laborers, soldiers, bouncers, bailiffs, boxers and pub heavies.

The latest statistics in modern Britain say that one in four young men will be in trouble with the police for drunken, boisterous and loutish behavior, now termed by psychologists as "footballism."

A Boxer's Hand

Many years ago, at his constituency office in Essex, Winston Churchill told me that in peacetime, fighters and brawlers were a menace to society, but when war comes, these violent criminal psychopaths were just what the country needed.

Reflexology tells of the foot and its relationship to the body as a whole. Palmists have, since ancient times, used similar techniques with the hand, and looking at this man's hand print tells us that the particular developed muscle groupings mean many years as a boxer. Boxers can make a lot of money, but they—like this man—usually die in poverty.

The British Medical Association's figures suggest an incorrect cause of death in 50 percent of death certificates, and complementary practitioners of all types are in demand as never before.

It is often the rule that these strong, physical men whom you would assume would be so passionate in the love arenas, are strangely usually very placid, and may not relate to other adults, but can relate well to animals, children and teenagers. Several boxers, footballers, and several top pop stars spring to mind.

This man is unusual because, statistically, the best athletes and boxers tend to be black men, but their dense bone structure means they are not good swimmers, so you rarely see a black swimmer.

This hand print shows a superstitious man, a man who with the combination of square palm, heavy knuckles, and short stubby fingers (Brachydactyly). This can often be the symptom complex of OCD (obsessive compulsive disorder), and he was famous for his pre-bout urges to perform a series of complex rituals, comprising both mental and physical acts. Everyone had to say three times to him that he would win and keep winning, and his hands were chapped and sore from the anxiety of constant washing.

The head line is no longer a line at all. It looks in the print like a white blotch, being thickened with constant blows, and finally broken at 36 years of age. Strangely, in the month of Aries, which rules the head, the white blotch, or gap in the head line, signals what looks suspiciously like a subdural hematoma, leading rather quickly to cardiac arrest.

Doctors have wanted to ban the sport since the introduction of brain scans, but punters say it would drive the sport back to the street corners as in the Depression and the dark days of WWII.

Thousands of pounds are wagered with each fight, and tragically it often pays better to lose than to win. The money angle attracts the gangsters, and they often fund promising young boxers who see only the bright lights, the applause and the pay cheques. This keeps men in the ring long after they should retire.

The London College of Psychiatry has a study on *Wernicke's Aphasia*, which links the neurological damage that gives the symptoms of using inapplicable words in a sentence, or constant verbal repetition, and the small vocabulary that often goes with head injuries, which shows in the hand's communications sector.

This formula brings several top boxers to mind.

Unfortunately, television and films regularly glorify violence, and parents send kids as young as 6 to Karate and Kung Fu lessons.

It was psychologists Carl Jung and Charlotte Wolfe who correlated that a non-appearance in a hand of the fate line, as in this print, was one recognized criminal marking, because its non appearance signifies a drifter, someone who cannot plan ahead, or keep a job, and regrettably, pugilism and

A Boxer's Hand

criminality often go together.

The lack of the fate line is a typical marker in the schizoid temperament, which shows poor social adaptability, common among career soldiers and boxers.

Some palmists claim the hand cannot tell you your future, as the lines change, but the lines appear on the palm on the first few weeks in the womb, and if changes occur in later life in the main lines, they are almost always of the secondary character, and at the line endings, relating to the emotional and intellectual infrastructure, not to the life purpose.

The only exception to this rule is the fate or destiny line, which runs up the hand center, to the middle or Saturn finger area, and this can change all through life. This man's life line goes on until his 70s, but is broken halfway through.

Pharmacokinetics is the science of studying the long-term effects of drugs on the body. This man's enlarged knuckle formations tell of the overuse of analgesics, to deaden the pain in his hands and fingers.

Confirmation is found at the root of the index or Jupiter finger in the gastric sector, and in the poor health line, which rides from under the little, or Mercury, finger to the life line. Its collision is at approximately 36 years of age.

The heart line (known to medicine as the upper distal transverse crease) speaks of heart failure at the same age, and the life line has a gap at around the same period. This man's constant need for "one more comeback," "one more fight" has cost him his life.

"Like a river small at first, narrowly contained within its banks, and rushing passionately past boulders and over waterfalls, gradually the river flows more quietly, and in the end without any visible break, the waters flow into the sea."

This print was taken with difficulty. His fingers curled tightly into his hand, had to be straightened and tied to the sole on his shoe, for the necessary rigidity in order to take the print.

That such a popular young sports personality should end his days in this way is indeed a tragedy. The venerable Bede in the seventh century described life as a sparrow which flies swiftly into a great hall through one door only to leave, almost instantly, through another.

9

Frozen Trauma

Palmistry is not primarily about people's futures. Often it's more about dealing with the past and sometimes unresolved problems which now affect the present.

This hand print shows someone with the symptoms of Frozen Trauma. Frozen Trauma is something from our past that we cannot deal with. It holds us back and handicaps us with our day-to-day duties, and statistically this is most often from childhood.

So what are the signs? Gestures of clasping, grasping hands, wringing hands and holding hands tight to the body.

COPING
Do you have things that you used to cope with so well that now overwhelm you?

RELATIONSHIP PATTERNS
Are you having the same relationship problems with different people?

ISOLATION
Are you lonely but feel safer and more secure on your own?

OVERREACTIONS
Do you think you have overreacted when faced with any recent problems, or have you experienced rage when it was not really called for?

ANXIETY
Is your threat response turned on all of the time, even when you know you are safe? Do you feel things are out of your control?

DEPRESSION
Have you had bouts of intensely low spirits? Do you wish you were not here or might resort to self harm?

Frozen Trauma

OCD
　　Do you keep looking fearfully in the mirror, washing hands, checking things, doors, windows, the gas, etc.?

EMOTIONAL EATING
　　Do you use food, alcohol or drugs as an emotional prop?
　　If you have said yes to three or more of these, you may be suffering from Frozen Trauma, often from a long time back.
　　The hand print shown has a spider's web of lines all over its surface. This shows the person cannot rest, that they are perpetually in fight-or-flight mode, highly strung and constantly on edge.

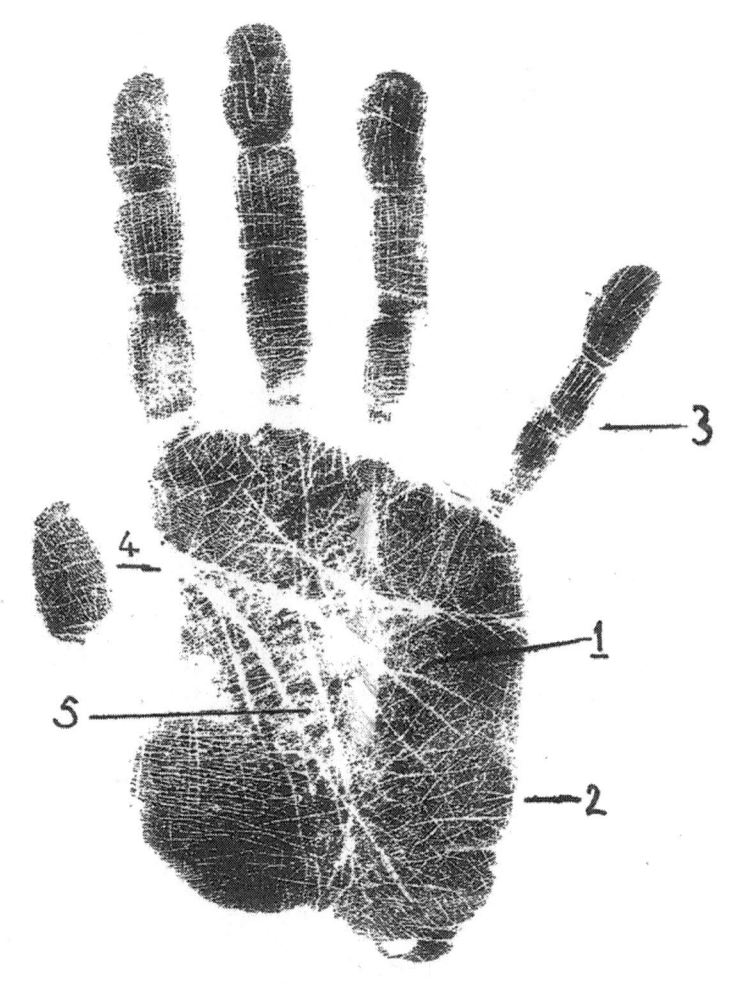

50 Case Studies in Modern Palmistry

A lot of tiny stars across the palm print shows the body's electrical circuit is on the point of burnout; the immune system is very low, and the deep lines on the fingertips are accepted warning signs of an imminent breakdown.

Incidentally, a mass of palmar lines is often seen in Cystic Fibrosis.

(1) The head line ends in a fork. This is the marking of actors and authors, someone who has to put themselves in other people's shoes, and because of this, it shows indecision: half the person will want to do A, and the other half B, causing a split, anxious mental state.

(2) The lines crossing the Luna mount and attacking the life line show unremitting stress and restlessness.

(3) This has affected all close relationships as shown in the Mercury, or little, finger standing away, showing that the sexual infrastructure is not harmoniously integrated into the rest of the hand.

The dermatic skin condition known as "chicken skin" on the hand print is medically called Keratosis Pilans; it is usually found with gluten assimilation problems, and is from a fatty acid deficiency. This is helped by Vitamin A and Omega 3.

The cause? If we look first at the life line in teen-age years (4), we see a barbed-wire type entanglement that shows prolonged bullying in school, this carried on into their twenties. The bullying was partly emotional, but largely sexual in nature, and over a long period.

(5) The formation of the long, unbroken fate line suggests that the difficulties were karmic in origin. The Indian palmistry schools would say, *"This is Parabhada karma, the sum of what you have previously done, and now lies in wait for you to experience."*

Professor Dieter Wilke of Warwich University, the author of a new report on bullying, has this to say: "Being bullied is not a harmless rite of passage, but throws a life-long blanket over the affected children's lives with great cost to individuals and society."

Children whose parents separate are twice as likely to under achieve at school, suffer mental health problems, become the victims of bullies, and struggle to form long-lasting relationships in late life. This is according to a recent study by the London School of Education, which highlighted seven major areas of concern after the large number of teen-age and twenties British kids took their own lives.

The report added that those bullied were twice as likely to suffer serious illness and three times more at risk of psychiatric disorders, were more likely to smoke and engage in risky behavior, such as getting drunk, drug taking, driving recklessly, and promiscuity.

Bullying is being recognized as a frequent major factor in suicide that at last the US Army is beginning to take notice, and is softening the army training, as harsh and excessive discipline can lead to anger, rebellion and retaliation.

The report showed many of those who bullied were lacking in several personality areas, and some were obvious psychopaths.

* The research published in the journal *Psychological Science* studied 1,420 children in the USA, between the ages of 9 and 16, and again from ages 24 to 26.

10

Misaligned Bite

This hand print is that of a lady who presented at the Alternatives Clinic, complaining of insomnia, anxiety and gastric restlessness.

This hand print well illustrates the Ectomorph body typology with all its established health anomalies.

It is estimated that 45 percent of children could benefit from teeth braces and possibly 75 percent of the population has a misaligned bite. This is highest by far with Ectomorphs, and also those of premature births, forceps deliveries, tonsil/adenoid problems and whiplash injuries, but mostly those who suffered intra-uterine malnourishment, or poor nutrition in the womb, or as young children.

This illustration shows the knock-on effects of being unable to eat properly due to bite difficulties. Over long time periods, the TMJ (Temporo Mandibular Joint) jaw connection to skull will ache, the nervous system will instruct the brain to compensate with the head and neck being used to drag the jaw into line. Such things as nocturnal bruxism (sleep teeth grinding) can disrupt sleep patterns and lead to anxiety and possible behavioral anomalies. Muscular fatigue which affects posture is common.

The jaw is a very powerful muscle. The bite is strong enough in normal people to hang from the jaw alone; this strength can have knock-on effects, such as to pull on the neck and misalign the spine, giving particularly neck aches, headache, spinal misalignment, dizziness, tinitis, neck and shoulder discomfort. Even hand tingling and arm numbness can all be long-term effects.

The skull contains 29 bones which normally knit together well as we grow, and unless good nutrition is employed, and bite anomalies rectified, this will exacerbate the inbuilt fragility of the Ectomorph body type skull bones.

Allopathic doctors continually spout: "With a healthy diet, no extra vitamins or minerals are needed," but they can't tell you what constitutes a healthy diet, as a pregnant woman will need a different diet to a grown man

Misaligned Bite

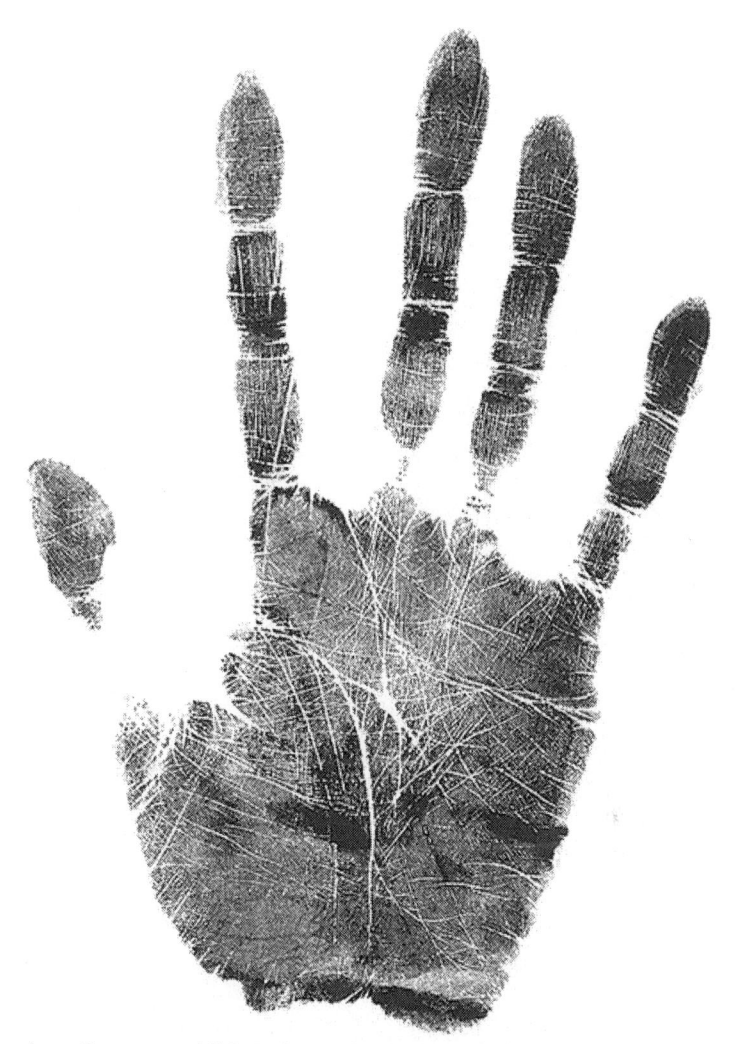

or that of a young child, and new findings show each blood type will have different nutritional needs.

Doctors have no nutritional training, and dieticians vary as much as nutritionists in what they say. Britain's flagship hospital, Addenbrooke's, still advises cow's milk for calcium, but most countries over the past 30 years say do not touch cow's milk as it has saturated fats, and studies carried out in Japan say cow's milk is liquid meat, which just gums up veins and arteries, bringing on possible later cardiovascular difficulties, and the sticky bonding agents used in industrial plasters and cements use casein from cow's milk.

Experts say cow's milk is fine for baby cows, but not human beings, and the mounting number of people with cow's milk allergies confirms the new thinking.

Each bottle of cow's milk can contain up to 20 chemicals comprising Niflumic acid, Mefenamic acid, Keteprofen, Diclofenac, Phenylbutazone, Florfenicol, Estrone, 17B Estradiol, Naproxen, Flunixin, Pyrithmethamine, Dicloforte, and Tricosian.

This number admittedly is rare, but the study was published in the *Journal of Agriculture and Food Chemistry*. Remember, what we eat and drink gets passed into the seas, where fish are now overdosing on Estrogen and Prozac, etc.

Serious alcohol drinkers will first drink a pint of milk, so the alcohol they drink through their evening out cannot be absorbed, because the milk lines the stomach. As it cannot be digested properly, it insulates the gastric wall against the alcohol, and the growth promoters fed to cattle pass through the food chain into humans and they then pile on weight as do the cattle.

Allergies are very common with Ectomorphs, and lactose intolerance shows as nausea, cramps, bloating, flatulence and burping, which begin 30 minutes to two hours after ingesting lactose. Visible symptoms include dark circles under the eyes, pale skin and slow growth.

Each body type is again different in its nutritional needs, and the four blood types all have separate nutritional needs, likes and dislikes.

Wisdom teeth problems are most often statistically found in this body type.

Professor William Sheldon, the constitutional psychology pioneer, allied psychological postures to the body types that develop from the three embryonic layers—Endoderm, Ectoderm and Mesoderm—and although several of the modern schools now reject his findings, much of this is still very apt, because scientific palmistry can predict from this information from the body typology, the psychological framework, and from that, how and what he will eat, social interactions, their taste in relationships and possible career choices; this is called Palmar Physiognomy, as it all shows in the hand print.

The many-lined hand as shown here can be indicative of long-term antibiotic overuse, and I advised the lady to have a live probiotic drink last thing at night and to take a daily B Complex, iron, Vitamin C and calcium, and one of the fish oils, and also to join a yoga or meditation class and try to wind down during the evenings before bed.

11

Karma in the Hand Print

"It is impossible to build one's own happiness on the unhappiness of others. This perspective is at the heart of Buddhist teachings."

— Daisaku Ikeda

Please look closely at the hand shown here before reading and notice any anomalies.

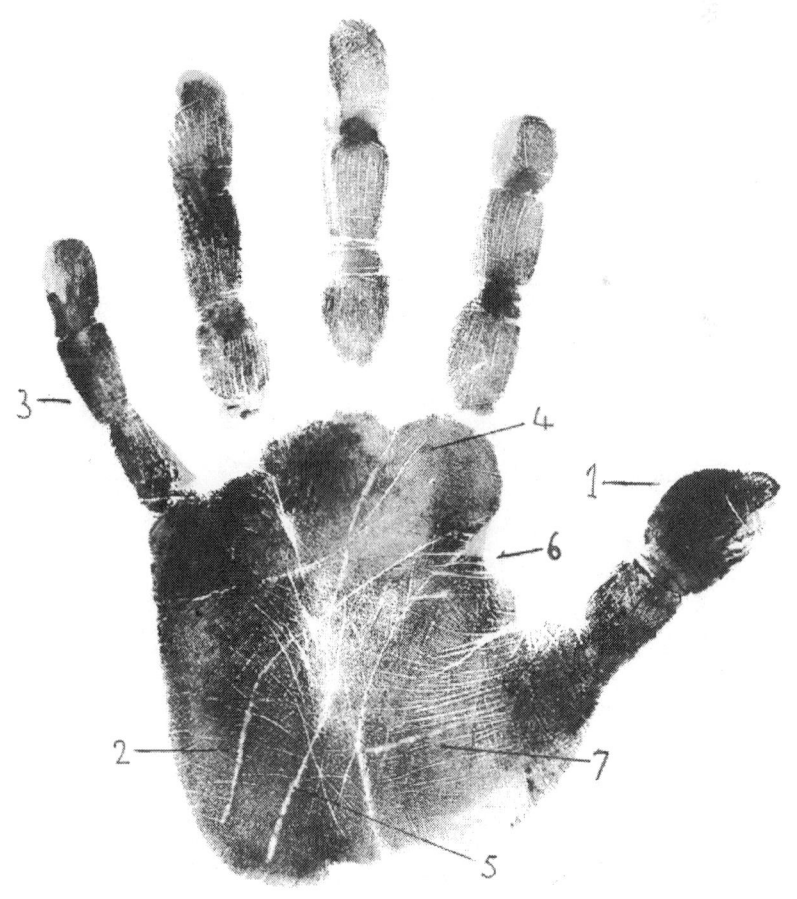

(1) the thick end to the thumb
(2) the head line plunging to the heel of the hand
(3) little, or Mercury, finger curved and thin through its length
(4) deeply curving heart line
(5) powerful Destiny line showing the whole way through the hand
(6) Influence lines breaking the life line at approximate ages 7, 10 and 12
(7) Influence line from Venus directly hits the life line at approximately age 50.

So what do we have? Remember, no sign should ever be read in isolation.

The thick end to the thumb shows a lack of self-control. These people often have bad tempers and blind rages. This does not come from out of nowhere, so we have to look at why. Psychologists tell us that "those experiencing rage usually feel the effects of high adrenaline surges in the body and this increase raises the strength and endurance levels while dulling the sense of responsibility."

Studies done with the help of the late Professor Henri Rey and me, in his anger management clinic, showed a far higher than normal ratio of these thumbs. In Medieval palmistry this was called the "murderer's thumb." It figures high in my own collection of murderers' hand prints.

This head line, which plunges low onto Luna, is always seen in artists, visionaries, mystics and often depressives, and these are usually affected most at times of the full moon. The London Metropolitan police, some years ago, commissioned a study when it was noticed some crimes peaked at full moon. These were crimes of arson and alcohol-related violence. Officers' time away was cancelled at these times.

The Mercury finger, thin and curved through its length, always shows a stunted sexual development through either abuse, conditioning or from an excessively religious home or school environment, where it is taught sex is a bad thing. For whatever reason, the normal energy flow is not going through this finger.

So that energy is being dammed up, and at some place or time will have to burst its banks. A Mercury finger shorter than the top crease of the next finger always shows a damming up of this fine energy, and coupled to a deeply curving heart line, shows the longing for a deep, committed love on all levels—mind, body and spirit. This is a marking of fire and passion, and when seen with the bulbous-tipped thumb and overactive imagination, can be a recipe for sudden outbursts.

Karma in the Hand Print

The destiny line here starts very low, early in the subject's life. There is much argument among palmists and astrologers over how to tell what is destiny and what is free will, but a long line like this, which is so strong it divides the hand in half, can only mean a predestined series of events which we see plainly marked along the life line.

The three crossing lines breaking through the life line in childhood show the life force being disrupted. The subject said she was brought up in a strict religious household, and she was taught that sex was sinful and babies born out of wedlock went straight to hell. Yet the pastor was secretly sexually abusing several of the children, including her.

The guilt and inner anguish over what happened affected her whole life in the way that only sexual abuse can. When she finally told her parents and family, no one believed her, saying the pastor was a fine and godly man. Carl Jung said, *"Inside each of us is someone we do not know."*

And on the day before the full moon, on January 16, 2014, at age 52, she sought out the pastor—now an old man—to demand an apology, and she killed him in a fit of anger.

I visited her in prison and took this hand print. The sentence was lenient, but in my view, she had already served her sentence in the years preceding the attack.

Everything in life is transitory, for life is as unstable as water.

12

Chronic Obesity in the Palm

A well-known and very accomplished author, with 20 bestsellers to her credit, contacted me for a reading, and below is her hand print.

She is a frequent personality on TV and radio, advising about health and dietary matters. It was very difficult trying to get my views on her hands across to such an expert.

Famous psychologist Carl Jung once said, *"The greater degree of learning, the narrower the horizons,"* and just as the last people to even consider new health treatments are doctors, so I could not get through to

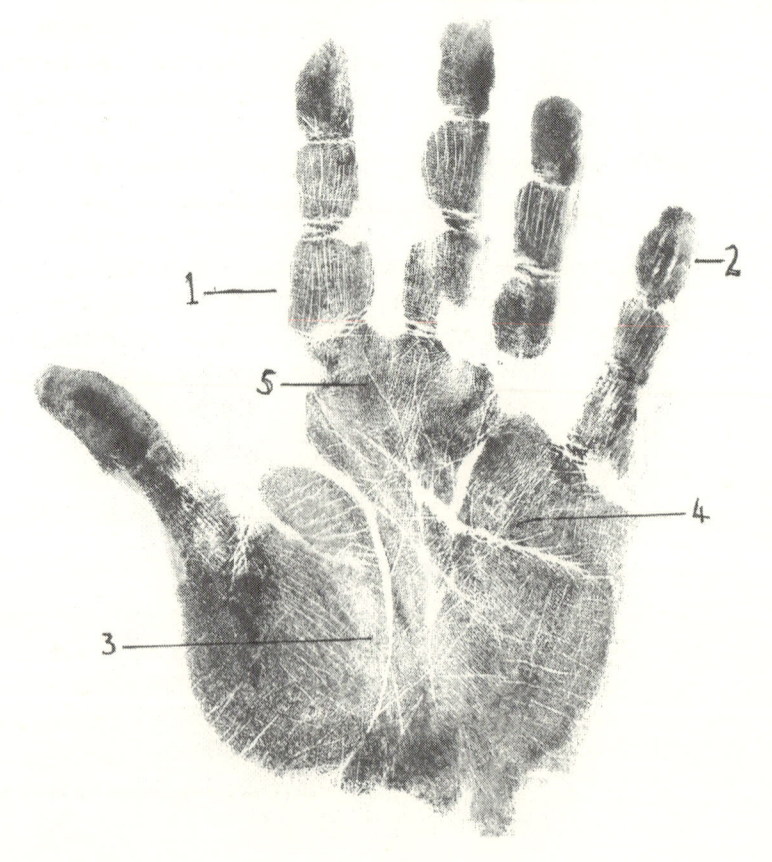

Chronic Obesity in the Palm

this health-conscious lady that the reason she could not get a man in her life was her enormous physical size.

Psychologists call it Body Dysmorphia, when people don't see themselves as they really are. This intelligent, articulate lady really thought she was slim. Men are very visual creatures. They won't eat a meal unless it looks right, and they are very much the same with relationships. If they think a woman cares more about the biscuit barrel than them, they will be off.

The *British Medical Journal* and the *New England Journal of Medicine*, in their articles to doctors, warn that the biggest killer this next decade would be from ramifications and side effects of long-term obesity. Recent court cases in England and Australia have seen overweight children seized from their families by the court and fostered out to families who will feed them less.

Chronic obesity has links to Polypharmacy, or the regular taking of more than four drugs for associated disorders, and thus suggests a shorter lifespan than those who are slim.

We used to see on our British TV sets Americans that were huge, and no one understood how people could do this to themselves, but this past seven years, food additives such as Aspartame, Monosodium Glutamate and growth promoters fed to cattle have seen English waistlines exploding, too.

The hand print here shows all the classic signs of overeating, coupled with malnutrition. How can it be that we are loading up on food and yet suffer malnutrition? The answer is the toxic ingredients which go into the food. Crops are given chemicals to force them up quickly, and have less than half of the nutritional value that was present in pre-WWII crops. GMOs are being forced on us, and are often hidden in other ingredients. Aspartame is non-digestible and stays around the gastric area. Aspartame has 92 registered side effects. Women who spent years on the contraceptive pill also pile on weight.

These signs in the hand are danger signals:
1) The fingers are separated into three phalanges, loosely Mind, Body and Spirit. When the sections nearest the hand are plump, soft and pudgy, this is telling you your diet is wrong.
2) The lines up the tip to the Mercury finger show thyroid imbalance. Tap water contains the two biggest thyroid disrupters, fluoride and chlorine. Even much of bottled water now has fluoride added.
3) If the pad inside the life line is soft and pudgy, this means you are physically not coping with the extra weight. This is often seen in couch potatoes, who binge on junk food. Notice the life line thins from

this point, showing the effect of the weight. It's often not what we carry outside, but what is packed inside around the organs that counts.
4) Look at the fragmented heart line. The line is stop-start. This shows the heart action is sluggish and not coping as well as it should be.
5) This is most interesting, and shows the fate or destiny line going right up to Jupiter. This is only seen in leaders, pioneers and those who blaze new trails, and our lovely but well overweight lady has had a great effect educating on the health and lives of others.

Experts advise two things. The first is exercise; start slowly, remember, and build up a little each day. Brisk walking is ideal for any age, and swimming uses all the muscular groups of the body and is a wonderful all-round toner. Secondly, cut the binging on snacks. They used to say "five a day," but now they say "take nine a day" of vegetables and fruits, instead of the junk, and your palmar lines will improve from the day you start.

13

Taking Care of Your Heart

An article recently appeared in the *Journal of the American Medical Association*, warning of the dangers of over physical exertion and pushing the body too hard. Even army training is, at last, beginning to take this into account.

Your heart beats 100,000 times in one day and it pumps 1 million barrels of blood during the average life, yet strangely men's hearts beat an average of 70 times a minute while a woman's beats 78 times. But anywhere between 60 and 100, while at rest, is normal. This is hampered if you are much overweight, especially if you are carrying what is called "belly fat," and remember, it's not what you see on the outside, it's what's *inside*—squeezing your organs and flowing around in your bloodstream—which is really important.

In an article called "Palmar Dermatoglyphics in Heart Disease," Dr. T. Takashina and Dr. S. Yorifuji showed that the displaced axial tri-radius of the fingerprints (shown in the triangle in the graph) appeared in 64 percent of those with congenital heart disease. The healthy triangle should reach down to the palmar base and be from the center of the apex.

If you have this marking in your hands, do not push the exercise envelope too far. Remember, all things in moderation—including physical exertion—and you should be fine.

After every large marathon run, it's pretty well guaranteed that one of the runners will have a myocardial infarction (heart attack), and as often as not, it will be a man at the coronary age. That is the time of the Andropause or midlife crisis, when waistlines are expanding and more alcohol is being consumed.

The heart line, which is the top crossing line on the hand, will show heart attacks. Most of these are silent, but are shown under the small Mercury and Apollo fingers, actually on the line. Feel along this line for any nodules under the skin, which is confirmation.

I used to be a student counselor and was shocked at the rubbish eaten by most young people—cola drinks, fast foods, saturated fats, and loaded

50 Case Studies in Modern Palmistry

with Aspartame and monosodium glutamate. It was unusual for these young people to eat fresh fruit and vegetables. A good diet is essential for good heart health as is *moderate* exercise each day.

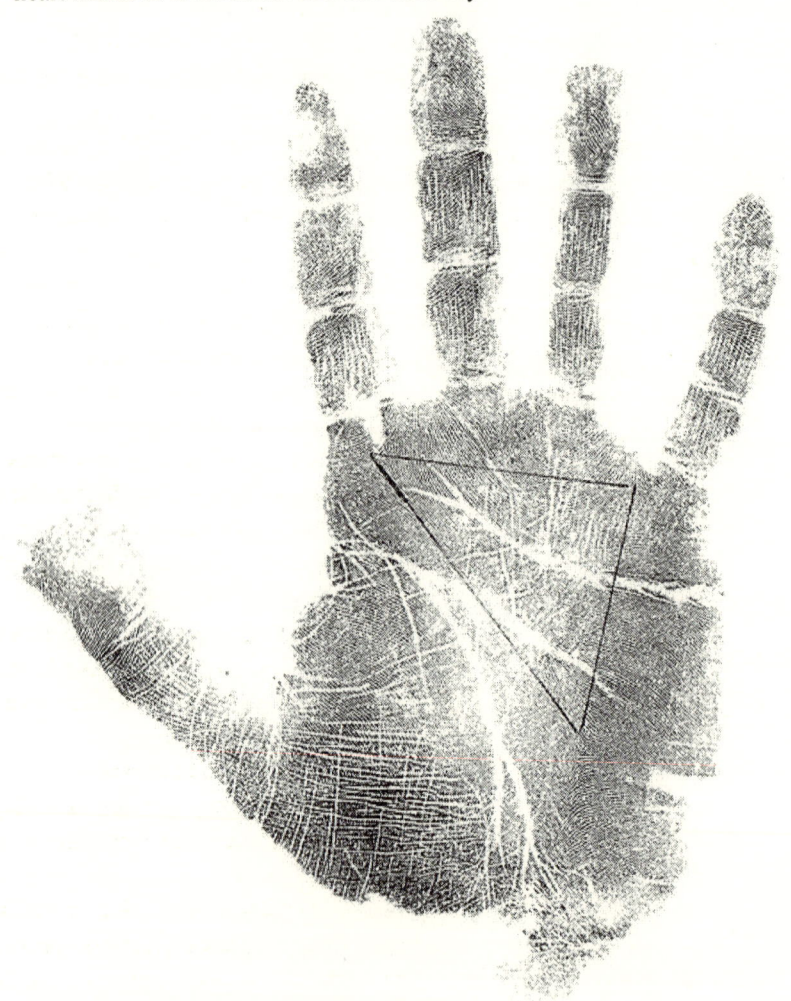

The fingernails have among their shapes what is called "a heart nail." This is small and roundish, often pale and not strong, which is an accepted congenital marker for a family history which will include some cardio-vascular anomalies. Fingernails should have what is called a moon. This is because the Moon rules all the tides of the seas and oceans, and of course all body fluids. A small or large nail moon, triangular or odd shape, can also give clues to heart health. And make sure the moons in the thumb nails are uniform. One good warning sign of a stroke possibility is a weaker moon in the left thumbnail.

I have often hoped my talks to the doctors at Whipps Cross Hospital in the '70s helped to save lives. In the USA, people trust doctors far more than they do in Britain, where people take more responsibility for their own health. But it helps to use the acupuncture type pulse taking used in Tibetan palmistry for heart checking. More on this in an upcoming chapter.

If you have a Girdle of Venus, which is a curved marking under the two middle fingers just above the heart line (this can appear with an islanded, ragged, broken heart line), it can tell of cardiac dysrhythmia or irregular heartbeat; too slow is Bradycardia and too fast is Tachycardia. Many of those I see with Atrial Fibrillation can be helped with Craniosacral therapy. Distance healing can also affect heartbeat positively as demonstrated with my old pal Harry Edwards (please google him).

Such things as palpitations, fainting, chest pain, chest pressure and mental unease can all help to trigger Atrial Fibrillation.

In Atrial Fibrillation, the heart rate may be over 140 beats a minute. Anxiety is one cause; another is nicotine and too much coffee. Studies have shown that some Americans drink 10 to 12 cups of coffee per day. Experts say to have just two or three cups a day because caffeine is a heart stimulant. So, unless you wish to switch to Decaf, please cut down.

Remember that a wide wrist-to-palm ratio is one sign of possible later life CHD (coronary heart disease), so cut down on the junk food, and remember to check your life line and also your health line for more information.

Hypertonia (Arterial Hypertonia) with its associated disorders such as stroke, heart attack, cardiac insufficiency and kidney disease, is a key disease factor in the developed countries. Prevalence is at a constantly high level of 10 to 20 percent.

Early detection of Hypertonia leaves much to be desired. It is one of the most frequent consultation issues at general medical practices, yet red blotching on the hands is a give-away signal, especially if you're overweight. In the age group over 60, only one in four people have normal blood pressure levels.

Cold hands on a warm day can infer later life cardiovascular problems, but can also be a sign of acute anxiety or thyroid imbalance. Check thoroughly. Only 10 percent of men and 21 percent of women receive the correct treatment as commercial medical doctors fumble in the dark, and only 7.5 percent of treated hypertonic diabetics achieve the recommended blood pressure level of under 130/80 mmHg. Blood pressure can be reduced by approximately 10mmHg (systolic) and 6mmHg (diastolic) simply by means of exercise and a healthy diet.

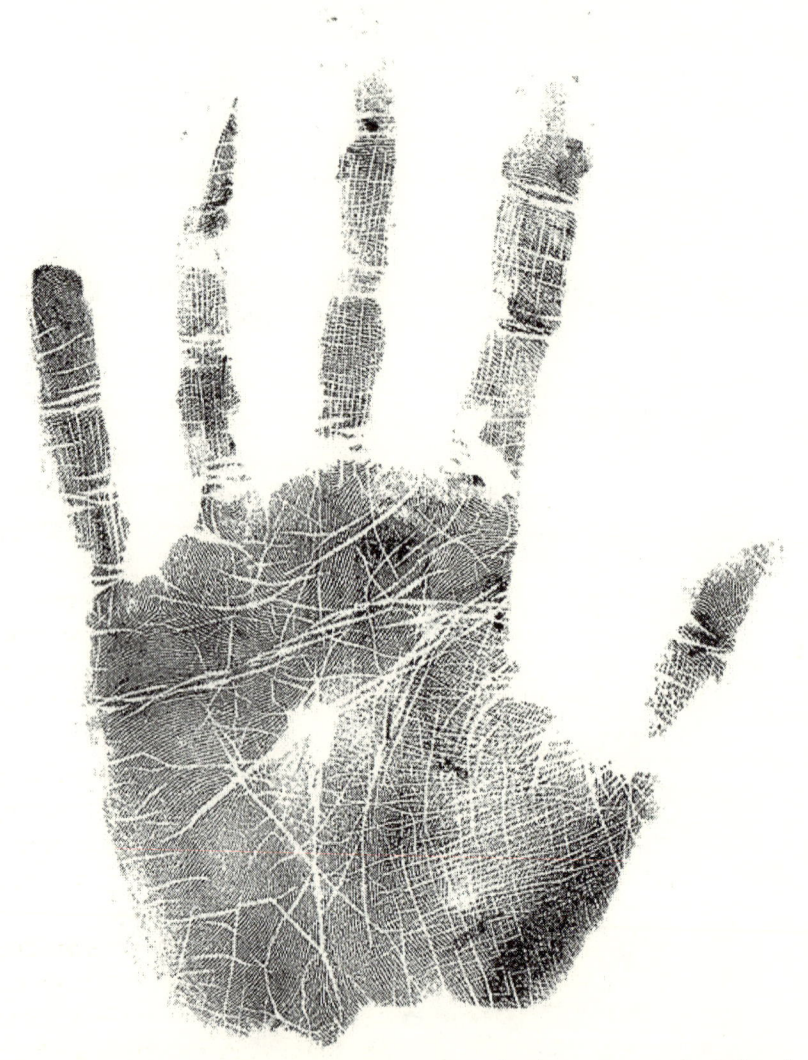

If you read the hands of friends, be gentle and diplomatic, please. If you suspect your heart rhythm, see your doctor for a checkup.

14

Tragedy in the Hands

Let's see what information we can give on the life of this hand's owner. She was found dead with no identification and no belongings.

First, let's look through what we have already covered in previous articles.

(A) This is an Ectomorph hand.
(B) It is an Air type.
(C) A shy, Introvert personality.
(D) Probably Caucasian heritage; the hand formation suggests Blood Type A, which is generally eastern European.

Death is very much a taboo subject with palmists and astrologers, and it needs very gentle handling. I have seen more arguments over this one topic than any other in palmistry. There are many differing views, even among palmists. I learned a valuable lesson regarding the prediction of death about 45 years back.

I was doing a charity fund raising for a hospice when one very elderly, overweight man came and sat down at my table. It was obvious he was very ill. He asked me to be honest and tell him how long he had. I skirted around his question, but he kept coming back to it, so I said "OK, at your present rate of decline, just less than a year."

The man was horrified and upset, and blurted out that he was counting on a cure being found at the last minute and did not want to die. My old friend, Elizabeth Kubler-Ross, once told me some people were in denial up to the very point of death. I upset this man terribly, and this was a bitter lesson for me. Afterwards, along with most palmists, I never cover this topic in any depth in personal readings. Tread very carefully, if you do.

The hand pic at (1) shows a very long middle or Saturn finger, which at (2) is set unusually high in the hand itself. This high mount, with a central apex as we see here, along with a strong finger, is always seen in Saturnine hands and is statistically seen most in Capricorn or January-born subjects.

(3) See the very thin Mercury finger. Mercury is the god of communications and everything from verbal to physical, even sexual, communication

50 Case Studies in Modern Palmistry

METROPOLITAN POLICE — Working together for a safer London
CENTRAL OPERATIONS

Lynne Owens QPM, MA
Assistant Commissioner

Room 1007
New Scotland Yard
Broadway
London
SW1H 0BG

Tel: 020 7230 2339
Email: Lynne.Owens@met.police.uk

13th January 2011

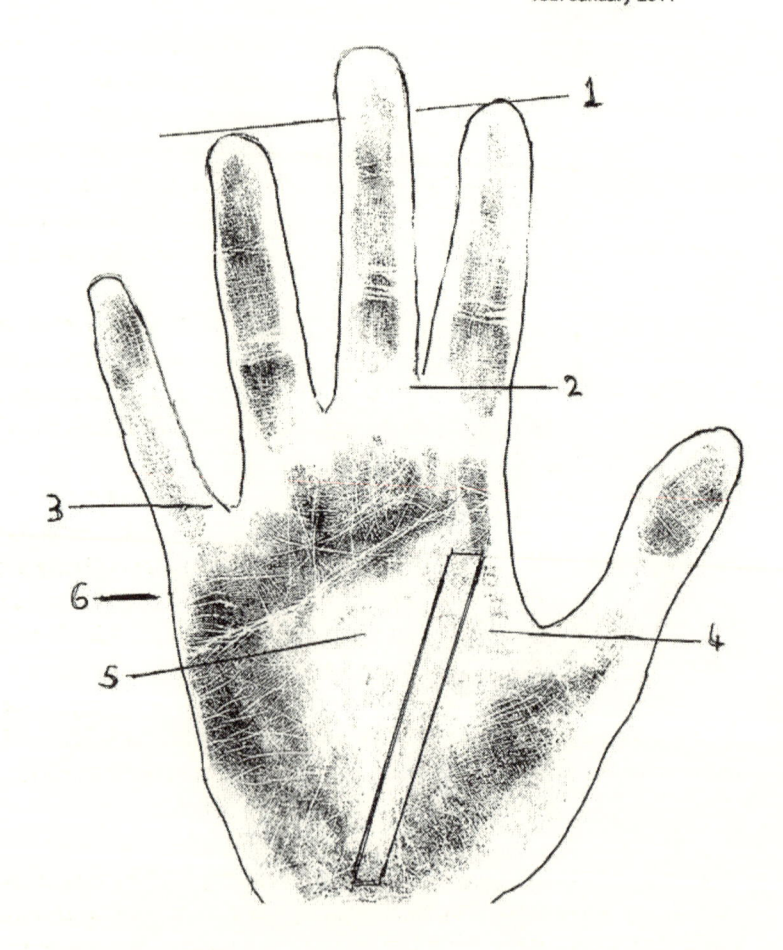

Tragedy in the Hands

is read on this finger. This shows that it looks withered and its low setting shows some arrested development in the sexual expression. This usually points to sexual abuse during the latency phase of childhood. If you see this, handle it gently, please. Every palmist should have some basis in counseling, and in this area it is vital.

(4) It is important to look at the beginning and end to the life line. Draw a straight line from one point to the other inside, then draw a parallel line at the outside and widest point of the life line. When it's as thin as this, it shows poor resistance qualities. This is being seen more and more now with the range of MSD (Multiple Sensitivity Disorders). It is a classic sign of a weak immune function.

A hand with this many lines is technically called a "full hand." It shows stress and anxiety. The broken and bitty heart line shows a nervous heart, particularly seen in Tachycardia and Da Costa syndrome. This shows gastric sensitivity, so remember 80 percent of the immune system is in the gut. Interestingly, the Max Planck Institute claimed that January-born children have a raised heart risk of 24 percent, indicating that January-born people are at highest risk of cardiovascular difficulty. This was because babies born in the first three months of the year are believed to have increased fat storage, which give later life problems.

There are several kinds of anxiety, and the anxiety in this hand looks like predictive anxiety. We all know someone who is a worrier, and if guests are 20 minutes late, will say "they have had an accident," "someone has died" or "the car has broken down," etc. This predicting is a kind of anxiety prevalent with Ectomorphs.

(5) The developed musculature of this hand is synonymous with dancers, and these always have leg and back problems. Many Ectomorphs also have spinal difficulties. We see the fate or luck line breaks badly at age 35; the lumbar, thoracic, sacral and cervical spinal sections all show sensitivity, with some possible kyphosis around age 35. Certainly, Saturnines suffer from bone and teeth weakness.

We also have at (6) a series of relationship lines ending, pointing downward, indicating unhappiness or failure. This is not an infallible sign, but with all the other factors shown, it indicates deep emotional distress.

SUMMARY

So, in analysis, I would say that we see a girl who was sexually abused, becoming a nervous, highly strung child. Her life line and travel sector shows movement in her late teens, so she could have come from the

Soviet Bloc about this time. She could have been a professional dancer, having to give up at around age 35 with spinal problems.

Wisdom teeth difficulties were indicated, and she had a very serious mindset. The narrowness of the energy levels of the life line are shown by the narrowness of the box drawn over it. Air handed people are always curious thinkers and theoreticians and famous for "what ifs." The spillover effect is the phenomenon where mental or emotional difficulties will eventually affect the physical body, and here we see a severely weakened physical body with some ill health caused by worry and anxiety. This will lead to insomnia and daytime listlessness and hopelessness, showing determination to end the life at around 35 years of age.

The hand print is included as it arrived with its Scotland Yard insignia. The police never acknowledge the help they get from astrologers, psychics, etc. All of our assistance is "unofficial" and off the record.

This poor tragic girl, someone's sister or daughter, was never named and was just given a number in the city morgue.

15

The 9 Types of Love

Falling in love takes 12 parts of the brain, all working together to release euphoria-inducing chemicals, mostly from the brain's ventral tegmental area. This gives us love's obsessive phase.

All relationships are built from two factors: attraction and attachment. Many women find they get addicted to the endorphin-releasing early phase and have difficulty bridging across to attachment, where the new love hunger morphs into the warm security of familiarity.

Research from the University of Padua showed that women experience emotional cycles, not just through the month, but in yearly phases, showing women's emotional fluctuation. A man's love is seen as stable, protective, predictable and constant. The old wives' tales about women being the weaker sex is untrue, since emotionally, women are far the stronger sex.

For some years, I was a college counselor. Because young love anxiety can be such a debilitating illness, many were students bedridden with lovesickness.

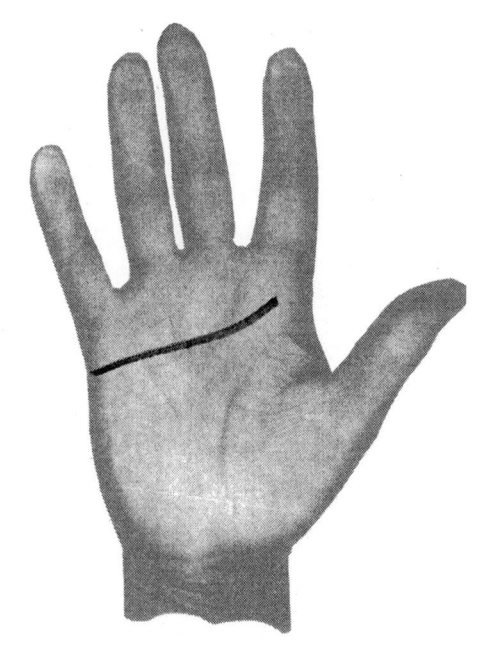

In the past, the public would see palmistry as the realm of gypsies and scammers, but over the past few decades things have changed. Top psychologists Carl Jung, Charlotte Wolf and Hans Eysenck all contributed to bring palmistry into the arena of counseling and psychotherapy. So what signs does palmistry say we should look for in a partner?

Although it's said opposites attract, the best partners statistically come from those who are similar to ourselves in culture, outlook, personality type and body type. Studies show more attraction to those from the same geographical area we are from.

Researchers, after a long study, have said there is not just one route to a loving relationship, but nine types or routes to love. These range from hedonistic, short, intense relationships to those based on mutual trust and those which develop into friendship once the fire of love has burnt itself out.

In the research tests, men and women were asked to rate a set of statements, such as "love is attempting to understand" and "love is a pleasurable addiction." Those which resonated to their own experiences were placed at the top of the list and the least resonating at the bottom. By examining these over a period of time, researchers were able to define nine love types.

Dr. Paul Stenner of Nottingham Trent University said people throughout the ages have tried to pigeonhole what love is, but the evidence says that love is culturally and historically variable. There is no one type of true love, but it's okay for love to differ across relationships and to change its character within a relationship over time.

The study showed that the participants aged from 18 to 59 felt that love should be based on mutual trust, recognition and support. The study published in the *British Journal of Social Psychology* comes at a time when divorce rates are soaring, and of the one in three marriages that survive, many were together just for the children or because they could not afford to move out.

The 9 types are shown here:

(1) Each partner endeavors to improve the other's life and helps the partner to maximize his/her potential.
(2) Love is based on physical attraction and intense, uncontrollable passion.
(3) Love is based on short bursts of hedonism, with fiery sex, which often burns itself out with no long-term consideration or commitment.
(4) Romantic love, the idealistic and far-away desires of wants the whole person, mind, body and soul.
(5) Realistic love is all about understanding, paying bills, differences of opinion, and learning to compromise.
(6) Unpredictable love consists of life-changing meetings and feelings, opening the door to opportunities and promises.

The 9 Types of Love

(7) Traditional love is where passion and desire turn into a steady, calm love-type relationship.
(8) Friendship love is a growing bond that starts with friendship and deepens and grows to form a true love.
(9) The relationship comes before each of the individual partners; the coupling is more than the sum of its parts.

Ideally, we should all be able to access these different love types, but very rarely can.

We can see, speaking generally, that although women can fall into the nine types, there are just two basic love types.

The heart line, which is curved and runs across the hand and up between the first two fingers, and those with straighter heart lines ending lower and well under the first finger.

(A) The women who have curved heart lines are go-getters. They are not shrinking violets. They are realistic and demonstrative and, if they like a man, they will go tell him and will not shirk at seducing a man. They are usually honest about who they are sexually, and are passionate and physical in their love natures. These women love from the heart chakra and are very warm and giving. They love good-looking, physical but youthful specimens, such as a boy toy, whom they see as prospective lovers.

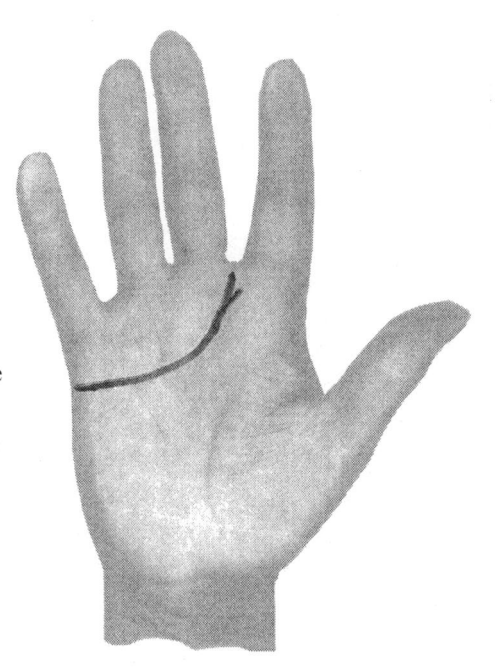

(B) Those whose heart lines lay flat across the hand like to be chased and wooed. They cannot make the first move, and are primarily head-centered. They like intellectual and amusing men, and these are the women who usually go for steady, mature, older men, where the physical side is not so important, but the sense of belonging is important. They are among the most loyal and these women are harder to sweep off their feet than the former.

Carl Jung described the first type as feeling women and the second as thinking women. This is just a general sketch. From the whole hand, you can tell where, when and sometimes whom a woman should love.

16

Timing of Events
The Golfer — The Big Vee

The most difficult aspect of hand reading is the timing of events, and each palmist has his own favorite method. Most are quite technical and complex, but here is a simple method from my first book published almost 40 years ago.

This man, a famous golfer, asks "When should I retire?"

This is a heavy square palm, with the lower base of the palm as wide as it is long, with a good life line reaching out wide into the hand. This is a man in vigorous health and is typical of the Mesomorph body type.

Wide palms across the base show brute strength and a love of physical rhythms and outdoor sports and activities, while the strength in that thumb and large mount of Venus suggests that this man uses his grip a lot. Those who continually hold fishing rods, bats and tools develop this musculature, so it is no surprise to learn this man is a well known golfer.

If we use a compass to find the exact center on the Venus mount, and draw a line from this to the central apex on the Mercury mount, where it cuts the life line, this is the exact middle of the life—except when the life line starts right round the side of the hand.

From this apex on the Mercury mount, draw a line to the Apollo mount, to Saturn and then to Jupiter. Ideally, this should be a perfect letter Vee, but it rarely is. It will show which mounts are high and which are low. The settings here will be of importance. This man has a highly pronounced Saturn mount, and with a fate line running from the apex to the Saturn finger, we see an active Saturnian. This man would be of serious disposition, sober, tall and gaunt with poor yellowing teeth and pale skin. The Apollo mount is low; this is known as an "affliction," and an afflicted Apollo will take away some of its good message.

If we look to Diagram 2, we see from the center of the Venus mount two more equi-distant lines coming to the life line, and this divides the life line into four equal divisions.

These divisions are from where the life line starts—Spring, Summer, Autumn and Winter, and visual examination and comparison of these will

50 Case Studies in Modern Palmistry

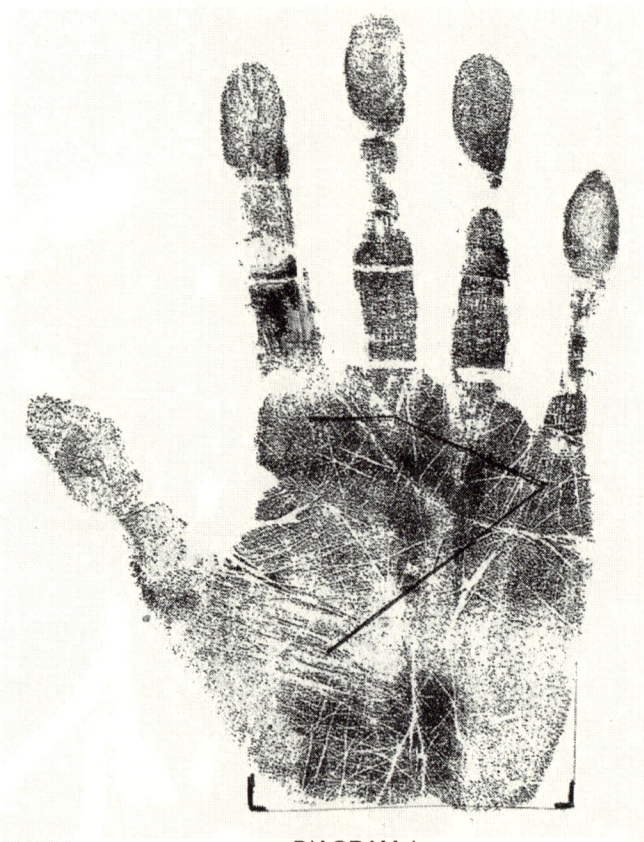

DIAGRAM 1

yield good results. Use your thumb tip to press each of the four divisions. Is one firmer than the rest? This will tell of resilience and power to spring back from adversity, and the best time to fulfill life plans, moves, etc. Scripture tells us that *"there is a time in our lives for sowing and a time for reaping,"* and so there is.

While softness under the line gives acceptance, lack of will and inability in the fight of life, some palmists see four divisions of line strength. Remember, wide thick lines infer sluggish systems and thin lines infer the inability to carry the life currents adequately. But most importantly, check to see that the quality and width of the line matches the other lines in the hand. If it does not and is alien to the other lines' formation, it's a "cuckoo line" and must bear closer examination. Also note if any parts have cross bars, gaps or islands—all of these are seen as derogatory markings.

Timing of Events: Golfer's Hand — The Big Vee

In ancient India, Ayurvedic medicine was used with palmistry to treat people's ills, and *Vata* was the period of early winter, *Kapha* was late winter to the start of spring, and *Pitta* was late spring and summer. People have their own seasons for ups and downs for illness and for health, and the hand shape and bone structure can tell you when you are firing on all cylinders and when it's best to tackle new projects or to wait.

So by dividing this man's hand, we can see the life line begins to fragment in the winter period, and by sub-dividing, we can say late fifties—probably age 57—is the year and the *Kapha* season would suggest February, and by using Numerology, we can often work it out even closer.

Aristotle said, *"The hand is the tool of tools,"* and Ralph Waldo Emerson said, *"The first wealth is health."*

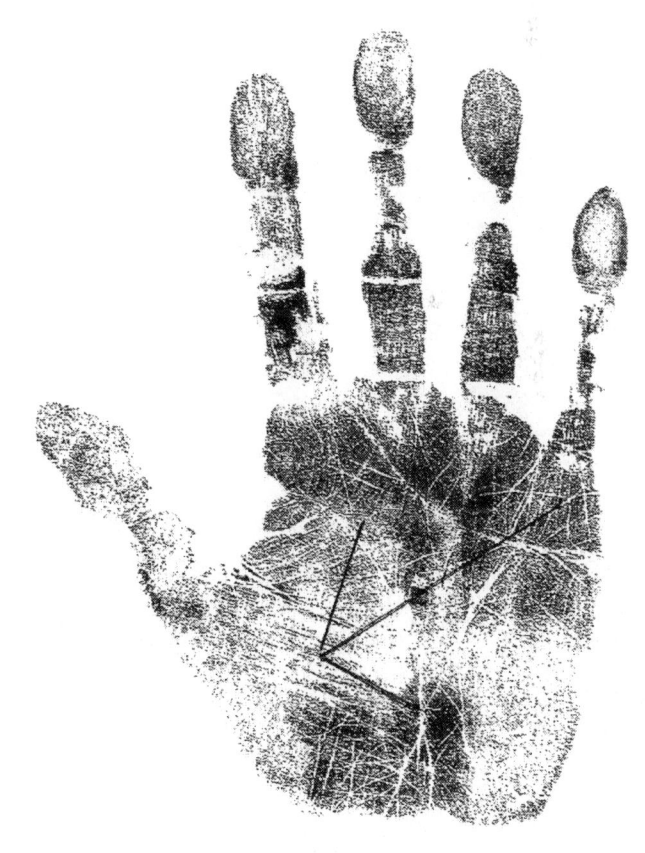

DIAGRAM 2

17

The Fermoy Hand

The Fermoy unit is a health facility for longterm psychiatric care, and this is a hand print of one of the patients. Permission to show this was only granted after much discussion, as patient confidentiality covers all from psychiatric assessment to psychic readings, and this comprises both.

The first thing to notice is the body typology, and this is an Ectomorph. Aristotle, the originator of psychology, studied the hand and said, "*I count him braver who overcomes desires, than he who conquers his enemies, for the hardest victory is over self.*"

A wrongly built hand as this shows a wrongly built mindset, and a dysplastic hand can hold life-long pain as does this, striving for victory over early trauma. The hand is split by experts straight down the middle along the fate line; the thumb side tells of the Conscious mind and the heel side shows the Subconscious.

The first, or Jupiter finger, represents the Ego, self-assertion, ambition and outward face, and should be the same size as the third, or Apollo finger. Notice how much thicker it is, showing forcefulness, an urge for power and a need for dominance. Compare this to the thin and wasted Apollo finger, and the small, low setting of the little, or Mercury finger.

Mercury was the god of communications, and if we look again at the Mercury finger, we understand that there are difficulties here. Communications start with speech, actions, gestures—even the sex act is only physical communication. But this finger stands away from the hand and hides low into the palm, showing damage in this area from long ago, and an inability to express this harsh inner pain.

William Sheldon was the man who allied body typology to psychological profiles, and Carl Jung the man who initiated psychology to hand types and astrology.

The close and ragged joining of the life to head lines in what is known to palmists as a "barbed wire entanglement" illustrates a very unhappy and insecure childhood. The stretching of the skin shown at this point is indicative of fear and anxiety neuroses, with its genesis in the latency period

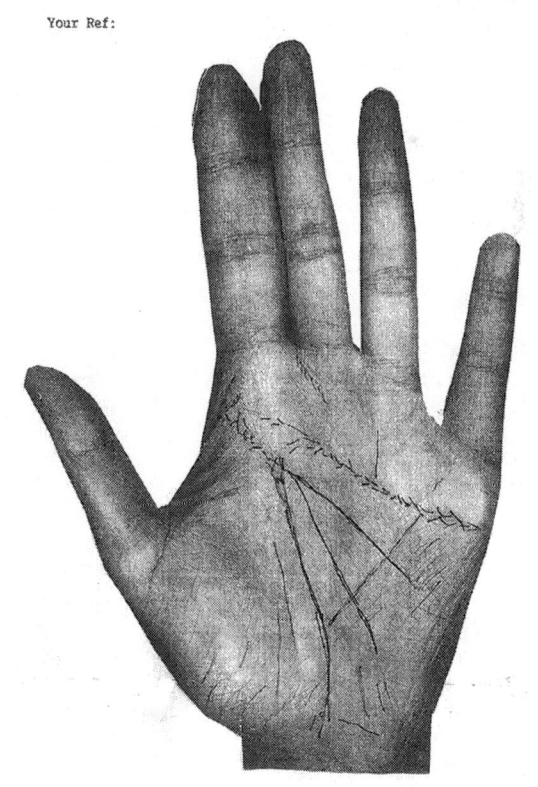

The Fermoy Hand

at approximately age 6.

The many-lined hand is called a "full hand" and is typical in sensitive, worrying types with its knock on physical symptomatology, and the wasted Apollo finger was known from Aristotle's time to signify the loss of the mother's love from the age shown in the hand.

Dr. Eric Berne described the Ectomorph as "brain minded and nervous," and the nervous system here has always been a problem and had resulted in many years in psychiatric institutions on a variety of medications and treatments.

The line running from the life line up toward the little finger is known as a "health line," and this shows gastric anomalies and eating disorders, which are confirmed at the thin finger bases and fleshless palm.

The lean of the Conscious fingers toward the thumb, in a grasping motion, shows an Unconscious need for security in outside objects. The lady in question has always hoarded small food scraps in her room.

The top line crossing the palm is known as the heart line to palmists, and Aristotle tells us thus: *"From this line we tell the warmth and care of how a person be."* This line is broken, ragged and pale. If we imagine the lines across the palm as rivers containing currents of energy which flow through, this is both sluggish and with deep emotional blockages, and the heart action is poor.

The Max Planck Institute found with studies that life expectancy relates to the birth month, with some showing high in depressive illness tendencies, and depression and suicidal thoughts have always been a part of her personality.

The Ectomorph mindset is one prone to stress, depression and agoraphobia. This poor woman has never trusted a living soul. The hospital cat has been her only friend, and she has only spoken a few times since the terrible ordeal in her childhood, and those were aggressive words to other inmates to keep away.

It turns out our friend here witnessed the Stalinist purges, and at dead of night they came for her parents, he a Polish officer, her mother a Polish schoolteacher. She, aged 5 and a half, followed at a distance and watched as thousands of people stood in front of trenches in the Katyn Forest and were shot.

She lived rough for several months, eating from bins and sleeping where she could. She was gang-raped by Russian soldiers, and was brought to Britain in a batch of half-starved children by the Red Cross, and has been institutionalized ever since.

I broke every rule there is as I stood up and held her close as she cried and shuddered deeply; she is reaching the end of her life, and this short human contact was all she had for many, many years.

True palmistry is about understanding and healing. We all at some time need another's help to pull us out of the pit, and many palmists use CBT type counseling, as talk through therapies have been shown to work better than pharmaceuticals.

Aristotle again: *"Some people are afraid of what they might find with too much analysis, but if you have to crawl into your wounds to discover where your fears are, once the bleeding starts, healing can begin."*

Further reading: *Katyn Forest Murders*

18

Dealing with Child Trauma

Any child with difficulties must be handled with great care, and just as the mannerisms and deportment can be very telling of an adult's state of mind, a child will be even more so. It is a well known truth in psychiatry that any mental disturbance will be accompanied by a disturbance in gait and gesture, and no gesture is more telling than those given by the hands. As the hand is the closest organ to the brain, this must be the first area for investigation.

While teaching many years ago, I would watch how the children held their hands, and often would ask a particular child to stop behind after lessons to chat, the first diagnosis of many problems.

The hand print shown is of a child brought into the clinic by the mother who found dealing with the child "stressful and difficult."

The Royal College of Psychiatrists says that for a child to be a fully rounded, complete human being, it needs three things:

(1) It must be born to a two-parent family, a man and a woman;
(2) Both must be seen to love the child;
(3) And it must be breastfed to the correct term.

This child displays all these characteristics, but deep trauma is clearly shown. The Royal College of Psychiatrists also says, in their instructions to counselors, that any problems up to the age of 6, known as the "latency period," are not easily resolved and can lay dormant within the psyche, and a later life upset will bring back the feelings of hurt and loss, which are then often transposed into other areas. Children with good early mental health were more likely to do well later in career, relationships and have happiness into old age, which they get from a stable mum and dad.

Modern fashions in child psychology are very different from 40 years ago. Gone is the "spare the cane, spoil the child" mantra. This purely authoritarian attitude, even in military training, has proved it does not work; it just builds later resentment.

This child is bereaved; the father was killed traveling to work. To the child around the age of 6, they cannot grasp that death is final and that Daddy is not coming back. They will ask questions such as "Can we go to see Daddy?" or "Is he having regular meals in heaven?" "Why can't he talk to us?" etc.

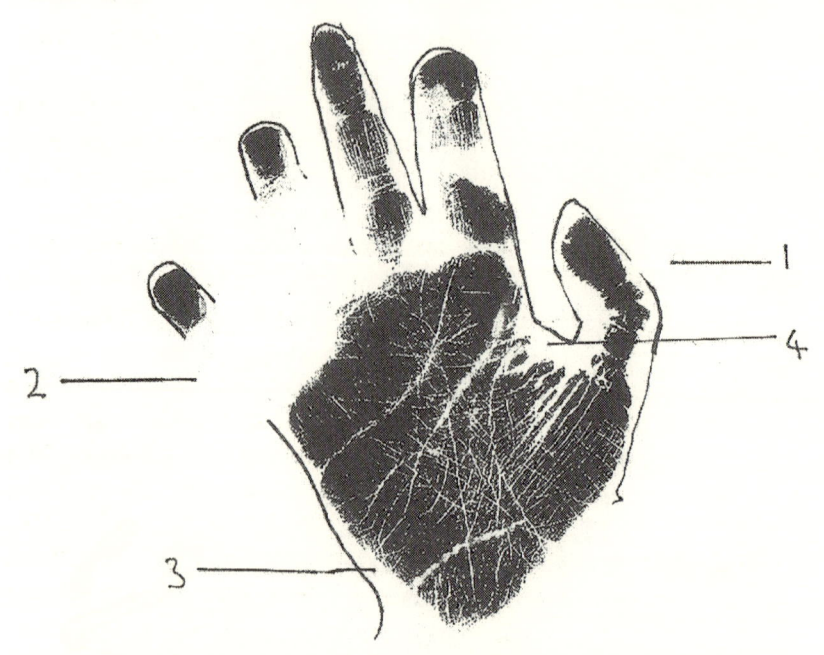

This poses a threat to the child, who needs to feel they are living in a warm, safe, familiar world, then see this as possibly happening to them. It is always best to answer their questions honestly but gently, as this helps them with the hierarchy of events later unfolding in their own lives.

Care must be taken in how the death is spoken of, such things as "Daddy is asleep" may cause the child to fear sleep, as then they may not wake up, and behavior may deteriorate badly as in this case, where bedtime produces screaming fits, mealtime is tantrum time, and screams for junk food is common, and the child is extremely disobedient and willful.

This hand has the thumb crooked at an angle (1). This unnatural pose shows acute anxiety and is often seen in child bereavement cases. Experts say 5 percent of children will need expert help and additional support. The other parent, too, is going through their own bereavement process and their needs are often overlooked. I often ask them to contact their religious organization for support.

The two fingers on the subconscious side of the hand are also slightly

Dealing with Child Trauma

crooked as the lower phalanges do not show in the ink (2). This shows deep emotional turmoil, which is not helped by the poison line crossing the Luna base to the life line (3), which is always seen with food and drug allergies, behavioral disorders ADHD and similar.

The large gap between the head and life line (4) shows that the thinking is not engaged with the life energies. These people are always impulsive and accident prone. This, coupled to the short index or Jupiter finger in the fully and many-lined hand shown, is the classic symptom complex for neuroticism and anxiety disorders, enhanced by the many breaks in the life line round the thumb, which shows energy and "life" disruptions. Yet, the hand is good in its long-term prognosis. But careful handling now is vital. Many parents find a scrapbook of the lost parent is a good method of externalizing the grief, where the child can write in things and draw pictures, along with a soft toy like a teddy bear to talk to about things. Also, good diet with fruit and vegetables is essential.

From around the time of puberty, children react very differently to close family deaths, as they understand more of the long-term consequences of loss, but they have to learn how to survive without the loved person. This trauma can re-emerge and manifest in a sense of isolation and loneliness, educational problems and self harm, with possible attempts at suicide. The other aspect is that early extra responsibilities may have to be shouldered after the loss. All youngsters show grief in different ways, and this can emerge at different life stages and have to be faced again. Elizabeth Kubler-Ross first enumerated the five stages of grief, which at some time we all have to undergo: Denial, Anger, Bargaining, Depression and Grief.

Please be mindful of this, and watch for each stage and deal with it sympathetically. Not all children make the excellent progress shown in this hand.

Further reading: *The Hands of Children* by Julius Spier. Julius was a pupil of Carl Jung's psychology and palmistry studies. The term Psychochirology refers to this branch of palmistry.

19

Decisions in Love

For anyone who consults a reader, one question is, above all, of the greatest importance—how can they insure that the reader is genuine?

In these difficult times, quacks, cold readers and frauds abound as never before, but there are certain safeguards you must employ.

First, tell the reader nothing about yourself. You are paying them to tell you, and just answer yes or no, and never have a reader visit your home, because cold reading frauds will look at your clothes, your furniture and photographs, etc., and they will ask you questions and feed it all back to you.

Do not have a Skype reading, as the last answer you give is often used for their next statement.

The only way the frauds cannot imitate is when you send hand photos with nothing else. They can't figure out how to fake this.

The hand print shown is from a lady who sent me a seven-page letter with family photographs of her home and life, and I was furious with her.

This hand print shows how her life had deteriorated to the depressed place she now occupies. Her big question was, "I am in an old, stale marriage, where my husband spends all his time at the golf club or at card games. I have had an offer from a lovely young man. What should I do? Go or stay?"

So what do we see?

    (1) many lined hand
    (2) Saturn and Apollo middle fingers unnaturally close
    (3) very long middle or Saturn finger
    (4) very thin Mercury or small finger
    (5) notice the double life line
    (6) heart line very long, ragged, with heavy girdle of Venus
    (7) lumps on the knuckles (not shown)

"Keep your face to the sun and you will not see the shadows."

— Helen Keller

Decisions in Love

Many lines infer an anxious, worrying temperament. Saturn and Apollo fingers tight together show depression or a feeling of impending crisis. Long Saturn finger, a serious, fretful disposition. Very thin Mercury finger throughout its length, a damaged sexual infrastructure, and these signs together infer childhood sexual exploitation and its aftermath of long depression.

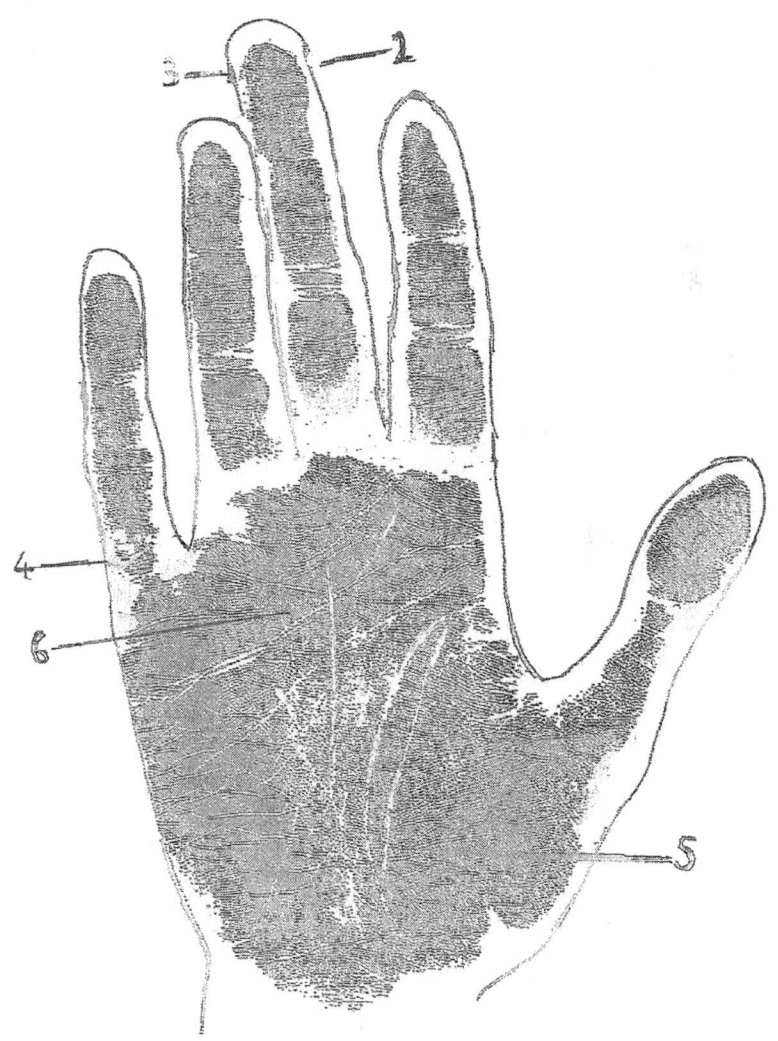

The double line of life is rare and they clash around 50 years of age.
This long, straight islanded and ragged heart line tells us of someone who has a lot of heart and who cares very much about the community

outside the marriage. This with the Girdle of Venus above means being loved is the most important thing in her life. She needs that emotional nourishment with physical love, but has a lot of emotional turbulence in her past.

The lumps on the knuckles were hard, yellow, fatty deposits and are familial hyper-cholesterolaemia, an inherited condition leading to very high cholesterol readings. People with this and the heart line shown can be at risk of heart attacks at any age. This kind of heart line infers arrhythmia, and compounded by many years without a break on the contraceptive pill, meaning she had to make several important life changes.

A father's love is more important to a young girl than her mother's for the child's development. In terms of parental rejection and acceptance, this shapes our later personalities and can decide on our choice of life partner. Professor Rohner's studies show that deep rejection affects that part of the brain with which we deal with physical pain. The early rejection and exploitation by her father was hugely damaging to the psychological bedrock of her personality.

This girl's background was very shaky indeed. She married, for security, a wealthy, older man who loved to show off her beauty, but could give no love, and she had had enough.

So what should she do? Stay in an unhappy, soul-destroying relationship, or leave for a man who genuinely loved her but was poor?

* It is never the job of a reader to make people's decisions for them, just to point out the pitfalls that can occur; this was described beautifully by the Greek philosopher, Epictetus:

"Remember that you are an actor in a drama of such a part as it may please the master to assign you for as long a time or as little as he may choose, and if he wills you to take the part of a poor man or a cripple or a ruler or a private citizen, then may you act that part with grace, for to act well the part assigned to us, that indeed is ours to do, but to choose is another's."

I get a Christmas card every year from a lovely lady who found love a little late in life. She found love and a blissfully happy relationship.

"There is no remedy for love, but to love more."   — Henry Thoreau

20

Danger Averted

These are two interesting palm prints taken from the same subject five years apart and show that when all seems lost, there are still times when Right Thinking, Right Eating, Right Living, and Right Action can save the day.

These four "Rights" were the mantra of Harry Edwards, one of the greatest spiritual healers of this century, and these two palm prints show how using Harry's four simple rules changed and maybe saved a man's life.

We see here a blotch of fuzzy lines in the palm centre. This we expect to see in some complex medical conditions, such as Cystic Fibrosis.

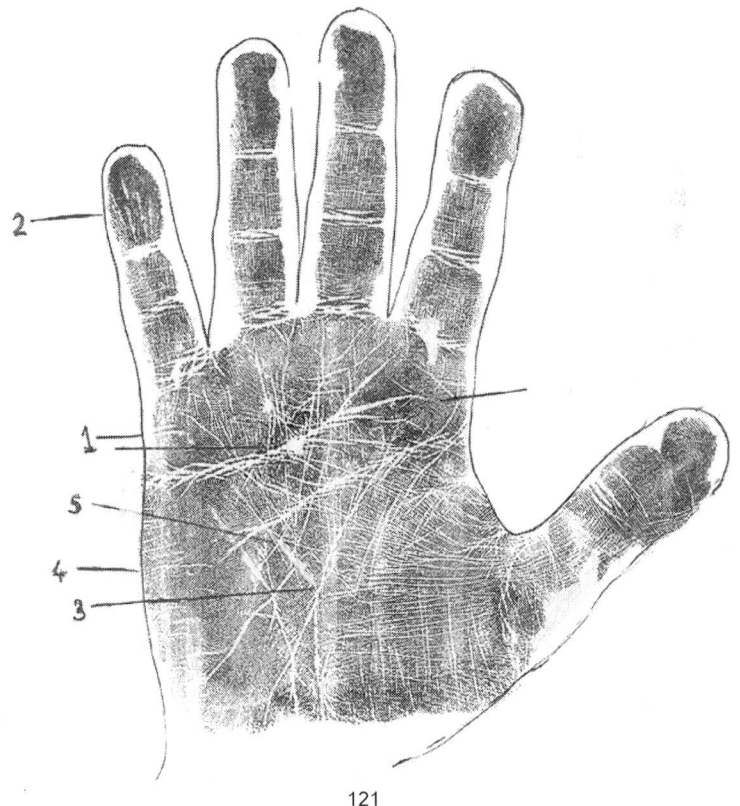

50 Case Studies in Modern Palmistry

The owner of these palm prints began having problems when he was skateboarding in a supermarket car park. A car speeding through ran him down, and he was off work for some time. As his health deteriorated, he could not keep up his mortgage as he lost his job and his new wife left him.

(1) See drooping relationship line and large, white blotch on heart line, showing emotional difficulties.

(2) His reaction to allopathic medication and pharmaceutical drugs upset his glandular system; the small lines on the tip of the Mercury finger show thyroidal imbalance.

He had also become addicted to prescribed analgesics (painkillers) which was seriously affecting his digestive infrastructure.

(3) The health line colliding with the life line shows the ongoing gastric problems, and his life line from this point takes on a weakened, thin and broken appearance.

(4) Lines on the side of the hand, called travel lines by some palmists, are actually restlessness lines, which are often at the root of much travel.

(5) Destiny line broken, fragmented and short; this is an ominous sign.

Shakespeare said: *"When troubles come, they come not singly but in battalions."* And this poor chap had seen his life collapse around him.

The second, more positive hand print was taken five years later.

The relationship lines had improved; in India, this drooping line is called a Mangli line and infers a problematic or difficult relationship with a negative prognosis. Thyroid problems had improved drastically with the addition of homeopathically prepared kelp, a seaweed rich in necessary thyroxin; he had also stopped using a fluoride toothpaste. The two biggest thyroid disrupters known to man are added to tap water: chlorine and fluoride. These were removed with the aid of a kitchen filter jug.

The health line—sometimes this can move up the hand from the life line and sometimes it can come down and attack it. Look to see which end of the health line is the thickest; this will show where it begins its travel. Note the age on the life line and its appearance after. This life line now is much longer and stronger.

It should be said that the damage done by prolonged antibiotics is only now being recognized. I urged him to take a live probiotic last thing each night, to replace the natural flora and fauna of the gut.

A live acidophilus yogurt is also beneficial; not the commercial yogurts, which are full of fake sugars (Aspartame) and preservatives, but buy the genuine stuff with real fruit. I also recommended an Omega 3 and mixed vitamin and mineral tablet each day.

Danger Averted

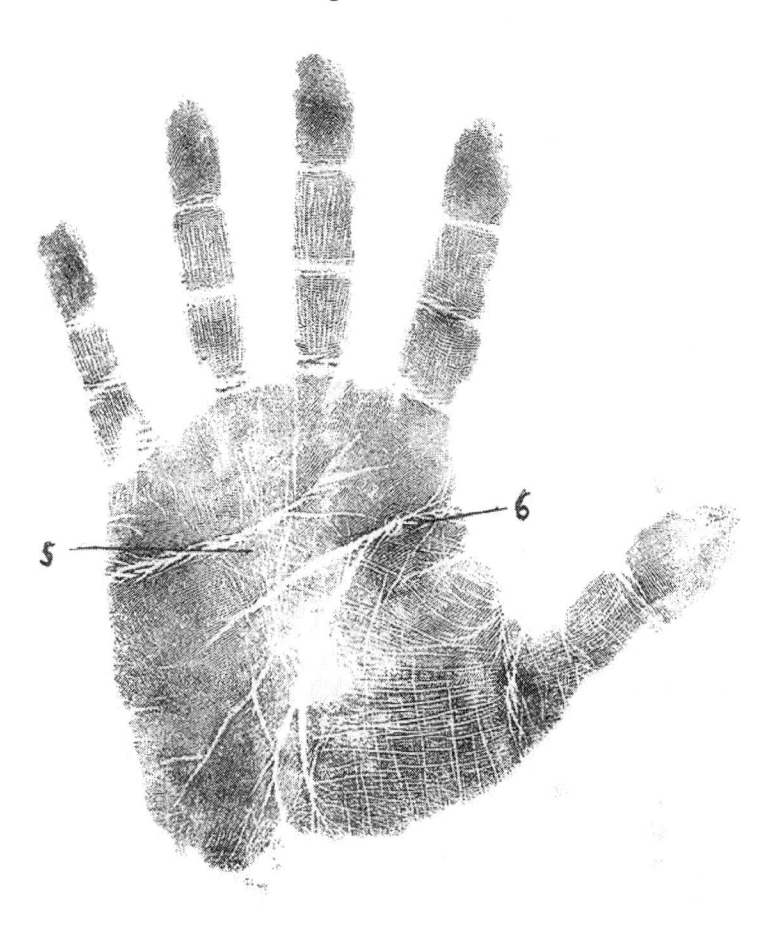

Travel/restlessness lines almost gone, but the destiny line up the hand is longer and thicker. There are also several protective squares on this now, covering the period after this man's illness. This is very good news.

The square is the most positive sign in palmistry. In Tibetan palmistry the square is called the *poi,* which means "safety of land," and when you see big squares like this, you know our patient has landed safely.

The Bible at Zachariah 2-1 says: "*I lifted up my eyes and there was a man with a measuring line in his hand.*"

The line of destiny was called the measuring line, and when the physician saw a strong measuring line as here, he was more positive about the man's recovery.

The early part to the life line now shows a small circle (6). This is the rarest mark in palmistry. I have seen this less than a dozen times in 60 years of hand reading, and this depicts the trauma of the accident and loss of his wife and home.

The meaning of the perfect circle depends on where it is seen, the type of hand and its direction of travel.

This man had taken on board the 4 Rights of Harry Edwards. He drastically improved his diet, cut out junk food and now bought his food fresh from the farmer's market. He meditates for 30 minutes at the end of each day, he walks to work each day, and still uses his skateboard, but runs for an hour on weekends.

If he can get his life back under control after such a crisis, so can you. Sometimes we need a little help. If you need it, remember to ask.

Harry Edwards died on 7 December 1976. His signing-in book contained thousands of people who claimed they were helped by his spiritual healing, and I never saw a single person who said they were not helped after visiting him.

> *Do all the good you can*
> *By all the means you can*
> *In all the ways you can*
> *In all the places you can*
> *At all the times you can*
> *As long as ever you can*
> — John Wesley

21
Are You Being Emotionally Abused?

I recently had a hospital doctor email me to say he always read my palmistry articles and particularly liked any mention of illness diagnosis from the hands, but then said I hope you don't discuss these points with your people as you are not a trained doctor. I replied that he should not discuss them either as he was not a trained palmist.

The Royal College of Psychiatrists claim that any mental illness will be accompanied by its own disturbance of gait.

The late great psychiatrist Henri Rey and I used to play a game on seeing a person with disturbed gait, to guess what the illness was, and in many cases you can determine the problem accurately from how a person walks, etc., and similarly, the way a disturbed person holds their hands will also give you many clues to their illness.

I used to work part-time in a health clinic and I could, by taking a quick look at the hands in the waiting room, usually tell what the problems were before speaking with them.

The hand shown has several distinguishing features. Can you spot them?

(1) Two fingers huddled together for protection
(2) Mercury finger leaning sharply away
(3) Head line ending high in the hand
(4) Thick tip to the thumb, which is crooked
(5) Lines of Apollo unclear and a mixed jumble
(6) First, or Jupiter, finger standing away

Just as you can determine the country of origin by the face (e.g., Caucasian, Negro, etc.), because of the underlying bone structure, the four bone structures (Caucasoid, Negroid, Mongoloid and Mesoid) also show the nationality from the hand, and this hand print was from the Indo/Pak subcontinent, which infers an arranged or forced marriage, which statistically can be prone to difficulties.

When the musculo/skeletal structure is put under stress over a period, the body will begin to compensate, such as in the thick muscly legs of footballers, and the hands here showed a thickening of the Scaphoid and

Lunate wrist bones as seen in longterm tennis players.

These are very difficult times, and many are suffering economic distress. This may lead to abuse of drugs or excessive alcohol use, and addictions can lead to erratic and inappropriate behavior. Any substance abuse often leads on to emotional abuse and a deteriorating relationship.

Emotionally abusive spouses want you all to themselves and they do not understand that you may want to see family and friends outside the relationship. It is healthy and normal for you to hang out with other people, so if your partner prevents you from doing so, this may be a sign you are in an emotionally abusive relationship.

An abuser will shout at what you have spent on the shopping, placing their anxiety at your door for what has to be spent on groceries. Some will even check up on where you have been. Men will often tell you what you can and cannot wear. Women are more subtle and will buy you clothes they want to see you in.

Your partner may call you bad names. Even if they say they are joking, this is meant to hurt and keep you in line. Abusers sometimes cover themselves by saying it's your fault and that you need to lighten up, and that you are way too sensitive. This is not true as a loving partner would not do this. Abusive partners have a way of making you think that this is normal behavior and that it is you who has the problem.

Abusive partners will use various control mechanisms, such as instilling fear. If you feel fear at any time, then there is something very wrong, and abusers may try to intimidate you with threats of violence, or dominating you with other power tactics, and in these financially stressful times, all this is happening with ever greater frequency.

A technique used by many women is the isolation technique, where they shut off and won't speak to you, or another controlling behavior is to shut off sex. Men are easy to manipulate as they quickly become sexually dependent in a relationship; this increases their anxiety and fear factor.

Abusers are great manipulators and will sulk, threaten to leave, and emotionally punish you for not going along with his or her idea of how things should be. They will try to make you feel guilty any time you exert your will and assert what is right for you. And at times the abuser may appear to be apologetic and loving, but the "remorse" doesn't last long. Abuse begins again when the abuser feels he or she has you back where they want you.

Women are usually the game players in relationships, as they know men can't cope with mind games. The result will be that he punches walls

Are You Being Emotionally Abused?

or doors, shouts, bangs doors, drives too fast, and you will witness displays of anger. This is the "tipping point." When you see this behavior, think deeply about what you really want. The World Health Organization says all relationships should be 50-50 equal partners in all decisions, but they rarely are.

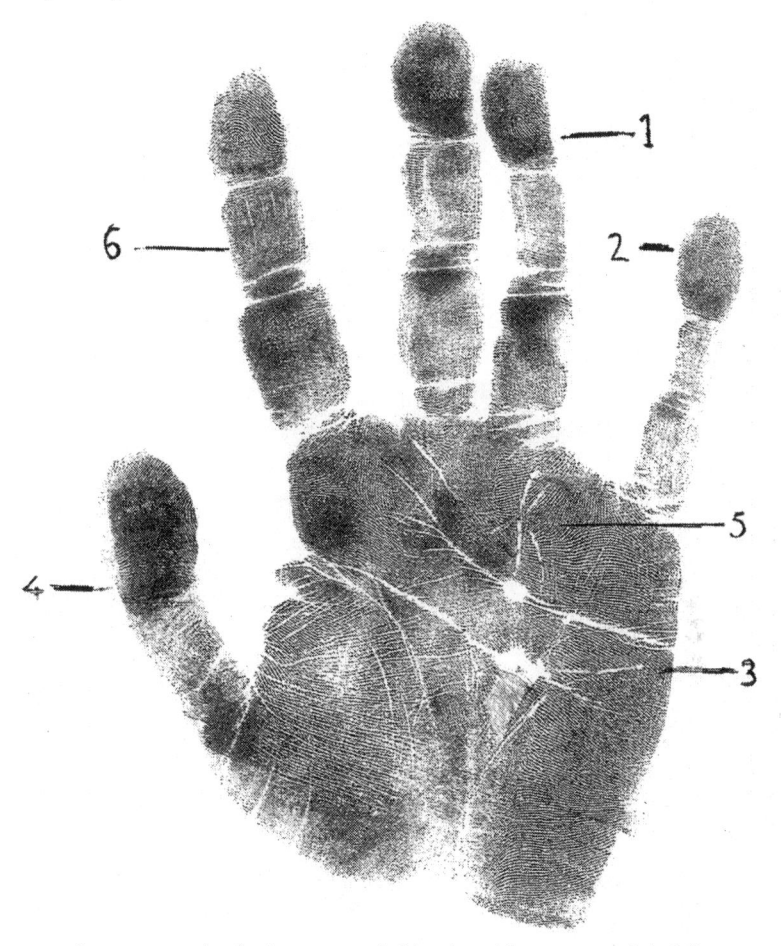

Some years back, I was good friends with a top model. Like many women who, through abuse, have retreated from relationships with men, she had instead 13 cats. You can tell the strength of the hurt by the number of cats. Another ex model had 25. Some retreat into same-sex relationships or none at all.

(1) The huddling together of the Saturn/Apollo fingers is a sign of despair and depression.

(2) For Mercury to be divorced from the other fingers and leaning away shows the need to escape the confines of the relationship, either temporarily or permanently. This person is just going through the motions and is not involved with the partner at a deep level.

(3) The head line ending high in the hand shows, among other things, the desperate need for economic security. Money has recently often taken the place of the security normally given by a warm, loving relationship.

(4) Thick end to the thumb shows bottled-up energies, and possible temper tantrums in frustration. In Medieval times this was called a murderer's thumb; the crooked thumb is seen in extreme anxiety cases.

(5) The lines under the Apollo finger can relate to money, and this arrangement is not a positive sign for financial health.

(6) Jupiter finger in this position shows unease in the career situation; in the other hand would mean the home situation, and this lady had both.

It turned out that our once extremely beautiful Indian lady had been a tennis player and a dancer and had been put in an arranged marriage with a wealthy man from an important family. The marriage had deteriorated to the point where she was on medication, and the results are here in the hand print, which tells us she was at breaking point. The husband had been threatening extreme violence if she went home to her mother, and had described most graphically what he would do to her.

If you are undergoing any of these signs listed above, you need to get help. Do not keep this in silence; these situations need the light of truth to shine in and only then can help be given and accepted.

* In memory of Fakhra Younus, murdered by her husband April 17 2012.

22

Protection Against Vampires

There have been several vampire films released recently, but did you know some people have a sign in their hands that a centuries-old tradition claims gives them protection from vampires?

This is the hand of a multi-millionaire Russian mafia boss now resident in Britain. He very proud of his protective mark.

Ex-Soviet people I have met have always impressed me with their warmth and generosity. They are family-oriented but very superstitious. Many of the Russian millionaire residents now in Britain have regular psychic readers at garden parties, weddings and family gatherings. Before any business deal, they will have a psychic present as protection.

The hand print shown speaks of the quality of parental relationships having a direct bearing on how a man reacts in key situations. Studies show parents have to be one of each sex for optimum mental and emotional health. The missing part of the small, or Mercury finger, is a sign of Mafia initiation. The name Mercury comes from the same root word as merchant, and mafia activities are about money and power.

This man has paternal relating difficulties from an overly strict father, which have colored his later life outlook with inferiority feelings as shown by a very short Jupiter finger (1).

The large, thick end to the thumb shows anger management problems, and in early lore was called "the murderer's thumb." (2)

The upturned branch of the head line toward the heart line tells that the intellect will take total control of the heart, at the age referred to by the life line (3).

The main lines crossing the ball of the thumb toward the life line from the family ring at the thumb base to the life line show family conflict and perhaps disapproval of the lifestyle (4). Hargett, the 19th century U.S. research palmist, spent his life watching these lines because they can, when seen alongside the relationship lines under the Mercury finger, tell about karmic loves.

The missing fate and Apollo lines is a rare joint marking and is seen with people who do not feel they are in the right place on life's path (or enjoy

50 Case Studies in Modern Palmistry

their money).

The life line at the palmar base, as it meets with the health line, forms a huge letter 'V'. This is seen in Eastern European countries as preservation from vampires and something they do not joke about. Maybe you have it, too? (6)

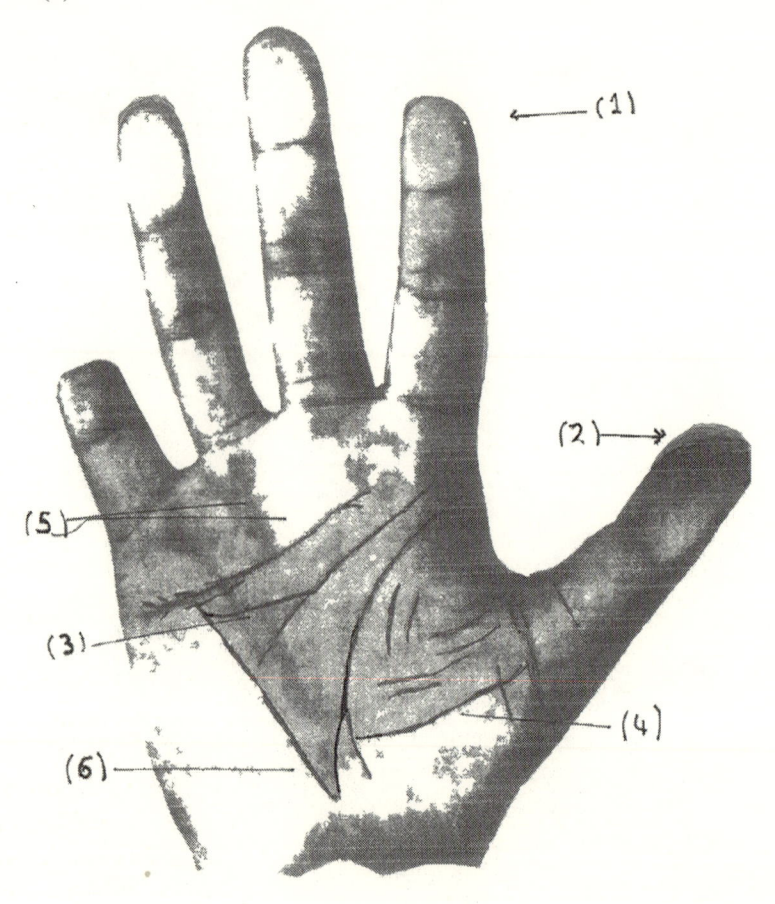

This world is but a canvas for our imagination.

23

Romance in the Palm

This is the hand print of a well known TV singer, dancer and entertainer. The Gesell model of human behavior says that behavior is a function of our structure. We behave in a way that results from the way our bodies are built. One look at an athlete tells you of their physical prowess. This being the case, we can read into the separate stages of bodily development, and discover many astonishing things.

The physical can be affected by the foods we eat and drink, the air we breathe; in fact, our total environmental blanket of home, work and play affects our emotional infrastructure, intellectual architecture, karmic landscape, health and longevity—every arena of our lives. It alters the lines on our hands from the 10th week in the womb.

Romantic advice was asked for this girl's disastrous love life. The line of heart, which is the upper crossing line (1), shows a deep need to love and be loved. The depth of the curve shows passion, a good physical response and a warm, caring, demonstrative, feminine nature.

Each dropping line from this line shows an emotional hurt, and she has several (2). She is changeable in her emotions.

Recent studies from the Italian University of Pavia have shown that in the first 12 months of a love affair, when palpitations are the norm, women can become addicted to the attendant bodily chemical responses, making them hunger for partner changes at 12-month intervals. This, coupled to the mood swings of P.M.S., can mean that during her cycle, she will in turn be attracted to wimpy types, fatherly types, rugged, unsuitable, rough macho men, then real compatible life partners, and lastly for a space, no men at all.

So her many-lined hand, which is technically called a "full hand" (3), goes with an anxious, sensitive, worrying, fretful and changeable temperament. She is an exciting and physical girl, certainly a head turner.

As Shakespeare said, *"A young man's love comes only from his eyes, and alas, many women are valued only for their external beauty."*

The long ring, or Apollo finger, is a sign of emotional, musical and artistic awareness. This, with the long, strong and straight little, or finger of

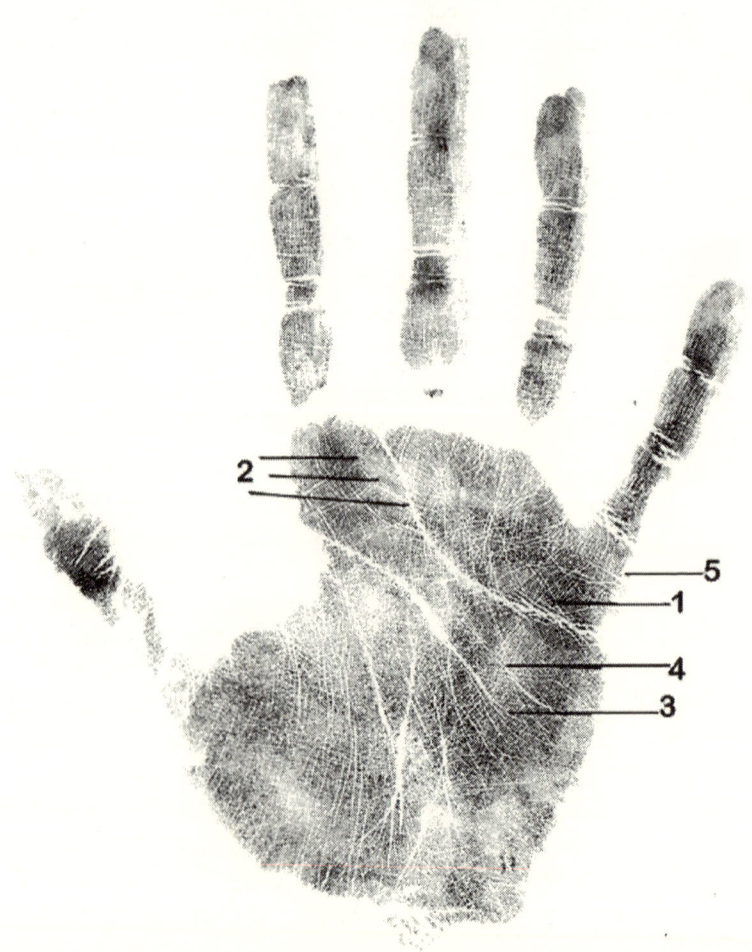

Mercury, means a good communicator with singing ability. These two added to the slightly drooping head line (4), among other signposts, and we have her present career in entertainment.

Her love line says that her first love was at age 18 and a "biggy" at age 21. Then, when she approaches her 27th year, her palm shows the best time for her to begin a family. So her new partnership looks very good indeed, for the support, drive and encouragement she needs.

The very flexible fingers can be a sign of later joint problems. Dancing has already taken a toll on her knees. This same palmar configuration also shows in Marfans syndrome and similar joint conditions. Statistically, this can mean conception could take slightly longer than the norm. But for this girl's nurturing nature, children are a must.

Romance in the Palm

The number of children can be read sometimes reliably, sometimes not—from the relationship lines down from under the Mercury finger, and she has three (5).

Because she has a love of all things artistic and beautiful, we can tell that her home would have the color, shape and form of an artist, as would her taste in clothes—pretty, fussy and feminine.

Carl Jung demonstrated that within each woman is a masculine element. He called this element the Anima, and we can describe from the soul imprint, and Zodiac sign, the kind of man who would attract her.

She does show some gastric difficulty that is considered normal with the eating habits of women dancers and singers. This could indicate either a Candida overgrowth or I.B.S. (irritable bowel syndrome). There is some indication of either extended use of the contraceptive pill or antibiotic overuse. The result is that she needs to replace the natural flora and fauna in the gut with a live acidophilus yogurt each morning, She also needs good whole foods rather than a snatched lunchtime Mc'burger. This would improve her overall metabolism.

To improve the imbalance with the stomach acid/alkali, she is advised to dissolve half a spoonful of soda bicarbonate into a glass of water as a start to her detox, then have a Saturday each week as a "just fruit" day.

This girl has an imaginative, romantic visionary framework to her emotional profile. She likes to share, but will not be told or bossed about. There is often conflict between heart and head. Jung called this thinking versus feeling, and if you compare the two lines that cross the hand, the heart is a mixture of splits and starts, showing uncertainty, moodiness and changeability, while the head line is crisp, straight and unbroken. This symbolizes the clear, straight thinking, intellectual function, impulsive yet methodical.

So, although a beautiful range of inner feelings is experienced, the end result shows happiness, security and common sense prevails, and my guess is a new man entering her life in April.

The romantic prognosis is good.

24

Awkward Client

Both doctors and psychiatrists agree that intuition plays a large part in how to interact with individual clients or patients (for all readings the technical term is *querent*), and that some people are easier and smoother to deal with than others. The teaching and cultivation of the intuition is an often neglected discipline.

Several psychologists have gone as far as to say all counseling should be intuitively based, and I confess that when I was counseling professionally, some of the worst practitioners were those with the best credentials, who could not intuitively connect.

Hans Eysenck, author of 70 psychology books, told me some years back that many psychologists hold the view that understanding the fundamental chemistries behind patient or client behaviors helps massively in initial bonding, communicating and the healing process.

Eric Berne, the originator of transactional analysis, was able to guess the professions of many of those who came to him, and came to respect the intuition in a way that not many psychologists understand.

Berne studied the way people interact with each other and identified three distinct styles: the Parent, Adult, and the Child, and he looked into the predominant state of communication from each. These he called *transactions*, and repeated transactions he called *games*.

Berne's work is now the cornerstone for training many in the orthodox caring fields, so for those of you who also work in the alternative/healing arenas, please be mindful that the first few moments that a patient or client arrives are vital in establishing a climate of trust, which is an imperative base for healing to begin.

This hand print was of a client who was actually very defensive, anxious and obnoxious, and I was on the verge of asking him to either lower his voice or leave the clinic. Remember, when confronted with people under great stress as this man, always speak slower and softer, so they have to concentrate. This has a marked calming effect.

Several atavistic markers show in his hand:

Awkward Client

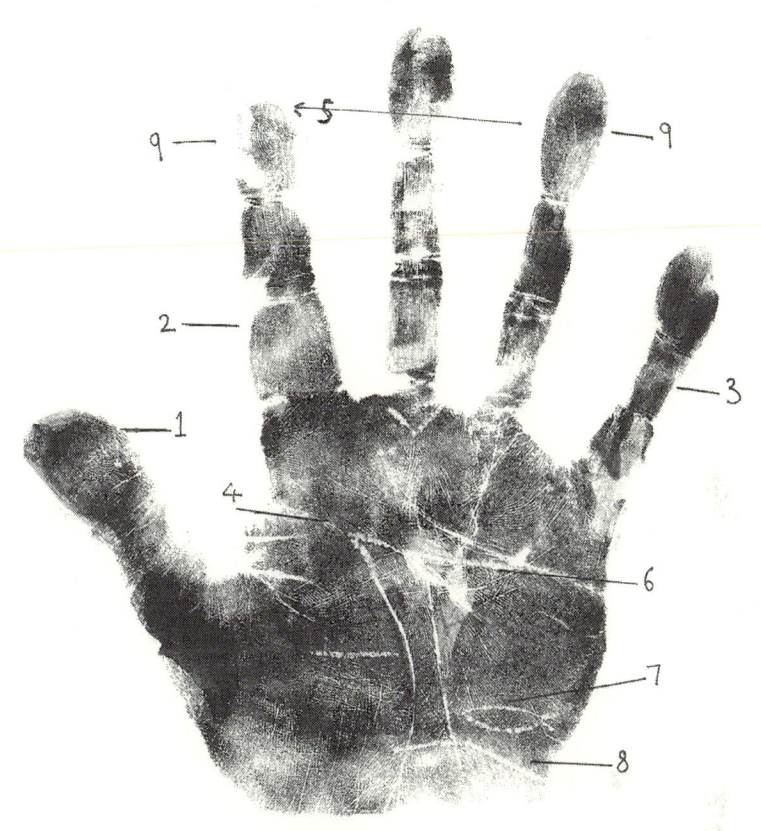

1) Bulbous tip to the thumb
2) Jupiter finger very thick in the third phalange
3) Mercury finger central phalange very thin
4) Closely tied head and life line
5) Short Jupiter finger
6) Head line close to heart
7) Sign of the fish attached to fate line
8) Allergy line
9) Several whorl type fingerprints, including one on the thumb

When this hand print was taken, several mosquito bites showed on his wrist. One in 10 persons are highly attractive to mozzies and they like specific blood types. They can home in on a tasty subject from 50 meters. These include pregnant or overweight ladies, and those whose skin smells of steroids or cholesterol, sweat or carbon dioxide. So, the large, overweight man, who was sweating profusely and gasping for breath, told me he had breathing problems, which is confirmed by the closeness of the head and heart lines at (6). This is an accepted sign of asthma or emphysema, but particularly late onset hay fever.

(1) The bulbous tip to the thumb is seen with those needing anger management or with uncontrollable tempers. In ancient times these were called "murderer's thumbs," and they are a common sign in my own collection of murderers' hand prints taken from British prisons.

(2) The basal phalange of the Jupiter finger rules stomach, intestinal and general gastric problems. In a good hand, it is one sign of the gourmet or chef; in other circumstances, speaking generally, it can tell in women of the emotional eater, and in men the problem drinker.

(3) Mercury (little) finger central phalange very thin in section signifies a difficult early mother experience, where the baby felt neglected or afraid. The London psychiatrist Ruth Seiffert* collated studies of CRD (childhood relating difficulties), which were the basis of much later work worldwide on this topic, which is of great interest to therapists.

(4) The close head and life lines is called in Tibetan palmistry, "the sign of the yak" because the yak is a slow-moving animal who will walk all day with the heaviest load, but hurried he will get obstreperous and anxious, and like this man, can only move at his own pace.

(5) Short Jupiter, or first finger, always is the sign of lack of self-confidence and often self-sabotage. Ideally, it should be the same length as the Apollo, or third finger, but rarely is (Prof. Manning studies).

(6) Closeness of head and heart lines means conflict between emotions and intellect. So well put by Carl Jung in his studies, this conflict creates the tension which often leads to breathing problems.

(7) The sign of the fish. This looks like it is a fish caught on the rod of the destiny line. I have only seen this mark possibly five times in 50 years. This on the Luna, or water mount, tells of a whole variety of facts, but in the main is a sign of a spiritual teacher or philosopher.

(8) Allergy line, called the poison line in ancient literature, because it shows food allergies and intolerances, from signals given in the Mercury finger and the bloated Jupiter. We see this as probably cow's milk allergy or intolerance among other gastric sensitivities. Obesity is linked to bacterial gut flora populations that differ tremendously from the norm, and these signatures have been allied to illnesses from immune dysfunction and depression, both shown in this hand. Each body type is different in its nutritional needs, and each of the blood types will have separate likes and dislikes in their food.

Awkward Client

(9) The whorl type fingerprint is usually seen on the Apollo, or third finger, but several together—as here—suggest Rubella or German measles while the fetus was small inside the womb. Incidentally, the man who owned this hand had both asthma and eczema, and when found together, they are often because of Cesarean birth. In pushing the baby down the birth canal, the baby is squeezed through juices produced by the mother which assist the birth process and help prevent asthma and eczema type disorders.

So we see the cocktail of events in this man's life, which brought him for therapy. He had been to numerous doctors and psychologists and was no wiser. The fact that for over 40 years I have offered a money-back satisfaction guarantee helped him make up his mind to come.

The hand is a microcosm of the life. Everything we have ever done is marked out, because the hand is the closest organ to the brain.

His early difficulties with his busy mother, who had farmed him out for others to bring up, had been magnified over the years, until brought to the surface in a mid-life crisis. He was abusing alcohol, being aggressive to his family, and generally being a real pain by withholding affection from those close to him. This is now a common aspect of the control mechanism and is called "intimacy nervosa."

Remembering the palmist's motto, "Do No Harm," I advised him with extensive counseling and recommended Vitamin E cream for his eczema, Vitamin B complex and zinc, and selenium with Omega 3, and much less cow's milk.

Many sufferers of eczema should try mashing a banana in milk and pasting it on the affected part with a small paint brush.

*Dr. Ruth Seiffert worked with great dedication at the Maudsley and Victorian Barts Hospital with sufferers of severe psychosis. This hospital was known as the "Rat Run" for its Dickensian overcrowding and high rates of violence. She was specifically interested in the hand gesture's side to palmistry. Dr. Seiffert had to be escorted to and from the hospital. Only her extreme political views held her back from the professional recognition she richly deserved.

25
The Hand and the Horoscope

The hand never lies.

Notice the hand shape, the psychological type and whether introvert or extrovert. Of the three body types, this one is Endomorph.

So, the hand here is:

    (A) An introvert
    (B) Psychologically Type B
    (C) A Pisces subject

Knowing this, one could already write a fair assessment.

(1) Notice the thin Jupiter finger with its pinched-in base. This is called by some experts the *world finger* and shows the ego. And a small Jupiter finger shows—when mildly short—a lack of self-confidence; right, though, to a very short finger, a full-blown inferiority complex.

The central phalange on Jupiter shows a negative early father experience, and all central phalanges being waisted shows abandonment anxiety from a poor father/daughter relationship in the pre-latency period. The tight bottom section usually shows that it manifested with eating disorders.

The result in our Endomorph friend here means she is uncomfortable in social situations and with stressful social interactions, and often with built-in feelings of inadequacy and worthlessness. The emotionally and physically absent father can subconsciously color a girl for life and affect her choices or partner and major relationship decisions.

An overly strict father will show in the daughter as a failure to make her own decisions. Alfred Adler, who discovered the range of inferiority disorders, said, "*We hold the trauma of our emotional hurt in our weakest organ,*" and we see in the early part of the head line severe chaining and a large drooping triple-pronged fork (2).

In some Indian palmistry schools they call the head line the mark of the Dragon, and they see a restless forked tail, as seen here, as troubled, and the triple forking, which is known as the "sign of the temple," is symbolic of inner anguish.

The Hand and the Horoscope

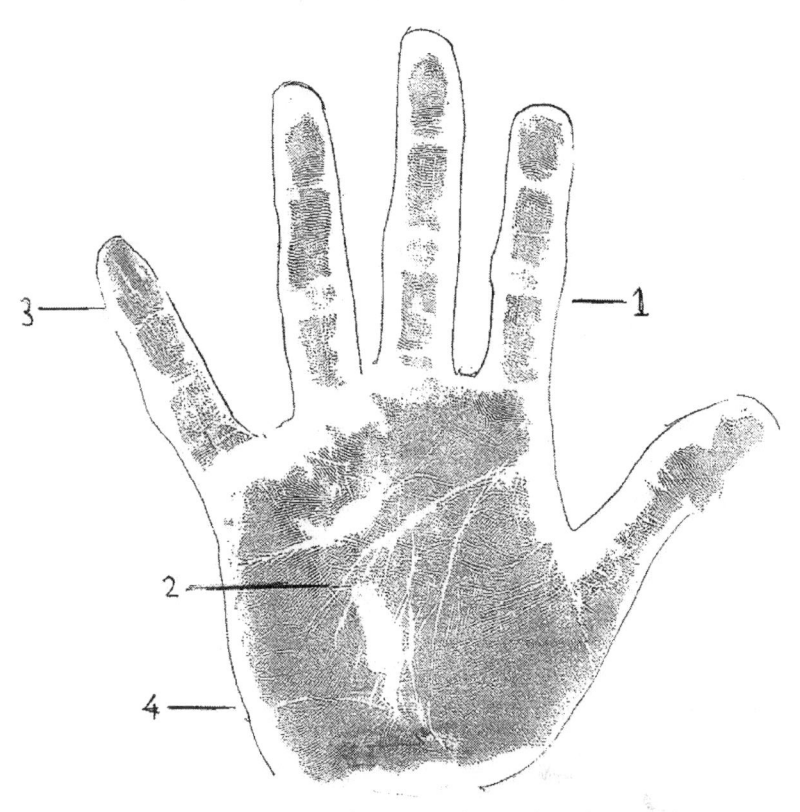

It's quite possible that the long-term depression hinted at in the head lines is from paternal abuse over strictness or neglect.

A recent article in the *British Medical Journal* questioned whether anti-depressants really work, and the fact that some family doctors are giving them for back pain and related conditions suggests they don't.

The new trials on Daffodil essence are far more promising with non-addiction and the side effects which have plagued the Benzodiazepans and Phenothiazines. Over 30 million Americans are on various anti-depressants and experience little relief.

The landmark book, *Noonday Demons* by Andrew Solomons, takes a much needed, fresh, independent look at the various depressions, in particular bi-polar disorders. The book is being hailed for its long and excellent research.

(3) The small, or Mercury finger, has tiny lines running up its tip, a sure sign of thyroid imbalance. The seaweed kelp is best here, while the Mercury finger, which governs communication and relationships, shows a

large knot at the lower knuckle. Any knots show a blockage of the expression of who she is sexually. This is the place where low self-esteem will best show itself.

The biggest thyroid disrupters are actually in the water you drink, Fluoride and Chlorine. A water filter jug will remove some of this, and also do not use fluoride toothpaste. Baking soda is good, provided it has no added aluminum. Do not cook with non-stick pans, which contain Perfluorooctanic acid, known as (PFOA). American manufacturers promise to ban this before 2016. Fast-food packaging also usually carries thyroid-disrupting chemicals.

The lady whose hand this is complained of knee pain when walking distances, and allopathic medication did not help. But after whipping her knees with stinging nettles, found she could walk distances without pain. Incidentally, Louise Hay, the well-known healer, says sore knees go with pride problems and unbending ego, as shown in her Jupiter finger.

Many studies show that a young girl's relationship with her father, called the "Electra Complex," is paramount to her later emotional development. Whereas a man's love is firm, protective and constant, a woman's will fluctuate up and down during the month and even during the year, and even a baby girl will absorb all this. And if the relationship is primarily one of discipline, as this one was, then she will have a negative view of what to expect from men, and will allow men into her life who are unworthy of her, leading to a miserable and unfulfilling love life.

She was also bullied by an office manager and this made her ill, and she lost her job. She experienced self-hatred and she self harmed. Her health suffered and she had serous gastric problems.

Those with the line across Luna at (4) should be wary of allopathic medication and addiction.

Hippocrates said, *"All disease begins in the gut."*

The Endomorph is particularly susceptible to gastric anomalies and does not cope well with the stress of office managers with terrible crushes.

> *Ring out the bells of Norwich, and let the winter come and go,*
> *And all will be well again I know,*
> *All will be well again I am telling you,*
> *Let the winter come and go*
> *And all will be well again, this I do know.*
> — Julian of Norwich

The Hand and the Horoscope

* Further reading: *Women Who Love Too Much*, by Robyn Norwood
I hate you, don't leave me.

50 Case Studies in Modern Palmistry

Part II

Famous People's Hands

50 Case Studies in Modern Palmistry

26

Lara Love

Birthday 8th February 1981

This hand print belongs to the celebrity Lara Oliver, better known as Lara Love. So what do her hands tell us for the coming year?

> *Tiger tiger, burning bright*
> *in the forests of the night,*
> *what immortal hand or eye,*
> *could frame thy fearful symmetry*

William Blake's words sum up beautifully the sign of the Tiger, which shows at (1). This marking shows a person who puts loved ones first and will fight like the tiger to protect her young. But it does behold an anxious and defensive temperament, and usually for good reason.

Before we look to the future, we must always look to the past, for the person we are now is the result of all that has gone before.

Professor Manning's recent university studies on fingers have confirmed much old palmistry lore, and in the womb testosterone influences the first, or Jupiter, finger and estrogen affects the third, or Apollo, finger, and we can see here early bonding difficulties with her mother, and an emotionally non-existent father, from the thick Jupiter finger (2) and the thin Apollo finger, (3) coupled to the low-set little, or Mercury, finger standing slightly apart.

If a girl's relationship with her father is loose or dysfunctional, this is often what is behind classic CRD (or childhood relating difficulties), because from the first man in her life she learns how a man loves. It should be a strong, unwavering, protective love that engenders the ability to build secure love bonding with men later on.

If she does not feel close to her father, this early bonding does not happen and she has no subconscious yardstick with which to measure the men who want to come to her in later life, and she will make mistakes.

These tendencies show primarily in the dropping lines from the heart line (4). The deep, early subconscious feeling of rejection by her father can leave like here, the painful feeling that they were somehow at fault, and

50 Case Studies in Modern Palmistry

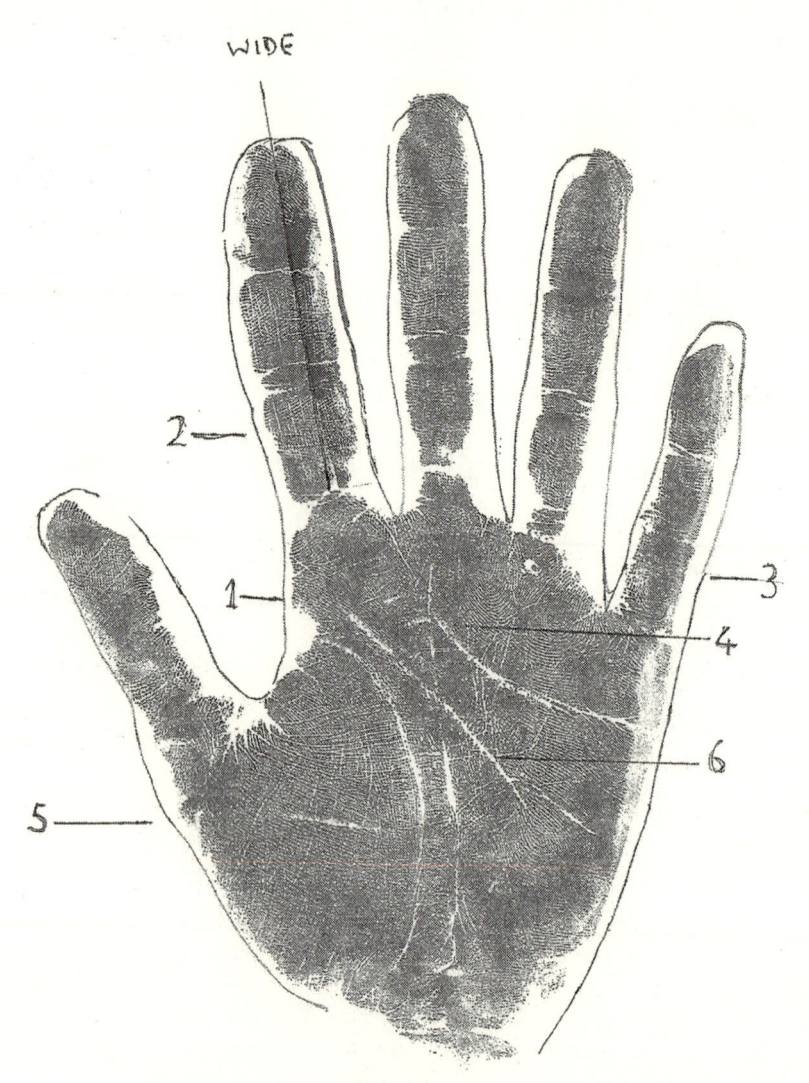

some possibly misplaced early childhood anger with the mother for allowing this. Teenage rebelliousness has its origins in this arena.

Lara has typical dancer's hands. Slim hands show a slim body, and a pleasant, uniform structure shows both in her hands and her body. And the ball at the thumb base (5) shows rhythm and tempo, essential for musicians and dancers. She has danced for some time with a well known dance team, and is now progressing well with both modeling and her girls' group. The long, rectangular hand with slim fingers is called the water hand, and is typical of the Ectomorph body typology, giving sensitivity, intuition and compassion.

When the fingertips have small perpendicular creases, this tells of hormonal changes, and is seen mostly at puberty, pregnancy and the menopause. But Lara had a baby recently, so some imbalance here is understandable.

The thyroid shows in the Mercury finger and here a little help with the nutritional seaweed kelp would be good to rebalance.

The strength of the fate line (6), that longitudinal line that separates the hand down the middle, is unusually strong, showing a good work ethic with promise for a good future and a career-minded girl, probably a compensatory construct for the missing, fulfilling, secure emotional life.

Lara is an Aquarian. Her birthday and hand corresponds to the "justice" card in the tarot pack. People with this, especially with the strong fate line, will be the instrument of justice for those who have been harmed or cheated. This can also mean she will meet a Libran subject as signified by the scales, as a life partner. My guess from the temporary lines on the fingers, in that part known to medicine as the "interphalangeal joints," that June and July is the big period for romantic meetings. A big strong type may sweep her off her feet. He may have black hair, and work in construction.

Her next karmic year is the pivotal year of 35. This coming year will hold much promise for opportunity, and she may surprise herself with how much she achieves.

27

The Hand of Psychiatrist Henri Rey

Henri Rey was the Chief Psychiatrist at the famous London Maudsley Hospital, until his retirement in 1977, during which time he radically changed the official view of mental illness.

His research papers were included in the "Universals of Psychoanalysis 1994," in which he showed his deep understanding of borderline and psychotic illness. When Rey left the Maudsley, he left behind a generation of psychotherapists and psychoanalysts who saw him as a special mentor and personal friend. But the main loss was to his patients. His understanding and generosity was remarkable and genuine.

He came to me out of curiosity after reading of Carl Jung's palmistry studies and comments by psychologist Hans Eysenck. He was curious about what extra information the hand prints would give, if any, on mental illness.

Carl Jung once said, *"Show me a man who is sane and I will cure him."* Henri Rey felt, as many experts do, that there is no such thing as a sane man, and man is far too complicated a being to be totally 100 percent sane.

Henri Rey used a variety of treatments to help his patients, including allowing soft, soothing music such as that of John Denver, to play at times. Also popular was the occasional bringing into the hospital grounds of dogs and cats. For many people who have lost their trust in human beings, animals are their only friends. Usually, the men went for dogs and women the cats. He also used good nutrition to create positive response. The diet for those in the hospital was very poor, and much mental and physical illness is compounded by wrong or poor diet.

Yet Henri could be cantankerous. He disagreed with Joyce McDougall, who had long been working at rehabilitating homosexuals. He felt the budget could be spent better elsewhere.

Henri Rey described the hospital as "The Brick Mother," since for many it was their first place of safety since the womb. He was very caring in gaining the individual's permission and trust to take their hand prints, because many had experienced such deep trauma that they were very

The Hand of Psychiatrist Henri Rey

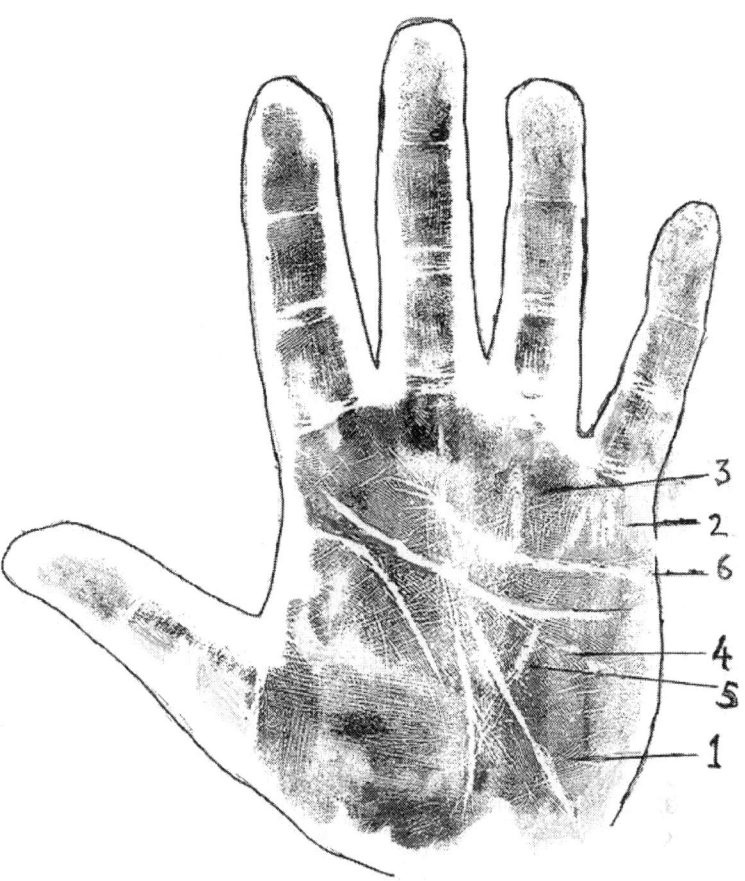

untrusting. Henri Rey longed to be back at his hospital, where he had so many vivid memories of times long past.

He wanted to collaborate on some short palmistry articles for a technical magazine at some point, but his death in January 2000 precluded this. Henri Rey gave me some 50 hand prints to analyze and write up reports, but it was just like him to hide among them this one of himself! On working through this one, it was so obviously him that I confronted him and he guffawed with laughter,

So what does his hand print say?

Although all the palmistry books you read tell of conic, square, spatulate or pointed fingers, in reality they are almost always a mixture as they are here. The first, or Jupiter, is conic, Saturn is square, Apollo is spatulate, and Mercury is pointed, or conic. But there is a feel here of a certain squareness to the fingers and a squarish palm. Remember that the interpretation of the palmar lines must always be filtered through the hand shape.

LIFE PURPOSE: The strikingly long, unbroken fate line (called the luck, fortune, *tey-pa* or destiny line in some schools) is a brilliant marking, which tells us of his karmic pathway. It lies unbroken from Luna to Saturn. This normally means the person's imagination, creativity or subconscious gives him his destined roadway. This line, unbroken, is always found in sound, well balanced individuals. The Hindus say when the fate line begins from the base of Luna, just as this one does (1), it shows someone who has been here before and has a mission, more a compulsion than a career. It also shows that he will be helped by the opposite sex. We can tell part of this by the prominent healing stigmata at (2). This kind of fate line in large, square hands gives a fate linked to the outdoors and to water. Henri's wish to take the mentally ill to the outdoors was constantly stifled by bureaucracy.

The medical stigmata, which is always seen with those who care for others, as opposed to those who do it for the money, is slightly closer to the Apollo finger than is usual. This shows a love of healing work. Where the sun line looks like a tree growing from the heart line as in (3), this traditionally is called a "money tree" and denotes success late in life. This fits the fate line's suggestion of great success doing what you love to do.

THINKING PROCESSES: His long head line at (4) gives an ability to plan and see ahead. His predecessor, Professor Heinz Wolfe, was the first to promote lateral thinking as an exercise. Henri's long head line in a broad, square palm shows his ability to think laterally. Since the time of Aristotle, it's been said that when the head line reaches from edge to edge, it is a sign that your work will be known abroad and is one of the signs of fame. Incidentally, the head line at its commencement under Jupiter and separate from the life line, shows ambition and thinking, which can be radical and not tied to the life energies.

This can make the subject impulsive and impatient. Heinz Wolfe used to refer humorously to people with this marking as "needing vitamin R for risk," since they enjoy risk taking and thrive on change, challenge and variety. They also are very independent thinkers. This kind of straight head line, ending high up on Mars, is symbolic of the rational, logical down-to-earth scientific thinking that we expect to see in psychologists. This particular formation has been called a "Sydney line" and has both genetic and health connotations.

If we use morphometric analysis of the four types of bone structure:

The Hand of Psychiatrist Henri Rey

Mesoid, Caucasoid, Negroid and Mongoloid, this is mostly Caucasoid, possibly originally from Eastern Europe and surprisingly quite typical of many Jews, not Middle Eastern. Genetically, we are more like our grandparent of the same sex than our own fathers. Now this gives us a big help; if we look at the illnesses and physical weaknesses of the grandparent, we know how to advise the person in terms of diet and lifestyle.

The slightly "S" shaped little finger, which is long, especially in the top section, would imply some early problem. The Royal College of Psychiatry suggests any trauma under the age of 3 is pretty well uncorrectable. Psychologist Heinz Kohut suggests an attack on the genitals (as in a non-anesthetized circumcision) is just such a trauma. It can mean a slightly distorted view of the person themselves and how they fit into society. This is not to be confused with conventional medical Clinodactyl interpretations.

The first, or Jupiter, finger, in Henri's case, is slimmer than the Apollo, or third finger, and suggests a remote or emotionally unavailable father figure. Many men who overdiscipline their children can destroy their self-confidence for life.

HEALTH: The health line is at (5), but health shows in all palmar aspects, especially in the nails. Henri was initially reluctant to try my simple cure for his arthritis, but when he agreed to glue two old pennies into his shoes and wear no socks, it helped him a lot. The hospital refused to allow him or the patients to walk barefoot on the grass in the sunshine, which I also recommended. Some arthritis showed in his five metacarpal and eight metacarpal hand bones. This prevented his enjoyment of horticulture in his later years, but he refused to take any herbs or plant-based medicaments.

He was shocked when I told him he was a heavy snorer, but his veins stood out prominently in his wrists and were hard and deep blue. This can be a sign of varicose veins, which are genetic, and also portend later life cardiac problems. The blueness is carbonic acid, which as CO_2, which is transported via the respiratory gas exchange. This tells us that the person is a shallow breather and is often seen in philosophers and intellectuals who think deeply. Stale pockets of air can gather in the corners of the lungs, allowing bacteria to develop, so I usually prescribe short bouts of deep breathing outdoors for this.

Incidentally, if you have varicose veins, I always suggest "essence of horse chestnut with butcher's broom," two old established medicinal herbs which actually strengthen veins and arteries. Put garlic in your food for two weeks, which acts as a blood cleanser.

Also seen is the doubled line of Heart at (6); an island here would tell of eye problems, and everything from cataracts to age-related macular degeneration is told here. Most common is simple eye strain or slight shortsightedness; however, the doubled line here was discovered by palmist Vera Compton in the '50s and relates to metal absorption. Henri was either eating from aluminum cookware or drinking water through copper pipes. I see this toxic metal absorption a lot now with the fashion for metal body piercing. The best thing to take is Chlorella, if you suspect you have heavy metal absorption or develop varicose veins.

GENERAL HEALTH: Some gentle criticism of his posture was necessary. Many who sit at desks or drive for a living develop a slouch. The 29 core muscles which regulate the trunk can become lazy and misshapen. The spine which shows up in the life line and the fate line, needs some corrective exercise, particularly in the upper lumbar region.

The tips to the fingers show mottling, as if they had been in water for a long time. This is most often seen in women at times, where the hormones are at unrest, but can be a sign of antibiotic overuse.

Remember, when reading hands, never go on one sign in isolation, and always be gentle and compassionate.

Further Reading

Murray Jackson and Paul Williams co-authored the book *Unimaginable Storms: A Search for Meaning in Psychosis*. It has been a most important source book for a whole generation of professionals.

Also read *Weathering the Storms—Psychotherapy for Psychosis and Noonday Demons,* Dr. Andrew Solomons, which is the newest work on various depressive illnesses.

28

Hugo Chavez

Hugo Chavez was born on July, 28 1954. Since ancient times, this day has been known by astrological occultists as "the day of the height of the sun." This tells us that every single day in the year has its own meaning, and the number of the date can give important information. Many dismiss this kind of thought today, but it has been recognized and used by heads of state and military strategists for eons. Winston Churchill in WWII had teams of people working to choose the most important dates in the war, and so have several US presidents in recent times.

Chavez was seen as an enemy to the USA and a hero to his own people because he refused to give the American oil companies permission to exploit Venezuela's oil. He, like Gaddafi, demanded clean drinking water for his people, but refused to allow the three huge water companies, who now own the world's water, into Venezuela because he knew that these water companies, owned by the World Bank, would then take over the government.

Instead, he worked on cleaning up the 116,000 different pollutants found in drinking water. He also spent money on social programs, state run food markets, cash extras for poor families, free health clinics and education. He refused the lure of spectacular construction projects that adorn the Middle East's oil-rich states and the offers of a palace and secret foreign bank accounts. He gave the wealth to the people.

Leaders who refuse foreign multinational and banking control are always demonized; take Gaddafi, Nasser, Assad, Ahmadinejad and Kim Jong Il. It was Hilary Clinton who said, "Chavez will play by our rules or will

50 Case Studies in Modern Palmistry

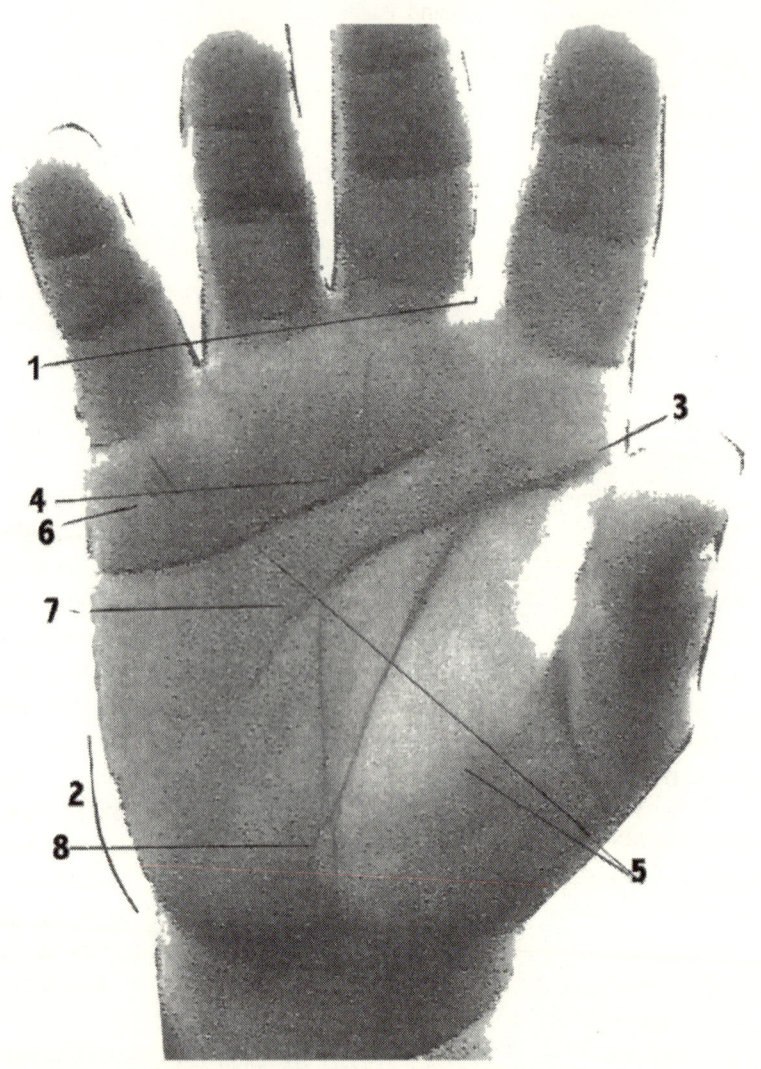

not play at all." Consequently, this was his main fear; that America would attack, rob and plunder Venezuela as they did Iraq, so Chavez increased the number of trained military men from 50,000 to 200,000.

Chavez was said to speak to all Venezuelans, *for* all Venezuelans, in a country which was said, by experts, to be a mixture of socialism and Marxism, but with an unusual face of democracy and freedom.

If we look at his hands, they tell us nothing we have not covered in previous articles. This is not the hand of a politician. Politics does not make good men and good men do not make politicians.

Remember, only one hand is shown here, and we really need both, since the brain crosses over and covers the other side of the body as well. This being his right or dominant hand, it tells of his outward face, and aspects of his future.

This is a Mesomorph hand and in the Cheiro/Benham system of 7, it is an elementary or earth hand. These are people who work with their hands: farmers, soldiers, sailors, people who make things, outdoor people who love nature. Chavez had been all of these.

He has a heavy hand with short fingers, corresponding to the fire category. These are people who work, often unknowingly, from deep-rooted, quick intuitive thought. We see the roots of the fingers all in line with a strong Mercury, or communications, finger (1). This is often seen with lawyers and people who can persuade or speak their mind, such as salesmen, orators and spokesmen.

The heavy curve at the heel of the hand we call Luna (2) tells of Physical energy. In fact, the whole side of the hand is curved and bulging with power, giving strength and endurance of palmistry's three worlds: Mind, Body and Spirit. The part of the palm ruled by the planet Mars is very strong indeed. This gives robust health and a strong immune system. The lower part, or Mars positive, starts under the beginning to the life line (3) and we see here the pugnacious spirit of a boxer, warrior, activist or soldier with plenty of strength, stamina and drive.

The heart line shape (4) is unusual in a hand of this type. One would expect this amount of drive and stamina to produce a man who would burn with physical passion and ardor, but there is much self-control. He likes intelligent, companionable women, rather than flashy, sexy, physical women usually preferred by the owner of this type of hand. Odd lines which do not fit the others, or the hand, I refer to as "cuckoo lines," as they can take precedence in the hand, and all other lines and markings must be constantly referred to this in the reading.

His two strongest mounts, or finger pads, are his Venus mount and his Mercury mount (5). Both are high and slightly red in color, showing activity. The strength of his Venus or thumb pad aligned to his strong Mercury, which contains the sign of the healing stigmata (6), shows he would care for and try to use his strength to heal his people.

His fate or destiny line almost stops at his head line at around 35 years of age (7), showing an intellectual or head-based decision to make a change in the direction of his destiny. Soon after, his fate line disappears altogether, which coincides with him accepting the leadership position of the Fifth

Republic Movement in 1997. This is a very unusual marking for a country's leader. Along with this, we see his strong life line cutting deep into his hand; this man is indestructible, but alas, his life line ends in a large egg shape just visible in the photo (8), and on March 5, 2013 his death was announced.

A long forgotten research palmist by the name of Walter Sorrel did many hospital studies and concluded that when the life line ends with a large egg shape, this often means cancer.

Do not confuse the egg shape with an oval, square or other shape. These all have their own meanings.

Incidentally, the name Hugo Chavez adds up to the number 8. The master palmist Cheiro says this about number 8 people: "They usually have deep and intense natures and often play some great role on life's stage, but one which is fatalistic for themselves and for others, and generally have some great government office or government responsibility often involving the greatest sacrifice on their part." The sacrifice of Hugo Chavez for his people was indeed in government office and was both responsible and fatal.

29

Princess Diana, Fated Destiny

Diana, Princess of Wales (Diana Frances Spencer, July 1, 1961 — August 31, 1997), married Charles, Prince of Wales, on 29 July 1981 at St. Paul's Cathedral. Her wedding to Charles, heir to the British throne, was seen by a global television audience of over 750 million. She was well known for her fund-raising work for over 100 international charities, and was an eminent celebrity of the late 20th century. She would have been 54 this birthday.

Diana's upbringing was very strict. This stifling of the natural personality and feminine ego shows in the index, or Jupiter, finger's slight curve to the Saturn finger at (1). This finger relates to the father and the Apollo, or third, finger, the mother and her relationship to both and their influence. The thinness in this section of the Apollo finger tells us her mother was not the most affectionate woman in the world. As a result, Diana believed strongly that she should be a "hands on" mother and not leave things to a nanny. This created problems, one of which was Diana's refusal to have the boys circumcised.

Diana's passionate nature is shown at (2), the rich, deeply curving heart line ending between the first two fingers. Diana had never had much love and wanted it now, but Charles' main duties were with his family.

Diana's fate line at (3) shows an independent woman who wanted to make her own way, a woman loved by all the men she met, but wanted and needed an emotional security that Charles could not give.

Diana, who was age 20 at her marriage, and Charles were rumored by footmen to have been pressured into the relationship by the Queen mother and Lady Fermoy.

When Diana met Dodi, the attraction was instant, and they spent much time together after her divorce from Charles.

Diana is the name of the moon goddess. In numerology, the name Diana adds up to the moon's number, which is a 2. Her title, "Lady Di," is also a 2. She was born in the sign of Cancer, which is ruled by the moon.

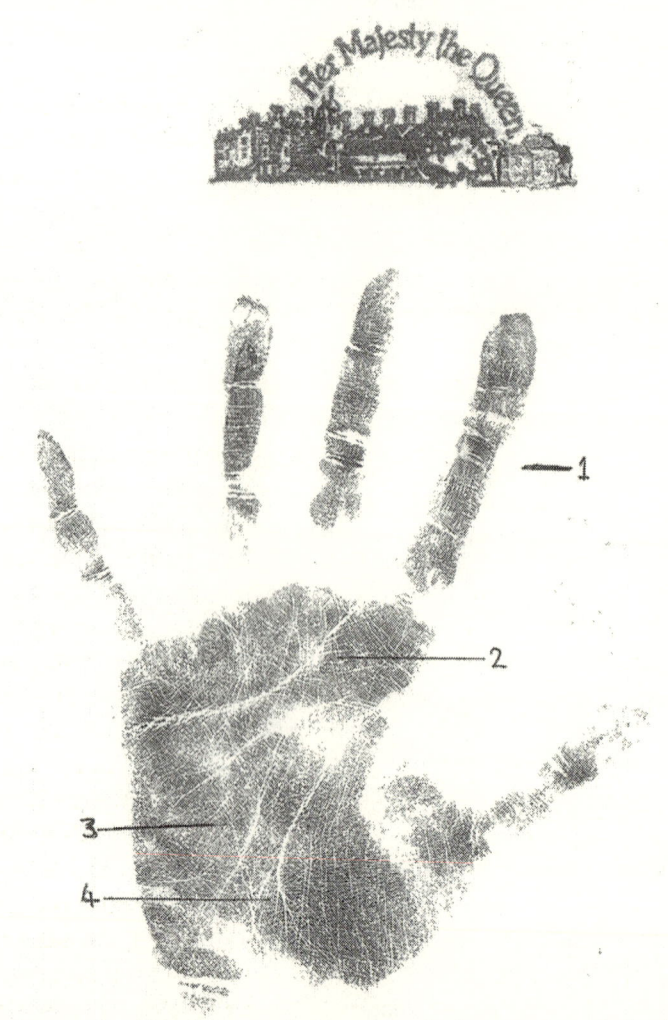

A close study of her life reveals the moon playing a major role in all her big life events, particularly the lunar eclipses at her marriage, birth of William, divorce and death. "House of Windsor" also reduces to the number 2.

The underpass where the car crash happened, "The Pont de Lalma" — which reduces to a 2 vibration, is on the same site as an ancient Diana human sacrifice temple.

Her death was on the eve of the Oslo Conference, in which 100 countries would discuss a land mine ban.

Diana pressed the United Nations, appealed to all the nations who stockpiled land mines, to sign the Ottawa Treaty, banning their future production and use. The problem with land mines was that they could lay in undergrowth for many years before going off. Being brightly colored, they attracted children and harmed a large number of them each year.

Diana, as patron of the children's funds, could not remain silent and campaigned across the world for the maimed children. Vested interests combined against her, and when she announced she would be visiting Palestine, that was too much. Her death at (4) tells us that it was no accident, and is echoed in all the other major lines. The success of Diana, in highlighting wrong use of land mines, meant her next cause—highlighting Israel's criminal acts, especially in Palestine. A personal visit for peace would seal her fate.

She was also about to appear in a documentary on the U.S. drug embargo, which killed 750,000 Iraqi children.

So, it was predicable that out of several high-risk moon periods, she would meet her end on 31 August 1997. The date's hidden numbers translate to 4+8+8, which finally reduces to the moon's vibration number 2. Westminster Abbey is also a 2 vibration, and 2,000 mourners were inside for the funeral.

Incidentally, the name Diana Spencer has 12 letters and carries the same vibration as the 12 of the Hanged Man in the tarot pack, showing the ultimate self sacrifice. The occult expert "Cheiro" says of the significance of the 11 vibration, which has here been reduced to the 2, and I quote: "This is an ominous number to occultists; it gives warning of hidden dangers, trial and treachery from others; its symbols are a clenched fist (aggression) and a lion muzzled (symbol of Britain with no voice, and corresponds to number 11 of the tarot pack). This also shows a person who will contend against great difficulties. It corresponds to the I-Ching sign for coming conflict."

Incidentally, Palestine also reduces to a 38=11=2, the same moon vibration, showing goal compatibility and a big coming success there.

The hand print shows her intuition to be remarkable. She was aware of the moon's effect on her destiny, and she knew she would not have a long life. She said she lived each day as if it was her last. She had a deep need to love and be loved, but for herself—not as a trophy, and knew time was running out for her goal achievement.

In Diana's hand, we see an intuitive and anxious personality, yet it is ambitious and focused. So is there any indication of her death?

"Well, only indications." With any forensic examination of a hand print, there is the danger of "fitting things in retrospectively." So to amplify data, we can superimpose the death horoscope chart onto the crossing lines

50 Case Studies in Modern Palmistry

of fate and head, and use this as a traditional mandala for focus, meditation and concentration, and to dowse the central cross, using for her, a moonstone on an 11-inch new thread, for information gathering. The central pole must align with the hand's fate line, under the Saturn finger. Her Saturn signs are very strong indeed, and remember, Saturn and Pluto are the signposts of death.

Several psychics did give the warnings about Diana's chart. Alas, I was not one of them.

The hand print was printed onto a sheet of Sandringham house notepaper, and I gave my word I would never show the hand print and tell of her secrets—a lovely lady who was cut off in her prime.

30

Priyanka Chopra

As a teenager, Priyanka Chopra lived for some years with an aunt in the United States. In 2000, her mother entered her into the Femina Miss India contest, in which she finished second and took the Miss India World title. She was then entered into the Miss World pageant, where she was crowned Miss World 2000 and Miss World Continental Queen of Beauty—Asia and Oceania, becoming the fifth Indian to win the competition.

Although Chopra, at one time, aspired to study engineering or psychiatry, she accepted offers to join the Indian film industry, which came as a result of her pageant wins. She has since starred in Tamil and Hindu films. Her beauty and intelligence have made her a firm favorite with men all over the world. So, what does her hand say?

You would think this woman would have it all, and yet here is a very unfulfilled woman.

(1) The right hand middle, or Saturn, finger is ringed and is unusually short with the fingers of either side leaning to it for strength and comfort. This indicates that early responsibilities weighed heavily, and she has a dislike of responsibility. This is a classic sign of insecurity for the future. She would like to leave off the makeup and have some freedom to run barefoot in the grass, in the rain laughing, or something similar. It also shows someone a little rebellious, who sees the funny side in everything.

(2) The tip to the first, or Jupiter, finger slants to Saturn. This shows an oppressive parental figure in childhood and indicates that the natural growth in the pre-teen and teen years was somewhat stifled and burdened

with responsibility.

The right hand thumb is held in a crooked manner, and this is a well known anxiety sign, and seen held close to the hand. This is a combination often seen with servicemen and others under prolonged stress. This is a long thumb, which shows a thinker. These people make good historians and psychologists.

(3) The small, or Mercury, finger is thin in the top two sectors and struggles to lean away from the collective comfort of the other fingers, and is slightly too short. Short little fingers are people on a short fuse emotionally. A mixture of inner insecurity and sexual nonfulfillment, coupled to bad choices in dysfunctional men, means she has not discovered who she is as a sexual being.

In the West, women have more freedom to discover what they need from men, and this helps them to grow in all areas, but a strict upbringing, which is very typical in the Indo/Pak subcontinent, can hold a woman back in these important areas.

She has some remarkably lucky signs in every area except the emotional sector; the Blessing of Shiva is a rare mark, giving balance and caution through the dance of life.

So Priyanka Chopra, whom you would think could choose any man on the planet and must be fulfilled, is really not. Her close relationships seem to have been short and not very sweet. Men have wanted her as a possession while she hungers for real, secure, lasting love.

Many women who seemingly have it all tend to find themselves with males with fractured egos. It's as if having the most extraordinary beautiful woman on his arm makes him a better man.

So, Priyanka needs to acknowledge that she is here to *live* and *love,* and face up to her feelings and thoughts, and make some emotional decisions, not just with her head. She cannot ask something of her man that she is not willing to do for herself.

Women need to stand in their own power and be enough for themselves, so that they stop hurting themselves unintentionally. Often the heart of a woman's issues is her own worth. She must stop looking outside of herself and start looking inside.

No man is worth the heartache she has been through. The lines on her hand were not clear in the photograph, but age 27-28 seems to be a time of great emotional difficulty.

This lady can really lose her temper; she is exciting and unpredictable and her best is yet to come.

Donald Trump

Donald's hands tell us so much about who the man really is behind the political mask. Born on June 14, 1946, he is a typical Gemini, a masterful communicator, a purveyor and salesman of theories and ideas. The flexible thumb set low shows a man whose morals are also flexible and changeable; he will no doubt sing to the gallery and say what the audience needs to hear.

Gemini is an air sign and air people exist primarily in the mind and the world of translating and communicating their thoughts. His hand is untypical of the sign; inasmuch as it is wide with a strong base, this indicates a physically strong, athletic kind of man, a powerhouse not just mentally but physically too.

Gemini is the sign of the lovers in the Tarot cards. Donald Trump and JFK, both Gemini, showed powerful sexual appetites. This means monogamy will be almost impossible, and like JFK his appetite is refreshingly normal.

He has a restless need for self expression and is a fluent talker on many subjects, but can be glib and has lived a double life in various arenas of his life.

Unusual for a Gemini, he loves the water. Over 80 percent of the human body is water and some people need to be near it. Donald would love the outdoors, especially if it's near water. He recently wanted to buy a large tract of land in Scotland near his mother's birth place, for a huge annual world-class golf tournament. This would have had a spectacular water feature included, but the Scottish people did not want it and vetoed the idea.

His low setting of his small finger, which is ringed and standing well apart, tells us that his subconscious motivation to succeed in business is that he needs to show his father he can do it. He needs to prove himself. This small finger of Mercury deals with communications across the board, from verbal to sexual. It indicates that he is a business and sexual adventurer, and that his libido is not being channeled through the bed-sheets, but is being channeled through his business world. Two problem areas, money and love, stand out when we think of Donald Trump.

The open gap between his head and life line indicates a gambler and a chance taker, and that he has proven himself to be.

Here in the UK, the many US military bases have a popular slogan, "Anyone but Hillary," and Trump seems to be popular here.

His promise to finally tell us the truth of why the USA allowed 9/11 and to investigate the awful US torture program, to work on stopping US wars on the rest of the world and sort the refugee problem is very popular with the UK. The big question remains, "Is he genuine with these promises?"

His destiny shows a divided path from age 68. Decisions made then, which was probably when he decided to run for the presidency, show he has two irons in the fire. One may be his bid for the presidency, but the other is furthering his business interests. These should be mutually exclusive.

Donald tells us he has made and lost four vast fortunes. This raises a red flag because no financier will sponsor a failed businessman more than once. To be able to do this four times suggests he is a puppet of the big money behind the scenes.

Rumor has it that when Hillary Clinton was going to smack Bill Clinton after the Monica Lewinski scandal, Sheldon Adelson, who allegedly bailed out John McCain's gambling and womanizing debts, told her, "You sit quiet, say nothing, and we will make you president." So the big question is, "Is Donald Trump a real contender or is he a Trojan horse candidate for the war-mongers?" A look at who his big backers are raises the hackles, but we were wrong with JFK and Jimmy Carter.

The Don's worst karmic crisis came in April 2001 and his next karmic crisis comes at age 77. December 2016 is a time when the chickens will come home to roost for Donald; let's hope he is the man we are all desperately hoping for; certainly he has the backing in the UK.

32

Imran Khan, 'The Shepherd'

Imran was born in 1952 on the 25th of November, just into Sagittarius, and in many ways he is typical of his sign.

An incredible sportsman, he is as much a popular star in Britain as his native Pakistan.

(1) His birth shows a tight-knit, two-parent family unit and he was breastfed full term. The positive knock-on effects throughout the life of a secure, breastfed baby over a bottle-fed one are too numerous to mention, the main one being in the ability to bond with others; this bonding process meant others loved and trusted him, and his strong communicative sector heavily amplifies this.

At the start to the life line, we see a deep, straight, masculine line of demarcation. This infers a powerful, paternal, male influence through life.

The hand is wide and heavy at its base, and this is always seen with physical athletes, and we expect to see the wide life line that is shown at (2).

(3) The Venus mount is full and hard, giving birth to a long, thick, unbending thumb, and he needs all the willpower and tenacity, for his fate or luck line starts early, showing in Eastern palmistry an old soul back on a mission. The purpose of that mission is revealed to us in the rest of the hand.

Just as the facial structure can tell the racial origin, so can the hand, but in these days, when the races are so mixed, this can be difficult. But Imran's is what we would expect from the Indo/Pak subcontinent. From the palmar structure, we can usually guess the blood type, and this looks like Type B, which is alcohol intolerant, and knowing the blood type is handy to know the correct dietary needs.

(4) The fate line stops at the head line junction, showing a head-based or "intellectual" reason for changing direction in life. This is when he left the cricket world after being Pakistan's greatest cricket captain ever.

(5) The Girdle of Venus and Girdle of Jupiter, along with the central Apollo phalange being thin, tell us of a conflict with the mother going back some years over his emotional and sexual restlessness, which with Jupiter's

50 Case Studies in Modern Palmistry

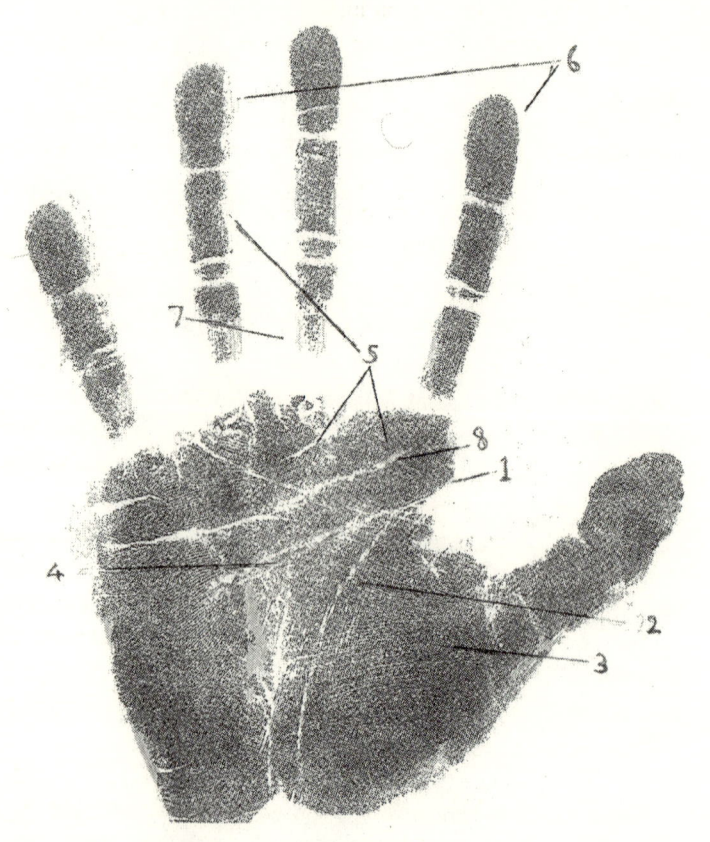

ring gives him magnetic and attractive qualities, and coupled to the persuasive abilities of a long and straight Mercury finger, we know that he was a playboy. This often involves deceit and is damaging karmicly.

Of the four types of karma, his hand speaks of *Parabhada* karma, which is *"the sum total of what lays in wait for him."* But he settles down, and what was surprising was his choice of partner, Gemima Goldsmith, daughter of James Goldsmith, the Jewish NWO financial speculator and currency raider. Nevertheless, Imran has put his own money into Pakistan's first cancer hospital, where most patients get treated free of charge; the only two cases of this generosity on record are both from Muslims, Imran Khan and Mohammed El Fayed, who offered to build a flagship hospital in memory of his son Dodi and Diana.

With men of power, drive and charisma, they have to monitor continually the direction of their drives, and Imran wanted to make a difference politically, to get Pakistan free of the IMF loans and the grip of

Imran Khan, 'The Shepherd'

foreign banks and a full ban on interest-based banking.

(6) The perfect balance and symmetry between the first and third fingers, or the "Jupiter to Apollo ratio," is evident of a natural but slow confidence. This Jupiter/Apollo=Saturn combination tells from his 53rd year he must watch for bleeding gums or gingivitis, which show systemic, oxidative stress, the signal for overall decline in health. Gum condition is an early warning of lowering health, and he will have later thigh/hip pain; something like Homeopathic Rhus Tox 30C potency is recommended.

(7) And the very slim base to the Saturn, or middle finger, means someone who over analyzes and over rationalizes before commitment. His life is his work, his work is his karma, and Kahlil Gibran says this about it:

"*Work that you may keep pace with the earth and the soul of the earth, for to be idle is to become a stranger unto the seasons and to step out of life's procession, that marches in majesty and proud submission toward the infinite.*"

Imran's hand is an Earth type. They resonate with the four seasons and with his very long, straight heart line (8), the heart line of a philanthropist, who knows when the season is right for sowing and when it's ripe for reaping. Imran Khan will reap a great harvest. His political plans need to be an immediate peace with India, as major banking powers are playing the two off against each other, in the same way they did with Hindus and Muslims, or Shia against Sunni. More conflict must not happen.

The combination of the Venus girdle and the long, straight heart line in a wide Mesomorph hand I have called at my lectures for over 50 years the "sign of the shepherd," a man who leads his flock, and Imran is the man to unite the people, and not just those in Pakistan with his Movement for Justice party, but people in other nations too.

The omens point to big recognition for him soon and his personal zenith occurs in June in his 61st year.

33
Jimmy Saville
The Man Behind the Mask

As a very small boy I realized I could look at people's hands and see visions of their later life. Using this talent, I made myself available for charitable events and anything from hospital open days to school fairs, raising money for every charity from animal sanctuaries to saving church spires across Britain.

It was as a result of appearing at a charity event that I was invited to a party to read hands. It was there that I met the famous DJ, Jimmy Saville, who was just one of the guests. Jimmy was very intelligent and claimed that he had good intuitive faculties himself, but said he did not have much time for this stuff.

Remember, Jimmy Saville was at the top of his profession, a national figure who associated with royalty, film stars and politicians like Prime Minister Edward Heath and Menachim Begin.

Show biz folk are very secretive about their private lives, and rightly so. Many a scurrilous journalist has wrecked the life of an aspiring performer. A palmist, medium or any psychic must obey the doctor/patient code and, like a priest or a psychiatrist, should not repeat any conversations, but Jimmy has broken his trust with the public, so I feel I can talk about the man beneath the mask.

His hand print at (1) shows a very difficult early life. Jimmy was one of seven children who was never shown any love or affection. Children who have had no love do not know how to experience it later. They cannot give what they never had. Sex often takes the place of love, if the bonding process is not formed up to the age of 6. The Royal College of Psychiatrists says that the damage to the psyche lasts the whole life.

Jimmy claimed he had never had a real relationship. He had dressed as a woman for a while and met men in public toilets, but could not connect with other human beings. Incidentally, the press has claimed Jimmy was a coal miner, but this conflicts with what he told me; in fact, much of what is in Wikipedia does not agree with what Jimmy said.

Jimmy Saville, The Man Behind the Mask

He did say that he was sexually abused as a boy, and he said this always affected his sleeping. He would often get up in the night and just drive about. This insomnia is echoed in his hand print. Psychologists say that when one is sexually abused, one can stay emotionally static at that point, and no matter how much older you become, you are still attracted to children of that age.

Let's take a look at his palm print.

(2) These two lines, the fragmented heart line, thin central finger sections and the two lines attacking the life line show the changeability and an unsettled emotional infrastructure. This always means sexual experimentation and a desperation to find the sexual identity and satisfaction. It usually ends badly.

The psychiatrist Ruth Seiffert worked with sexually disturbed people such as this at the Maudsley hospital. I advised Jimmy to chat with one of the experts there.

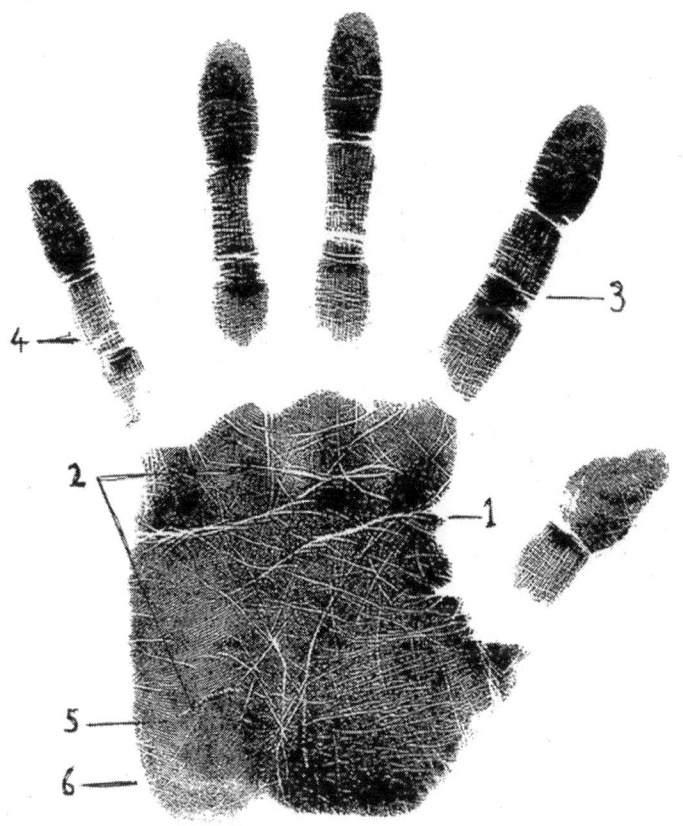

50 Case Studies in Modern Palmistry

The jumble of palmar lines known to palmists as a "full hand" shows someone who runs on nervous energy, and Jimmy's manic stage antics were legendary. The fact that he used cigars, shell suits and heavy jewelry is known in psychology as "affectations," but these were just stage props behind which Jimmy could hide.

Jimmy had an Ectomorph body typology, which is the body type for runners, acrobats, cyclists and distance athletes. Jimmy did all these at various times.

(3) The forward thrusting first, or Jupiter, finger in the right hand, with Jupiter as the highest mount, shows Jimmy was concerned about his career future at that time. Although confident, he was anxious to know which direction to take. The little, or Mercury, finger, divorced from its colleagues, shows his sexuality was divorced from the rest of his personality.

(4) The thinness in this section of the little finger and a sharp opposition line cutting right through, along with other palmar signals, are strong abuse signals indicated on his life line at around age 12 to 14.

This particular life line formation in Tibetan palmistry is called the sign of the Tortoise, and shows someone with a hard shell but is quite different inside, soft and sensitive, but someone who can negotiate all obstacles, albeit at their own pace.

I advised Jimmy that his sensitivity in the gastric arena meant a vegetarian diet would suit him better, and he would later on become very well educated in all dietary aspects.

Age 40 shows a landmark time when Jimmy became despondent and reflective. Although people have come forth and said Jimmy was their friend, since boyhood he had never known a real friend, and when he earned big bucks, he did not really trust anyone.

His head line shows a rational, practical-minded man, and the head line kinks upwards at the end like a scorpion's tail, often seen with Scorpio sun signs like Jimmy's, showing a deep, inbuilt fear of being poor like his family. This longing for financial security often shows as a substitute for love with those who never had the emotional security that many of us take for granted.

(5) The Andropause, or male menopause, can be a difficult time of readjustment for men, and Jimmy really began to slide downhill from this point. Others colluded with him to conceal his abuse of children and vulnerable adults.

Jimmy suffered this kind of abuse himself and passed this on to others in the most horrific ways, yet the large square shown at (6) indicates his

Jimmy Saville, The Man Behind the Mask

secret was kept safe within a box. The square is the luckiest sign in palmistry and his lasted almost until his death at age 84. Jimmy's death was the signal that people could now speak out. Those that protected him know that this is at last coming to the public eye.

34

Show Biz Advice

Those connected to show biz are the most superstitious people you ever meet. Many take readings very seriously indeed, and yet getting permission from them to print their hands can be very difficult. This may be because film and theatre people, like sports personalities, are often here today and gone tomorrow, and they are terrified of any unwelcome publicity.

They often open up for the first time in years and use you as a confessor, but doctor-patient rules on confidentiality are as important here as in the confessional, because you are often a mixture of both counselor and priest.

So, this interesting hand print of a celebrated author must remain unnamed.

(1) The forked head line is the sign of someone who can always see the other person's point of view. This forking is slightly more active in the lower branch, showing imagination, and the large forked heart line at (2) shows her preoccupation with matters of the heart.

The shape of the hand tells that she is an intellectual thinker and communicator, and we see here a famous British romantic novelist.

The forking is known as the "sign of the fish," as it is like a fish's tail, and is seen as a sacred marking in Christian and Hindu literature, and to a lesser extent in Islam. The fish is exalted in water signs and enhances the indecision seen in forkings.

The heart line, in particular, shows one branch to Jupiter—showing idealism in loved ones and the love of public figures, while the lower branch shows that she reaches out in a philanthropic way to the lesser privileged and has donated large sums to charity.

The fate line at (3) starts from the moon again and is extra emphasized in water signs, as the moon rules water and the tides, and shows that imagination will bring her much success in every sphere.

But if you follow the fate line up the hand to the Saturn mount, we see a girdle of Saturn blocking its path and interfering with the line of sun. (3)

Saturn is known as the Greater Malefic. It is the teacher who says we

Show Biz Advice

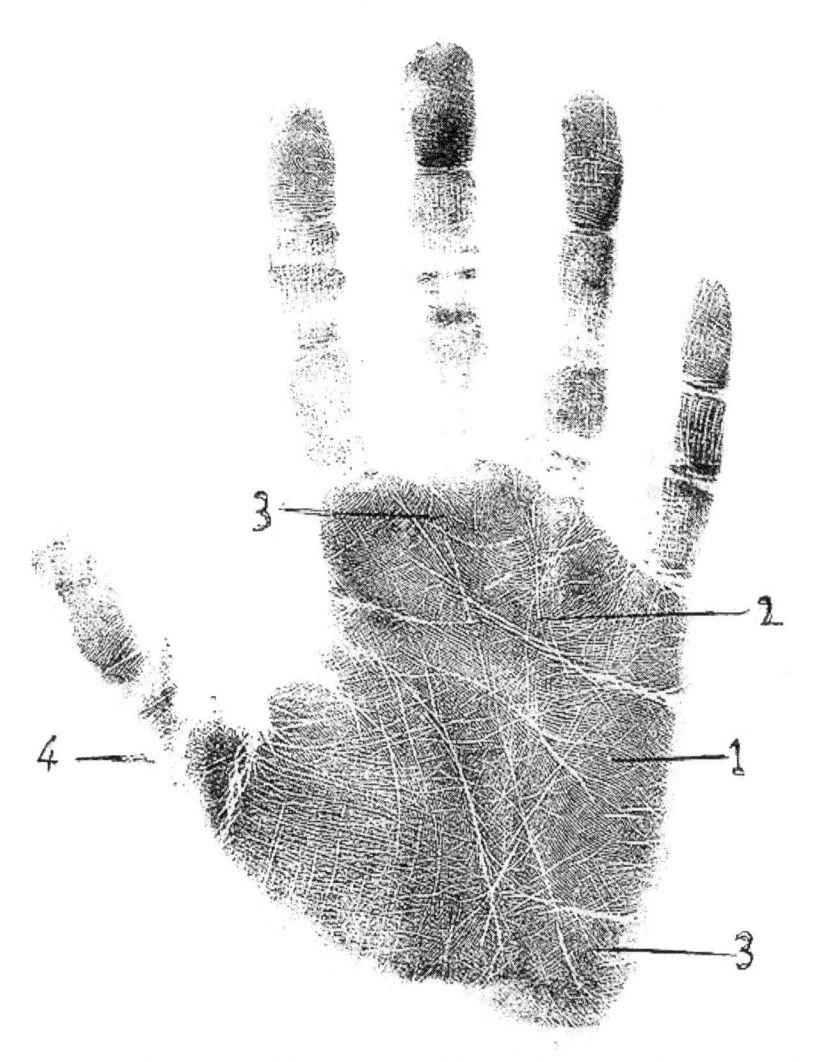

learn best through painful experiences. This can be a scandal or some bad investment decision, and she explained that she was being sued over copyright on a story, which was why she came for a reading.

It may surprise readers that well known show biz stars are often the loneliest people there is; they can trust no one. This lovely lady was desperate for love, but felt she would be seen as a wealthy prize rather than who she is inside.

When you see a fate or destiny line so powerful—and it cuts the hand in half as this one—it shows you someone who will feel that they experience a lot of pre-destiny in their lives. I see fate lines like this as a train line.

You can stop at various stations, but you have difficulty moving off the line itself. At times, people will board our train—friends, workmates, lovers, etc., and they may get off at various stops on our journey, which will be unknown to us and will bring us joy, sorrow and help us experience so much.

But we must accept gracefully when people leave their seats and leave our carriage empty.

The thumb marking (unclear) at (4) tells us that the wisdom of Ganesh will be with the subject, to always make the right choice.

* I have deliberately not mentioned the many small signs and marks in hands as, first, every other book mentions this, and second, reproducing hand prints with small detail is not easy.

35

Margaret Thatcher, the Iron Lady

Baroness Margaret Thatcher, (née Roberts, 13 October 1925 — 8 April 2013) was a Conservative and longest serving British Prime Minister this century, from 1979 to 1990. The Soviets called her the "Iron Lady," a nickname that became associated with her uncompromising politics and leadership style. As Prime Minister, she implemented policies that have come to be known as Thatcherism, the basis being "the open market economy." This means you buy from the cheapest source, no matter what.

This practice meant the closure of Britain's industrial base, since everything could be bought cheaper abroad. Ship building, steel, the mines, motor cars and motor bike companies all closed down, and a crippling VAT tax was applied to all small industry, closing that too. Many of those thrown into unemployment are still unemployed 30 years after, since the government has first priorities to employ immigrant labor. Incidentally, Adolf Hitler wanted Britain to keep both its Empire and its industrial base, but the Rothschild banks, who funded Britain's war effort, demanded it all be dismantled and allow, in mass, immigration which has destroyed Britain's unique character and cultural heritage.

As I write, the news media eulogizes her while the people hold street parties to celebrate that she's gone. This is similar, in fact, to Churchill's demise. There is public uproar at having to pay for these huge funerals for politicians who never served the electorate. The people want the bankers to fund her funeral, since she worked primarily for them. Stalin called those who worked against their own "useful idiots."

Please take a close look at her hand. The most noticeable aspects are the strength, length and thickness of the Jupiter, or Index, finger, the strong, straight thumb and the low, small, bent Mercury finger.

(1) Long, thick Jupiter fingers always show us someone who wants to be in charge. This means authority, responsibility and leadership. When as long as the second, or Saturn, finger as this, you have what my friend the late chief Psychiatrist Professor Henri Rey would call a confirmed "superiority complex." In males these are usually military or sport leaders. In women

50 Case Studies in Modern Palmistry

HOUSE OF COMMONS
LONDON SW1A 0AA

4th June 2008
Our Reference. AD/HCB/ /05/08

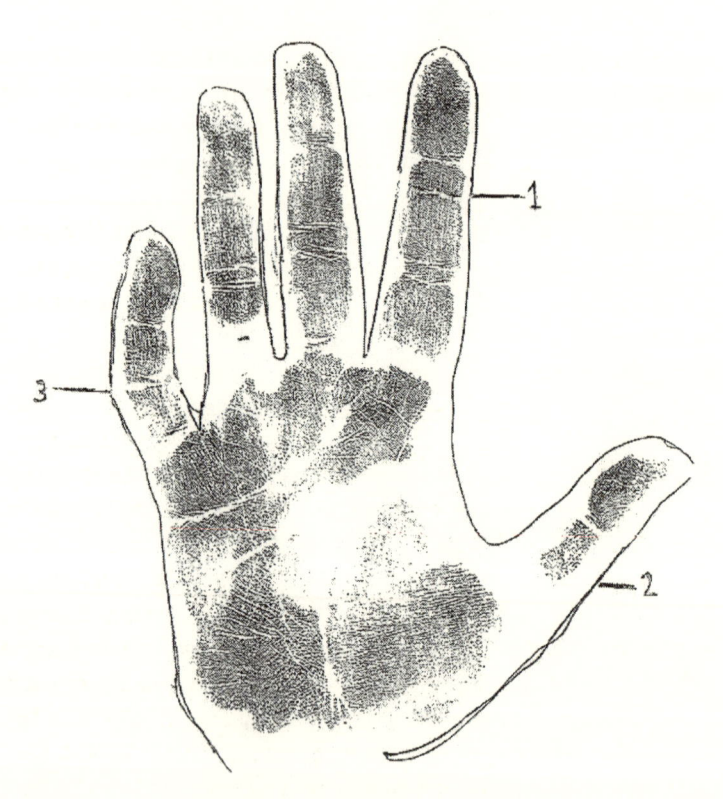

they show a dictatorial attitude. With religious or political leaders, in this, an Ectomorph Caucasian hand type, we have an inherited, purely intellectual leadership. In India this is seen as a reincarnated master, come back to show the way.

It should be said that the fingers develop in the womb and an imbalance between estrogen/testosterone will show an over-large first finger. These people always have developed ego structures. Margaret Thatcher would

Margaret Thatcher, the Iron Lady

brook no opposition and said on record, "This lady is not for turning." These people are convinced that they are always right because of their huge reserves of self-confidence.

In a woman's hand you can expect to see difficulties with menstruation and breast problems in the early life, and more serious issues around the time of the menopause. This is especially true in women with mercury amalgam teeth fillings.

(1) The large Jupiter finger with a small, underdeveloped Mercury finger denotes the power, which should have been channeled sexually, went instead to construct her outward world, and to controlling it. This would be a compensatory act for the lack of and inability to give or accept sexual closeness. Margaret was known to exist on two hours sleep, not conducive to any sort of marital life. Because the Mercury fingers display every facet of the communicative faculties, this tells its own story right back to babyhood, and explains Margaret's untrusting nature in being unable to experience the joys of the bonding process.

(2) The long, powerful, straight thumb we see here, with a strong head line, shows an unbending will—stubborn and self-obsessed, with much determination. When the head line goes blurry at the end, this can be a sign of dementia.

(3) The Mercury Finger low set, small and bent. When this print was taken, the condition was just becoming a nuisance and is known as *Dupuytrens Contracture*. Most Caucasians are descended from Neanderthals, who became the Vikings. Margaret's crooked Mercury finger is seen on Neanderthal skeletons, and her skull shape confirms this inheritance. The Hueguenots, who moved from France to England, had also inherited this characteristic, which was called a "weaver's finger," since the bent little finger was ideal to hold the threads of the looms. Eventually, the tendon will pull the finger into the palm. Several types of surgery exist to correct this, but the French method is best because then it does not reoccur.

The palm print was taken at a birthday dinner in 2008 as her health was failing. She had many regrets, but treated the palmist there for the evening with respect and kindness, squeezing my hand in a vise-like grip as she asked about her final years.

36

Reincarnation As Seen in the Hand

Have a good look at the palm print of this top British spiritual healer. This is actually a woman's hand, but the largeness of it suggests a certain masculinity. This always manifests when young as a "tomboy." The lines themselves, however, are very feminine. This can result in inner conflict problems developing as "identity crises" or the teen-age feelings of unhappiness with one's physique, known as "body dysmorphia." Certainly anxiety over this is shown in the linear formation, at age 10 and at approximately age 20. [See figure (1) and (2).]

A feeling of alienation with either gender or body type is often a sign of subconscious memory patterns from a previous life, or normally a run of these lives, showing through to the conscious mind.

Ecclesiastes 1-11: *"There is no remembrance of former things, neither shall there be any remembrance of things that are to come, with those that are to come after."*

If there is something that always goes wrong in a life, and it seems to form a pattern—particularly in the emotional arena—it is usually karmic in origin. The two main areas in the hand to examine, to look for clues for what is known as a "constant recurrent," are the beginning of the life line and the line that runs around the thumb (1). Note its genesis at the side of the hand, and what medical anatomists now call the "main longitudinal crease," but which for hundreds of years palmists have called the fate or destiny line. Although destiny is not confined to any one particular area, this is the place to start (3). In the hand print shown, the destiny line is what palmists call an "enfiladed" marking [see (3).] This, according to the dictionary, is: "A number of things arranged like beads on a string."

Indeed, this sums up the events of the destiny, which is read from the hand base upwards. The "things on a string," of course, represent the main events of the life.

The most noticeable thing on the illustration is the roadway that the heart line cuts geographically through the hand map.

Any line that is malformed or out of place deserves special attention.

Reincarnation As Seen in the Hand

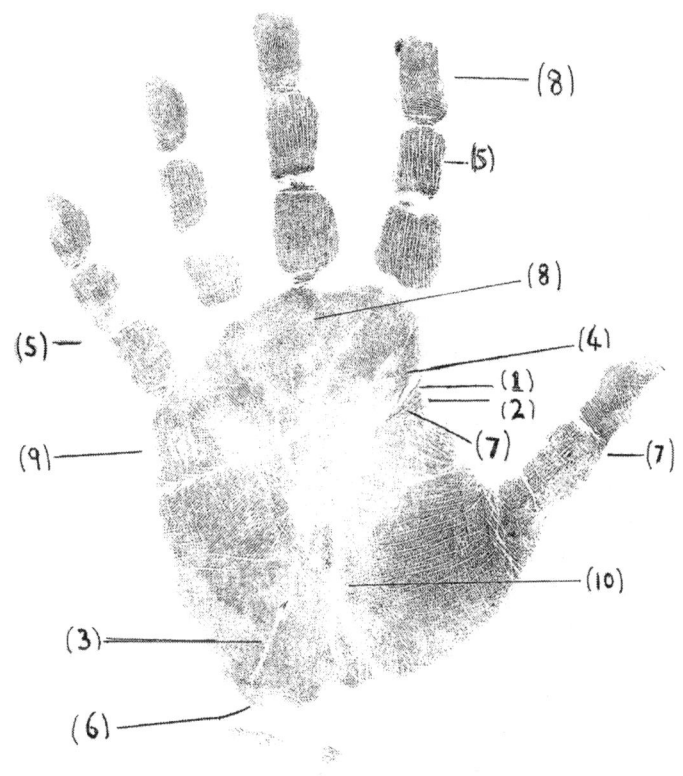

It has always been called at my lectures a "Cuckoo line," and we can see that this person's life lessons are emotional, as the heart line lies low, and is unusually marked (4).

Notice the markings on the life line at age 19- 20, which are confirmed on the line of heart. This can only mean a karmic marriage, and I would guess from finger patterning, to either an August or June birthday (5).

There is a passage in Hindu scripture, which says, *"There is a special place in hell reserved for the man that spurns a woman's love."*

That special place, I believe to be an internal place of suffering until realization is digested and the debt repaid, often in another life. The poet John Masefield wrote:

> *I know that in my lives to be,*
> *My sorry heart to burn,*
> *and worship unavailingly,*
> *The woman I used to spurn,*
> *and shake to see another have,*
> *The love I spurned, the love she gave.*

Any ill treatment of another, including the seeking of revenge, creates a karmic debt, which at some time must be paid (Sanchita Karma).

The correct attitude—but a difficult one to maintain—is as Jesus, and Gandhi suggested, "*to turn the other cheek.*"

Often we daydream that we are in a particular period in history, and we feel we are in clothes of the time, and really feel part of the zeitgeist. This is because there may be unfinished business here. Meditation is of great value in the understanding of who we are and why we are here, and what tasks we have to tackle in life.

The holy Koran tells us "*God sends back the souls of men time and time again until they are ready to return to him.*" Belief in the return to the godhead is called "Remanation." Some people believe we can come back as animals; this is called "Transmigration." There are no proven cases on record, and I believe the argument is unsustainable. Its origins are based on mistranslations of ancient Indian scripture.

Christianity teaches "metasomatosis" or physical resurrection, which is again theologically insupportable. The horoscope taken at the time of death can give pointers to the next birth.

Science tells us we are 90 percent water, and "entanglement" is the scientific name given to the fact that once water has been in contact with something, it forever carries that recognition and connection. Many believe Homeopathy works on this principle.

It would also account for much of the Law of Attraction with reincarnated bodies.

On the hand print shown, the destiny line starts from the wrist, or upper bracelet line, in the lunar sector. This tells of both karmic health and emotional responsibilities, which must be worked out (6).

The stiffness of the thumb always speaks of stubbornness and resistance to change, reinforced by the closed formation of life and head (7).

The heart line is long and flat, yet lies low in the hand, and shows signs of restricted emotional expression and passivity, with the head faculties strongly leading heart, which tells us of someone emotionally unconfident—but why?

Both the destiny and heart lines end their journey under the first, or Jupiter, finger (4). Traditionally, Jupiter represents power, authority and religion, so we see the area to search for past-life conflict.

Some schools of palmistic thought say that, where the heart line ends, shows the qualities of the planetary type they are attracted to. This one ends on Jupiter, which rules Sagittarius. Amongst experts there is perhaps more

Reincarnation As Seen in the Hand

arguments about the line of heart than any other. Certainly this person would value Jupiterian characteristics.

There is a pointed Jupiter finger and an unusual fingerprint pattern centrally positioned, under Saturn, or the second finger, the planet of karma (which incidentally is the highest mount in the hand). These clues added together give what is known as a "cocktail effect," and tell of some predestined link to someone with spiritual connections (8). The ending of the destiny line on Jupiter's mount is an accepted sign of a fated promise for a position in power or authority. For the bearer of the mark, this allied to the healing lines under the Mercury or small finger, and we have an inbuilt sense of pride in care for others, and the ambition to achieve this (9).

This is a strong finger of Saturn, with its central knuckle being shaped like a human eye, implying Saturnian seership. Remember, Saturn returns to our birth position at ages 30 and 60, and it is these times for the window of karmic opportunity to play its part, the seeds having laid dormant for millennia.

My experience here is that when events conspire at these ages, a "road to Damascus," or sudden change of attitude, takes hold, perhaps a new face in our circle of friends, bearing some aspect of Jupiter, such as a Sagittarian subject. It is as if the life suddenly finds purpose. A good example here is Eva Peron, who drifted through life experiencing feelings of failure and unhappiness; but come the destined time and she came to prominence, with her spirit inspiring a nation, and there are similarities here to our own Princess Diana.

Surely is it said, *"There is a time in our lives for sowing, and a time for reaping."* This hand print speaks of both travel and an expansion of artistic and emotional horizons, the reaping of the harvest climaxing at age 63. Isaiah 49-16 says: *"For behold I have engraven thee on the palms of my hands,"* a pointer to both past and future relationships leaving their mark.

That masterpiece, *The Tibetan Book of the Dead*, instructs us that just as a bird will rebuild its nest in the same old way time after time, so does the soul rebuild its body in the same old way time after time. Maybe this is how we recognize others from a time long ago.

The subject was not sure about fate, but agreed there had been a lot of strange coincidences in her life. I reminded her of psychologist and palmist Carl Jung's teachings that there was no such thing as coincidence, that all things were linked at a deep level, and this he called "synchronicity."

Book of Job, 14-14: *"If a man die shall he live again?"*

"All the days of my appointed time will I wait until my change come."

50 Case Studies in Modern Palmistry

I am perhaps asked at my lectures more questions on past lives than any other subject.

This view represents just one facet of the diamond, and not all experts are in agreement.

"We are such stuff as dreams are made of, and our whole life is rounded with a sleep."
— Shakespeare

37

Sonny Liston
World Boxing Champion

Charles "Sonny" Liston was born May 8, 1932—although this is disputed. This would make him a Taurus subject, and Taurus is extra strong in Mesomorph elementary hands.

Sonny's father was a cruel brute of a man, who beat his son regularly, as they lived and worked on a farm. Sonny grew up with no shoes and pretty well no education. Even as a schoolboy, Sonny was big, and being basically illiterate, he soon turned to crime, and at one point was apprehended by police, who broke their nightsticks over his head in an altercation. As a result, two needed hospital treatment, and Sonny was sentenced to five years in prison.

Sonny told us it was the only time in his life he ever got three meals a day. While in prison, he was encouraged to train as a boxer; his career when he left prison was meteoric.

A tough, strong, powerful man, 6 feet 5 inches tall, with huge hands and a reach of 84 inches meant he won 50 of his 54 fights. His bouts with Cassius Clay (later Muhammed Ali) attracted worldwide attention, as on paper he should have been an easy winner. Many say Liston had to throw the Clay fights, under threats from the gangsters.

Liston constantly got bad press and was labeled as the Gorilla. He was a man of few words and was gruff and monosyllabic, unlike Clay, whom the newspapers loved, who would make up rhymes for the reporters.

The writer for the *Sports Illustrated*, Gilbert Rogin, described Liston's body as "awesome, having arms like fence posts and thighs like silos."

His hand shows a powerful, solid, Mesomorph body type as most boxers are.

(1) The mark of the tiger in Tibetan palmistry, his open life and head lines show instant, impulsive reactions with no thought or caution; yet his fingers are slightly longer than I would have expected. He had broken almost all his fingers in fights, both legal and street corner, bare knuckle bouts. But long fingers show a thinker. His are midway between short and long, which means he could plan a fight and think it through.

50 Case Studies in Modern Palmistry

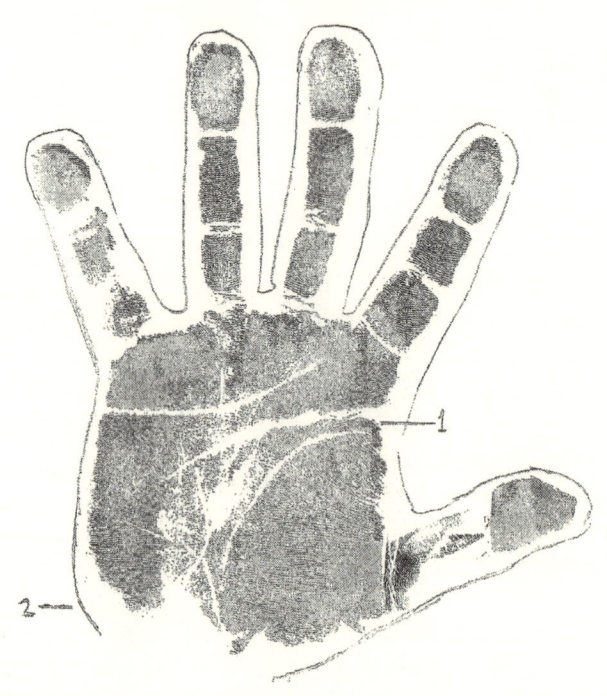

When Liston became heavyweight champ, the newspapers turned on him, and with his past involvement in crime, even President Kennedy was against him.

(2) A wide base to the hand shows immense physical strength. Liston was afraid of no one. His fist measured an amazing 14 inches in circumference. His hand was hard and both Mars mounts were firm and high, the mark of the warrior. When under the start to the life line is firm and high, this shows someone made for physical combat.

It is not generally known that he could sing; he said he would sing when working in the fields as a boy, and he still felt anger over his tough childhood and the ridicule for his lack of education.

Sonny had been an enforcer for the crime syndicates, and had done some bad things, yet he was an incredible fighter who died early. Many say he was killed by the gangsters who run boxing.

Of all the sportsmen and boxers' hands I read in the '60s and '70s, Sonny stands out as perhaps the most memorable.

Sonny Liston, the boxer's boxer, died December 30, 1970 under mysterious circumstances, aged just 38. He is interred in Paradise Memorial Gardens, Las Vegas. His headstone just says simply "*a man.*"

38

Peter O'Toole

The death of actor Peter O'Toole on December 15, 2013, at the age of 81, brought an end to an era.

Peter never knew where he was born, but genealogists say he was born in Yorkshire on August 2, 1932 to a strict Irish father, and Peter was brought up to love his Irish ancestry. Yet he was rejected by the Dublin's Abbey Theatre as he was seen as not Irish enough.

Peter was educated by nuns and he never forgot the harshness of their early treatment. The nuns would scold and beat children who were left-handed because this was said to be the devil's hand. The term "left hand path" is synonymous with evil, and thus children who were left-handed were called devil's children. O'Toole described these nuns as being in total denial of their womanhood, adding what god would ask such things of his finest creation.

His father was anti-British and several members of his family were sympathizers to the German cause in WWII.

He starred in many films, but as he said about himself, he woke one morning famous as hell. It was after David Lean cast him in *Lawrence of Arabia*, which became a worldwide smash, that he gained notoriety. He is described as a great actor in a great film, capturing the essence of who Lawrence really was.

Lawrence was used by the British in WWII, to tell the Arabs if they fought for Britain, they could keep their lands, while at the same time the British were promising the land to the Jews.

He achieved stardom playing T. E. Lawrence in *Lawrence of Arabia* (1962), for which he received his first Academy Award nomination. He received seven further Oscar nominations—for *Becket* (1964), *The Lion in Winter* (1968), *Goodbye, Mr. Chips* (1969), *The Ruling Class* (1972), *The*

50 Case Studies in Modern Palmistry

Stunt Man (1980), *My Favorite Year* (1982) and *Venus* (2006)—and holds the record for the most Academy Award acting nominations without a win. He won four Golden Globes, a BAFTA and an Emmy, and was the recipient of an honorary Academy Award in 2003.

He was expected by everyone to win the award that was given to Ben Kingsley for *Gandhi*, and many insiders said this was fixed, as almost everyone thought O'Toole deserved the award more.

His hands from the picture shown here describe a man, who with a head line ending low on Luna, signifies an imaginative and creative man. The long fate line is an omen for a good career, but very much the tool of fate. The right hand, Saturn finger with a ring, indicates deep-seated insecurities which concern his future. The long little, or Mercury, finger tells of

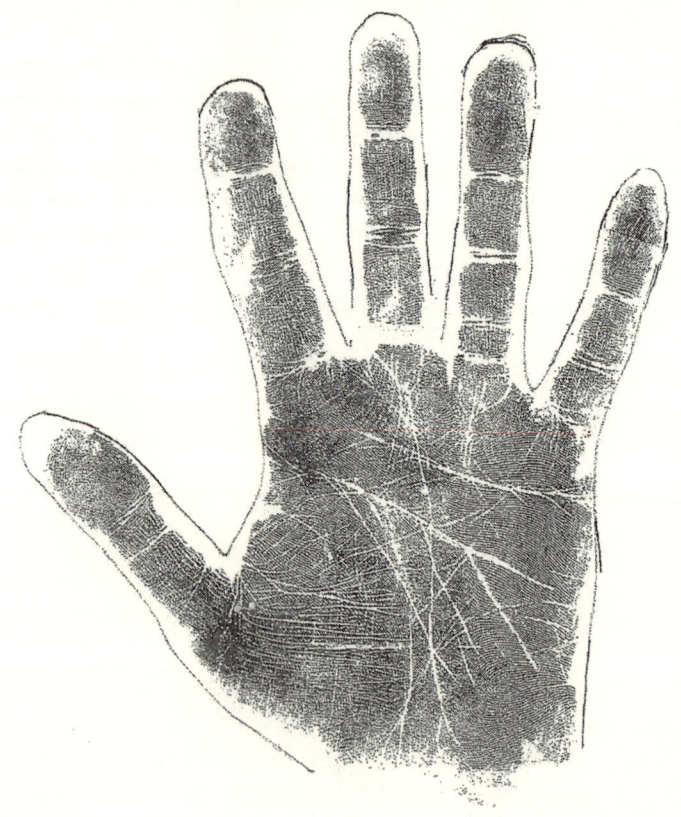

Peter O'Toole

communication and the ability to reach people, essential qualities for any actor. The first, or Jupiter, finger is the father finger, and just as we read the mother on the third, or Apollo finger, so Jupiter tells us here of a difficult early life with his father, his lifelong battle with excessive alcohol consumption, his emotional and violent outbursts, his risk taking, his inability to remember his wallet, keys, etc., are all part of what is now recognized as PTSD (Post Traumatic Stress Disorder). Alas, the strict father and the cruelty of the nuns scarred him for life.

The psychologist Hans Eysenck said that early-life instability or cruelty will give a very damaged later personality structure, and Peter O'Toole battled with his demons all his life. He suffered for his craft. The world lost a great actor on the day of St. John of the Cross, December 14, 2014, the day of Peter O'Toole's death.

The numbers to Peter's name are 75259 and 626635. These two names both add to 28, which reduces to a 10=1. The balance shown when first names match the last name gives what is called a seesaw effect, and the later life will balance out the first. It is often seen with bisexuals, or those who are midway between male and female, and ironically, the tarot card depicted at his death is the number 14, which warns of Temperance, which means all things in balance and moderation.

Peter O'Toole never did anything in moderation in his life; wherever you are, Peter, raise a glass for us.

39

Marlboro Man

Take a good look at the hand print shown here. This man was, for some years, a very successful male model and one of the best known TV faces in advertisements. What can you see in this hand?

The life line on its journey round the thumb (1) suddenly thickens at around age 30, indicating sluggish life energies from that time. The low-lying, straight, frayed and fluffy heart line starting under the Saturn finger shown at (2) is an indicator of both an unusual outlook toward relationships and possible later cardiovascular difficulties.

The deep flame-like line of health, which attacks the life line at around age 58 (3), tells of both chest area and digestive weakness. In Medieval times, the health line was known as the liver line or the hepatica. Its primary function was diagnosing in the digestive area.

Medical scientists at Sapienza University in Rome have recently confirmed that by measuring children's wrist bones and comparing the measurements to insulin levels, which if high can lead to heart problems in adulthood, is a better predictor than the BMI (body mass index) tests. Several studies showed that Athero-sclerotic cardiovascular disease, caused by narrowing of the arteries, begins in childhood.

To the palmist, the eight wrist bones, when thick as they are here, should also be read alongside the heart line for any weakness, and compared to the nails, nail moons and the finger pads, where the fingers join the palm, what medical anatomists call the lower inter-phalangeal joints.

In this man's hand, which is a Mesomorph type Earth hand, the bone structure suggests Caucasoid ancestry.

For each of the bone types there is a correct blood type, a positive and a negative, and some experts claim a correct diet for the blood type. This man's diet was awful. He has been eating fast foods since childhood.

Professor James Tanner was the pediatrician who identified the effects of the immediate environment on the growth patterns of children and adolescents with over 300 published papers. His work underpins the routine

Marlboro Man

monitoring of modern child development, which shows that poor diet—both in the womb and in childhood—can mean much later ill health and a possible early death.

So this man was born extremely handsome and irresistible to women. He told me he was actually a quiet, shy, reserved man, who never learnt to cope with female admiration. He went on to say that this had ruined all his relationships. He said that even though he was so happy with the woman he was with, she would become insecure with him and have a hard time dealing with bunches of flowers getting left on the doorstep, love notes put through his door, women's underwear left on his windshield, and the phone calls.

It always happens like this. Next come the accusations, the arguments, and then "I am single yet again."

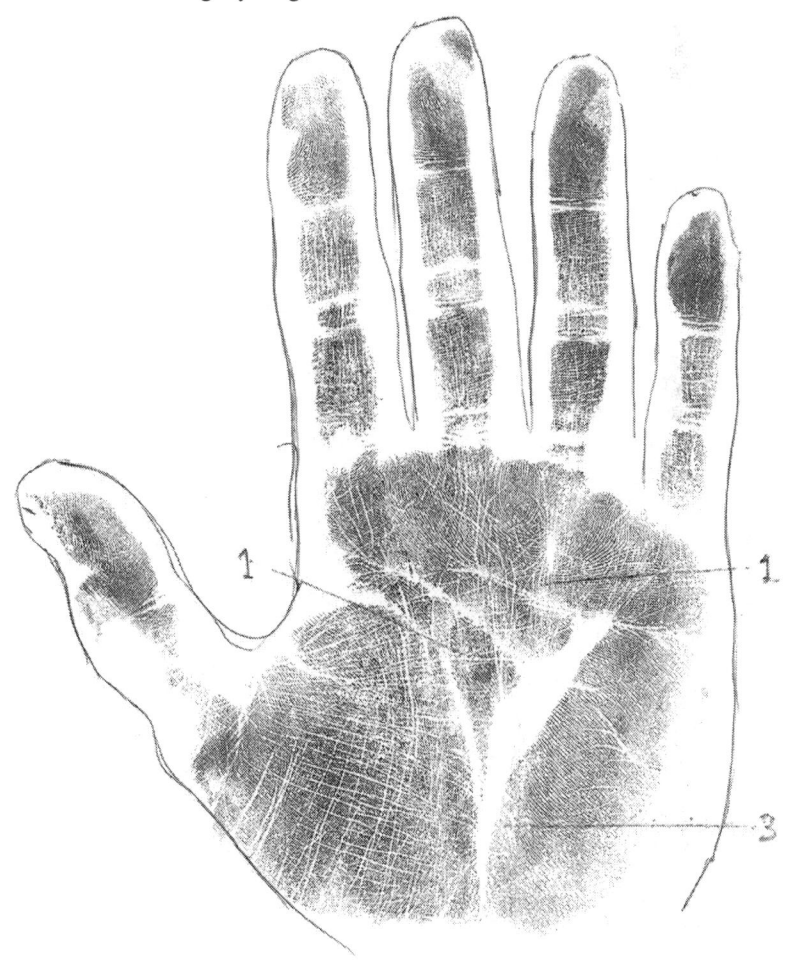

He explained that a motorcycle accident left him badly injured at 32 years of age, and he never really got fit afterwards. He began drinking beer more heavily, hence the sluggish life line.

He applied to be in an advertisement, and so many women rang in, they extended his work contracts into other ads too. He got busy and fitted in fast food between work assignments. This man was best known for cigarette advertisements, and the company would post him a carton for free each week; thus he became a heavy smoker.

It is tragic that as this man reaches his 60th birthday, alcohol and cigarettes with fast food are destroying his heath, and leaving him severely depressed.

Ayurvedic medicine claims moods and immunity are influenced and controlled by your digestion, so I recommended a total change of diet, to a vegetarian one with ginger, garlic and thyme, which help digestion. I also suggested that when he is feeling low, to have some elderberry syrup and Tulsi tea, since they have been shown to neutralize eight types of seasonal virus. This is to be taken with a daily multivitamin and mineral, with extra Vitamin B, because this nutrient is depleted with smokers and drinkers.

The good news is, he is actually enjoying the new diet, and now has a more positive mental outlook.

40

Robin Williams
The Day the Laughing Stopped

Robin McLaurin Williams (July 21, 1951-August 11, 2014)

July 21 is a cusp between signs of Fire and Water, and Williams epitomized the internal conflict of opposites. The heavy joining of life and head lines shows extreme sensitivity, shyness and caution, not typical in a show biz comedian (1).

His death on August 11 is perhaps fitting as it is the day of Saint Clare, who as a penniless vegetarian, lived her life working for various charities and other people.

Williams was an American actor, comedian, film producer and screenwriter. Starting as a stand-up comedian, Robin was an instant smash hit in England with the TV series *Mork & Mindy* (1978-'82). Williams went on to establish a career in both stand-up comedy and feature film acting. But in the film *Good Morning, Vietnam*, Britons took him to their hearts. All wars are unpopular with the people, but the Vietnam war doubly so.

His manic style was, to some extent, based on the British comedy actor Spike Milligan, whose YouTube video, *Pakistani Daleks,* is a timeless classic. Like Williams, Milligan's depression was at the core of his work.

Drooping head line at (2) shows creativity and depression. He also had the hairiest hands I have ever seen. The hair can show energy leakage.

Williams was nominated for the Academy Award for Best Actor three times, and won the Academy Award for Best Supporting Actor for his performance as therapist Dr. Sean Maguire in *Good Will Hunting*. He received two Emmy Awards, four Golden Globe Awards, two Screen Actors Guild Awards, and five Grammy Awards.

In 1986, he teamed up with Whoopi Goldberg and Billy Crystal to found Comic Relief USA, an annual HBO television benefit devoted to the homeless, which has raised $80 million as of 2014. Williams made benefit

50 Case Studies in Modern Palmistry

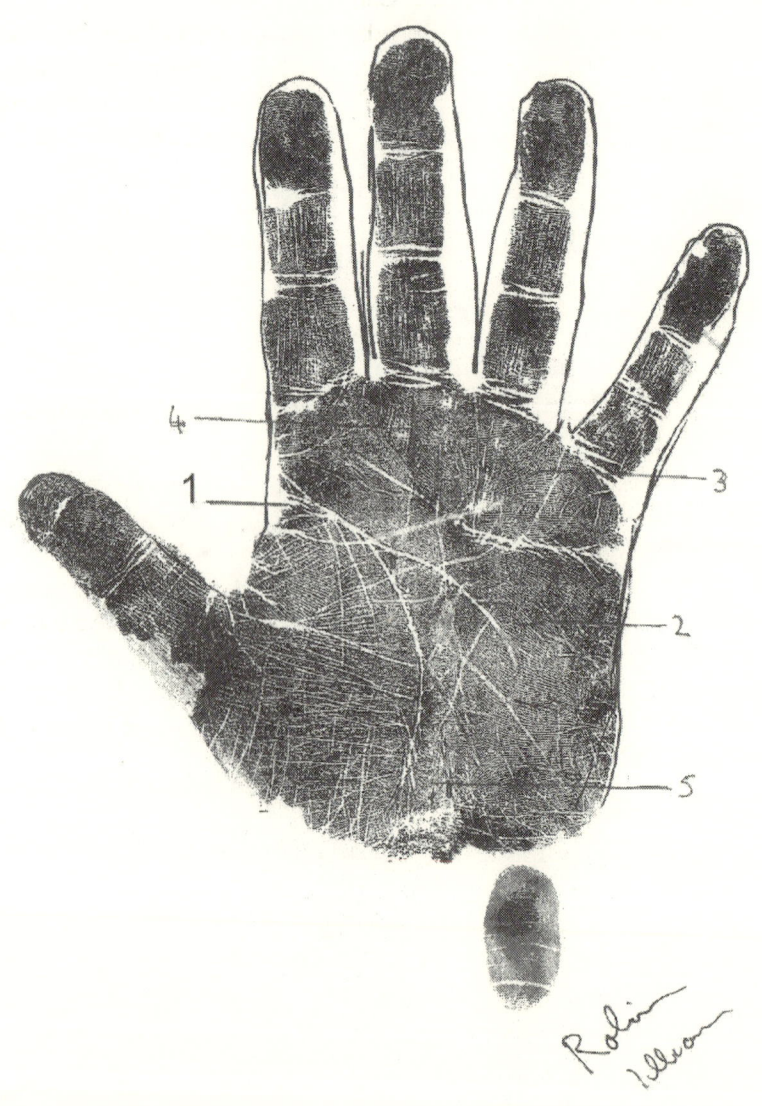

appearances to support literacy and women's rights, along with appearing at benefits for veterans. He traveled to thirteen countries and performed for approximately 100,000 troops.

Williams and his second wife, Marsha, founded the Windfall Foundation, a philanthropic organization to raise money for many charities. In December 1999, he sang in French on the BBC-inspired music video of international celebrities doing a cover of The Rolling Stones' *It's Only Rock 'n*

Robin Williams, The Day the Laughing Stopped

Roll (But I Like It), for the charity Children's Promise.

In response to the 2010 Canterbury earthquake, Williams donated all proceeds of his "Weapons of Self Destruction" Christchurch performance to helping rebuild the New Zealand city. Half the proceeds were donated to the Red Cross and half to the mayoral building fund, and he supported St. Jude Children's Research Hospital for several years.

Williams was hospitalized in March 2009, due to heart problems. He postponed his one-man tour for surgery to replace his aortic valve, and the surgery was successfully completed on March 13, 2009, at the Cleveland Clinic (4).

Williams' publicist, Mara Buxbaum, commented that the actor was suffering from severe depression prior to his death.

The sun line up Apollo's mount is missing, showing that he felt he was not a success, and he was not good with money (3).

Williams' wife, Susan, stated that in the period before his death, he had been sober, but was diagnosed with early stage Parkinson's disease, which was something he was "not yet ready to share publicly."

Williams died on the morning of August 11, 2014, at his home in Paradise Cay, California. In the initial report released on August 12, the Marin County Sheriff's Office deputy coroner stated that Williams had hanged himself with a belt and died from asphyxiation (5).

Shakespeare: *"He was a man and taken all in all we shall not see his like again."*

41

The Palm of Michael Jackson

The Avon and Somerset police force in England is the only one in western Europe with a computer laid out for just palm prints. The use of fingerprinting may soon be eclipsed in police cases by the hand print, and although graphologists regularly assist in police cases, the police use of psycho-chirologists (palmists) is rare in Britain.

Michael Jackson, "The Prince of Pop," seemed to have it all. The only stain on his long career was a charge of sexual abuse connected with his friendships with young boys. At age 50, Jackson was found dead in his bed. Entertainment news website TMZ, which broke the story of Jackson's death, claims the singer received an injection of painkillers at 11:30 AM on the day of his death. Later that afternoon, the singer was pronounced dead at the UCLA medical center.

After Jackson was acquitted on child molestation charges in 2005,

The Palm of Michael Jackson

prosecutors argued against returning to Jackson items including syringes, the drug Demerol and prescriptions for various drugs, mainly antibiotics, in different people's names. Lisa Marie Presley, briefly married to the pop icon in the mid-1990s, said he had confided to her 14 years ago that he worried about facing the same tragic fate as her father, Elvis Presley, who died of a drug overdose at age 42.

Brian Oxman, a former Jackson attorney and a family friend, said Friday he had been concerned about Jackson's use of painkillers and had warned the singer's family about possible abuse.

What does his hand actually say?

Michael's palm is the large, thick and solid type as known to experts as the Earth hand. As seen in the "Mesomorph structure," this always goes with athletic, strong and physical specimens.

Unusually, the fingers are small and thin, giving the impression of too much power in the palm, for them to carry. Here I would use the analogy of a racing car driving with the handbrake on.

Put simply, the index, or Jupiter finger, is both short and stumpy, and it shows damage to the psychological landscape in the early latency period. Michael must have suffered emotional bullying, or physical and possible sexual abuse from what appears in his latency period, which dates on his life line at approximately age 7 building to 11 years of age.

The short index is always a sign of an inferiority complex. This is compounded by the short, bent Saturn, or middle finger, with the ring or Apollo finger towering over it, showing an urge for compulsive, compensatory, irresponsible behavior. Incidentally, this is a common configuration with chance takers. The exact course this takes can be gathered together from other palmar indicators. Michael is certainly a gambler.

The most telling aspect is the little finger set apart from the other fingers, telling us that the qualities represented by the finger are not integrated, and are a separate entity. This tells of a personality construct that represents a separate fabric in his psychological weave. This little, or Mercury finger, is the finger of communications, governing all from verbal to physical, from his singing voice to his sexuality. Remember, psychologists say only 7 percent of communication is verbal.

His Mercury finger is not an able conduit for channeling the strength of libidinal power in his hand, resulting in huge blockages, which can only be from a botched or late circumcision, or regular abuse revolving around

50 Case Studies in Modern Palmistry

the central Oedipal hub building to age 11.

His life line speaks of an identity crisis at age 20 and again at 29, which deepens his sexual choreography into uncharted and unwelcome waters. Many years of writing psychological assessments for youngsters going to court leads me to say the combination of the inferiority complex gives low self-esteem. This means the drive for a partner cannot be achieved, and the inner feelings of worthlessness are incompatible with an equal basis partner, hence the youngster companions.

Surprisingly, many actors and show business types have low self-esteem, and build other personas with which to escape themselves, as do spies, and sexual deviants. The mask in Michael's case becomes a permanent feature, because literally "he cannot face himself."

By a combination of both psychological and occult methods, we deduce the mindset at the crucial time when Michael saw the power over children by "Ronald McDonald," the make-believe figure in the burger advertisements, and his persona remodeling began from that point.

Age 38 is for Michael crisis time; here he knows he is on the slippery path. Many abused children become "locked" at that point. Michael, in a man's body, is inside emotionally a small boy aged 11, still seeing children of that age his equals, and his possible partners.

His hand print shows a dysplastic or wrongly built hand, which shows a dysplastic mindset. Carl Jung said, *"The maintenance of secrets within the psyche is a poison that alienates the possessor from his community."*

Among the assessments I would write were for abused children taken into care, and Michael's palmar signposts are horribly familiar. This poor man had it all, yet had nothing. His hand says his 47th year is when the chickens come home to roost, and from this day he is on borrowed time. This day has been a long time coming, but feel compassion for the soul who may never grow up, for his life was over when he first stepped on the slippery slope, that awful day in his 7th year. Jackson died, reportedly awash in about $400 million in debt. "The greatest wealth is health." Jackson had lost that as well.

In Numerology, Michael Jackson has four even numbers and 10 odd numbers, showing an odd personality all round. They add up to 52 and he was approaching his 52nd year, pretty close to where his health line collides with his life line.

The "Prince of Pop" is dead. His contribution to music is beyond measure. We pray he finds the peace in death he could not find in life.

42

The Dalai Lama

This is a truly exceptional hand. In Tibetan palmistry this is the "hand of the Tortoise." The tortoise moves cautiously and slowly, and unfailingly negotiates many obstacles on his journey and eventually reaches his destination, no matter what obstacles lay in his path. He is a shy, peaceful creature, whose main life focus is internal, and his hard shell belies a soft interior.

The squareness of the palm is only broken by the high Jupiter mount, showing responsibility and a born leader. To determine which area of leadership—religion, politics, industry or sport, we look to a combination of palmar signals, and he is both religious and political. The finger bases all in a line suggest balanced abilities, and each finger being the perfect match for its neighbor, excepting Saturn or middle finger, which is slightly short, showing irreverence, self-depreciation and humor—traits we associate with Tenzin Gyatso, the revered 14th Dalai Lama.

In 1950, the Chinese invaded Tibet, and although the spiritual leader wanted to stay with his people, he was urged to leave and make the perilous trek through the mountains to the safety of India. This traumatic event shows on his life line at 15 years of age. (1)

Like many young teenagers, my introduction to Tibet and its spiritual legacies came through the famous '60s author, Lobsang Rampa, although many claim him a fake. His books, *You Forever, Doctor from Lhasa* and the biggest selling *The Third Eye* are still absolute classics and ones I insist must be read by all my students.

This hand shows at the life line start one branch to Jupiter (2), giving the Jupiterian characteristics of ambition, enthusiasm and leadership. The other branch, from exactly midway between thumb and Jupiter finger, starting right round the edge of the hand, which in Indian palmistry means a reincarnated soul waiting some time to be born, and this, with the straight long Mercury or little finger (3), gives a straight, communicative ability. This, with a tied head and life line, always means the caution and sensitivity of the tortoise, and with the same sizing of the Jupiter to Apollo finger (4) shows, according to Professor Manning's studies, remarkable balance

50 Case Studies in Modern Palmistry

between a structured ego and emotional desires. Not many men can cope with celibacy, but he has managed extremely well.

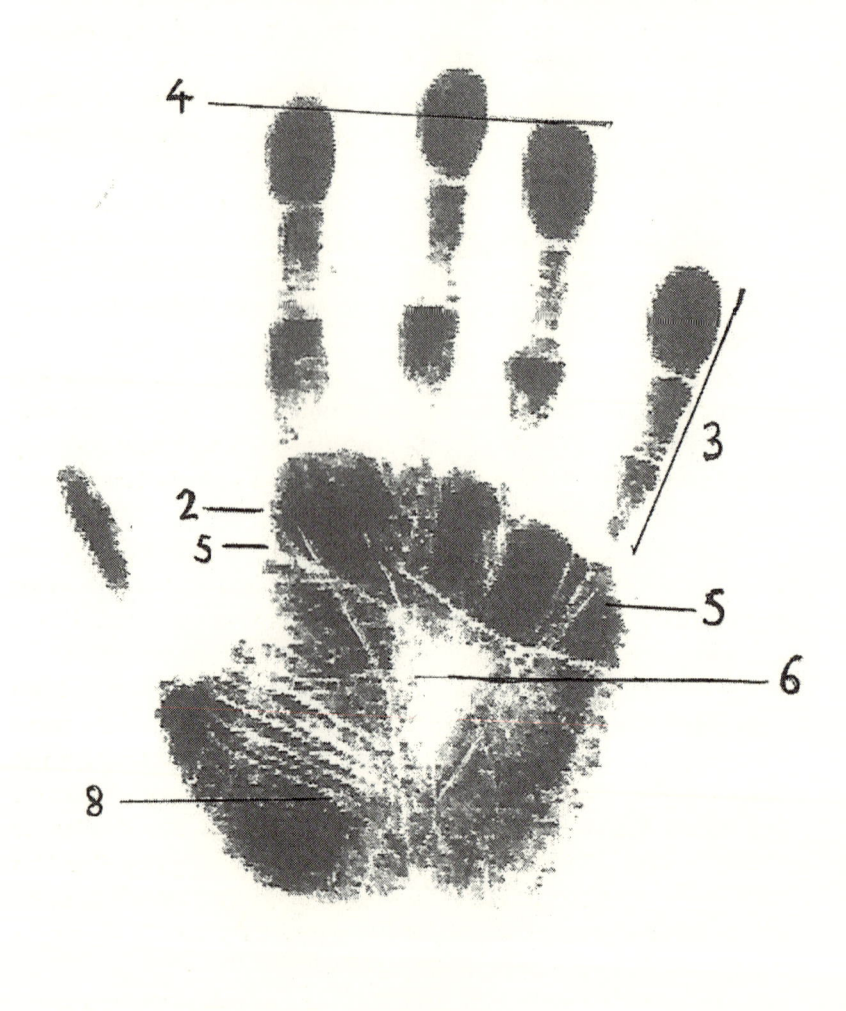

Polls across the world show this man, from a devastated and occupied country, to be the most respected of all spiritual leaders. There is no rich trappings such as jewels or gilded cloth or pointy hats; just a plain saffron robe, and in exile in India, he is as much at home with the Hindus as with his own Buddhists, yet the Chinese have a long-running hate campaign to discredit him and his many different religious followers.

The healing stigmata shows under his Mercury finger at (5). The four tiny, upright lines in a square palm confers his concern for the land, the outdoors, and for the people's identity, welfare and religious freedom, the promotion of basic human values, and ethics for the future of human happiness, and the fostering of inter-religious harmony and non-violence (*ahimsa*) across the world.

The tortoise equates in the Western system closely to the earth hand, and this is a sensitive earth. The lean of the fate, or luck, line towards Jupiter at (6) confirms the authority of a spiritual leader, and the heart line shows an idealist. So we have a man who has always dreamt of a free Tibet once again.

His thumb bears the rare elephant's eye marking. The elephant is a sacred animal in India, and this mark confers the memory and spiritual wisdom of the elephant. Ganesh, the elephant god, is one of five ruled by each finger, and his gifts are that he gives intelligence and education, and like the tortoise, is a peaceful remover of obstacles.

The only health indicators we see are a health line running from under the Mercury finger down to the life line at age 79-80, which looks like colon or intestinal niggles, which is unusual in vegetarians, and January 2012 was a month to be extra careful.

A long-running back problem also shows the spine is separated into four sections by experts—the lumbar spine, the thoracic spine, the sacral spine, and the cervical spine—and he shows cervical spine stiffness, which is not surprising for a man of 77 years of age. His life line ends where the fate line starts, showing his birth/death cycle to be very tight, and as the life line sweeps out wide into the palm towards Luna, showing he will end his life away from his homeland, but in emotional peace and tranquility. As the line ends in a square, the most protective sign in palmistry (8), we see his realization of the good karma of his life's work.

For truly doth the prophet say: "*Tomorrow belongs to the righteous.*"

Please see *www.dalailamatrust.org*

43

Jawaharlal Nehru
A 'Voice of Prophecy'?

Jawaharlal Nehru was the first prime minister of independent India, born on November 14, 1889 in Allahabad, now Uttar Pradesh, to a Brahmin lawyer and politician.

His mother claimed that Brahmin astrologers foretold a brilliant future and a great destiny for the baby boy. He later studied in England, at Harrow School and Trinity College, Cambridge, and became a barrister. This gave him a deep, life-long love for Britain.

He would fascinate his fellow students with his thoughts on Indian politics, Theosophy, yoga and vegetarianism.

In 1919 he joined the Indian National Congress, the national pro-India "stand alone" party, led by Mohandas K. Gandhi. This led to him being imprisoned many times by the British between 1921 and 1945.

He wanted to bring an end to Indian poverty, divisiveness and social inequality of the caste system.

The civil disobedience movement was launched, and Congress adopted a program of "No rents," the withholding of monthly tithes against rich landlords and money lenders, to bring matters to a head.

With the outbreak of WWII, the British declared India to be a belligerent nation because both Nehru and Gandhi—both men of peace—refused to be involved with the war effort. He had said that British and Indian involvement in a war was unnecessary, and the whole Congress assembly was then unjustly imprisoned.

Churchill had his revenge by refusing India help with the famine that killed 4 million people, while sending huge shipments of food and arms to Russia, whom our Intelligence services said, "*were more dangerous to Britain than Germany.*"

Churchill, with Ali Jinner, created the first Muslim state, Pakistan, after the division of India.

Sir Earnest Cassels, financier to Edward VII, as part of the Rothschild syndicate, pushed and bribed Churchill to declare war on Germany, and

Jawaharlal Nehru, a 'Voice of Prophecy'?

wanted India punished for its peace overtures. It was Cassels' granddaughter, Edwina, who was married to Lord Mountbatten. Edwina was the longtime lover of Nehru. Nehru was kind and loving, while Mountbatten was cold, aloof and harsh.

Nehru was a great statesman and orator, and his speech, "*Tryst with Destiny*," to the constituent assembly of India in August 1947, was reported worldwide.

His great fear—that India and Pakistan would become nuclear rivals—is seen by some as becoming "a true prophecy."

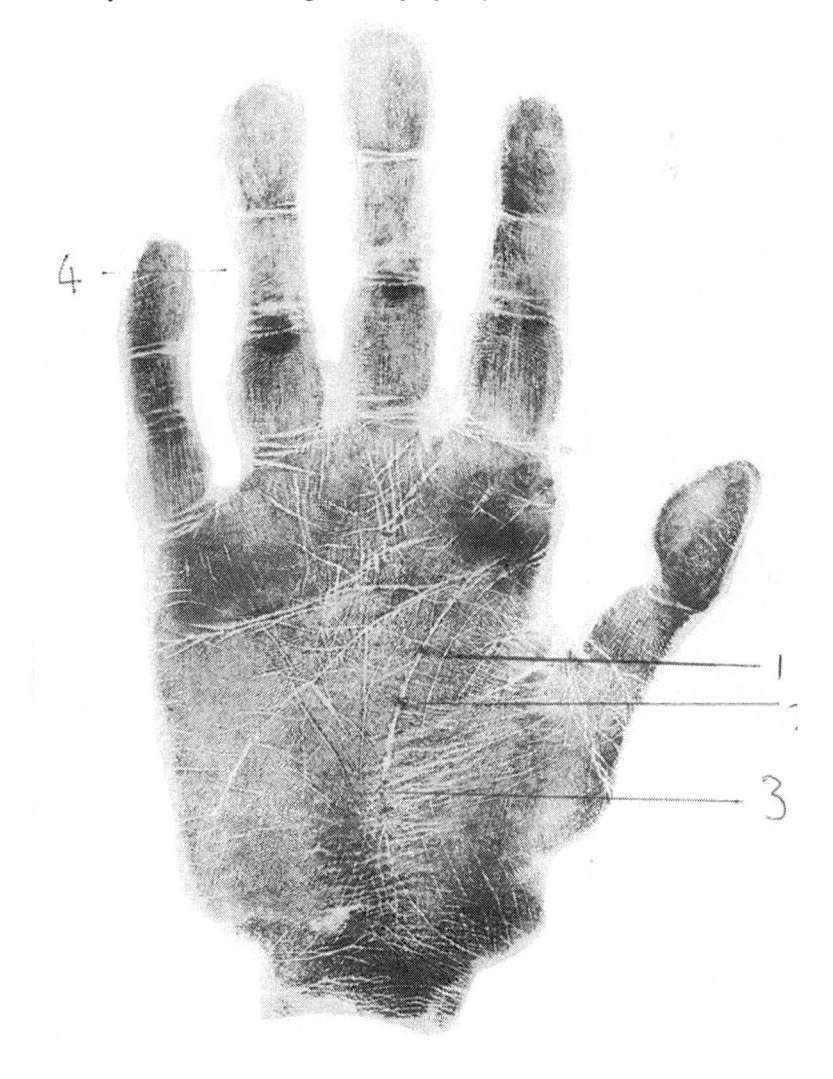

A man much loved, both in Britain and India, he died on May 27, 1964. His daughter, Indira Gandhi, succeeded him in 1966.

"Life is a game of cards, the hand that is dealt to you is determinism, the way you play them is free will." — Jawaharlal Nehru

What does his hand print say?

Always a cautious, sensitive and caring man, some early trauma is indicated in the slight, inward curvature of the little finger. This shows that he was born into a wealthy, two-parent family, both of whom loved him, and that he was breastfed, which finished abruptly. This can initiate various degrees of the oral complex, but seem to have given him a deep need to care and work for peace and others' welfare, and this shows primarily on his life line at age 30, with his joining of the Indian National Congress. **(1)**

He experienced a deep feeling of empathy for those less fortunate, and wished to teach them how to escape poverty. This shows in the teacher's square on the Jupiter mount, the general heart line formation, and is again confirmed on the life line with imprisonment preferred, rather than lower his standards, at age 35 **(2)**.

Outbreak of WWII in 1939 was a critical time for Nehru, when he was split between his loyalties and duties, both to Britain and to India, with both promises and threats from Churchill. Extreme stress shows for him **(3)** at around age 50, when the print was taken, showing thumb position, many lines, hand shape with anxious, gastric anomalies.

The waisted central phalange in the ring, or emotional finger **(4)**, is usually a sign of difficulties in the motherly attachment process between the years 1 to 5, and prognostic results are well documented, but often lead to overdependence on females in later life.

He always tried to take the "middle road" and tried to be seen to be impartial between both Hindus and Muslims. He was often appreciated more abroad than at home, for his warmth and sincerity.

His death in 1964 brought one newspaper to republish his piece on Mohandas K Gandhi's death:

"The light has gone out of our lives, and there is darkness everywhere."

44

Zulfikar Ali Bhutto
Prime Minister of Pakistan

This is a superb example of a politician's hand.

The closely tied life and head lines give caution, thoughtfulness and the ability to hold back (1). Hindu palmists call this "The blessing of Shiva," while in Tibet this is known as the "mark of the Tortoise."

People who have this marking do nothing hastily and without careful thought and planning. The long, straight head line shows a rational, non-emotional "feet on the ground" type approach. The three head line endings are called in the East the "sign of the trident," giving a balanced and several-sided way of seeing things (2).

The thick line under the end of the head line is an adjunct to the head and is always seen in those who study, and Zulfikar studied at Cambridge University, where he was very popular with other students.

The strong, stiff thumb shows a stubborn perseverance, and the smooth fingers an instant, intuitive grasp and appreciation of others' motives.

The destiny line begins from two places, one from Luna and the other from the life line. Luna shows a public favorite, a man able to tap into the Zeitgeist of the people, while the life line branch shows family help, advice and assistance. It veers toward Jupiter with three lines leaving the travel. This shows three distinct positions in authority (3).

In 1957, Bhutto became the youngest member of the Pakistan delegation to the UN, when just 29 years of age (4).

Bhutto, already a charismatic figure, wanted a mix of Socialism and Democracy. His mantra, "Islam is our faith, democracy is our policy, socialism is our economy, and all power belongs to the people," was an instant hit with the public.

Bhutto tried to steer a course between the major powers, but President Lyndon Johnson wanted him removed by any means, as he felt he was moving too close to China and Poland, both Communist countries. Agitators stirred up trouble between India and Pakistan, and Zulfikar insisted on Pakistan having its own nuclear program. He said they would build their

50 Case Studies in Modern Palmistry

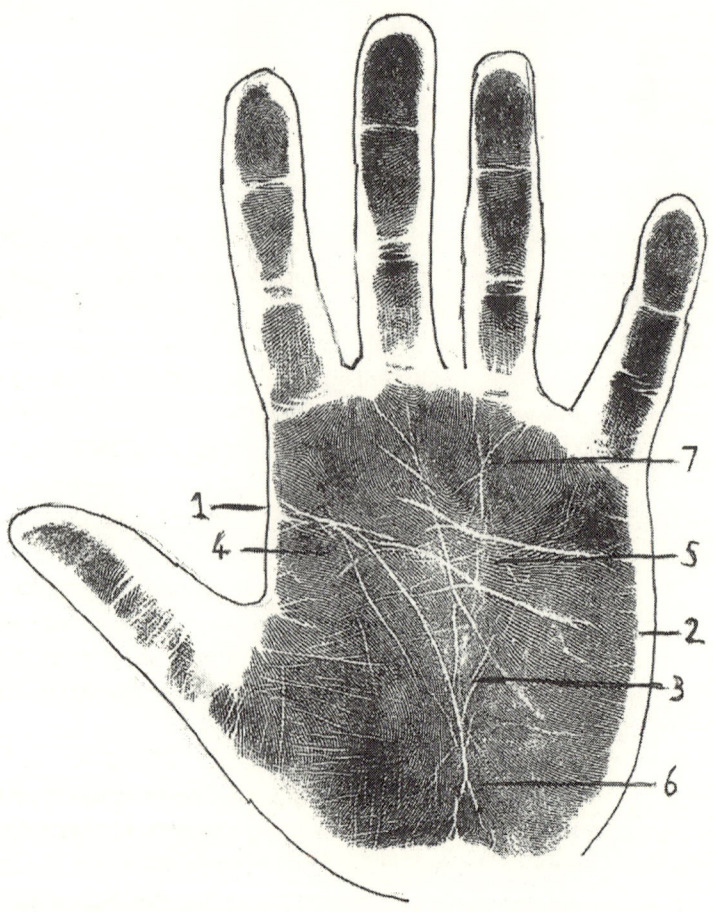

own nuclear defense, even if the people have to eat grass to get it.

A protective square on the destiny line is known as the "sign of the flag," and joins the destiny line with the head line, a great sign for showing good thinking with career decisions or destiny at the time shown by the square (5).

The frayed and broken life line at (6) is reflected at the bar crossing the Apollo line (7), showing bad luck and possible disgrace.

The Apollo line is shaped in the sign of the scissors. This in Eastern palmistry shows a cutting through or ending, and this is confirmed by the early truncation of the health line.

A popular and likeable man, Zulfikar Ali Bhutto was sentenced to death and killed at age 51.

45

Famous Footballer

Erwin Shroedinger's book *What is Life?* claimed that one of life's urgent criteria is the storage and transmission of information, e.g., a code that transfers this information from parent to child, and was both complex and compact enough to fit inside a single cell, and this code had to be at molecular level. Scientists believed Shroedinger's genetic code was carried by the DNA.

Insurance companies claim that by an examination of the DNA, they can tell not only what diseases a person will suffer, but *when*—even claiming to know pretty closely the length of life. They would do this, primarily to know whom to accept for life insurance and who not.

This information would also benefit employers, and preparatory documents exploring this have been discussed by the C.B.I. (Confederation of British Industry). The scientific establishment accepts and supports these findings quite readily, yet has balked over the centuries when palmists have made the same claims.

It is actually quite amusing for serious research palmists to have had their research vindicated by something as dubious as insurance companies, and under the counter back-street Dr. Mengele-type genetics laboratories.

A recent edition of the *British Medical Journal* ran the head line, "No one can predict the future," but each day the weather forecaster does just that, the stock exchange does it daily, the futures market sells produce years before it has been grown.

International money dealers do it months in advance, and sales projection graphs in companies are built on it. Remember Nick Leason, gambling millions of pounds of monies not yet even earned because these claim they can predict future buying trends?

The old Soviet Union ran university courses on it. The KGB used it as a departmental tool, so why is it impossible to predict the future? A specialized knowledge in any field must give prior knowledge. Albert Einstein, a believer in prediction, said, "Random systems eventually produce predictable patterns."

Theoretically, an expert studies his material until he sees this pattern, and it is upon this pattern that he builds his estimation of future trends.

Such old establishment names as the BBC, Proctor and Gamble, Marks and Spencer, and the Society of Cosmetic Scientists subscribe vast financial sums to what are termed "futurologists" for future prediction. In fact, the Soviets took so seriously such predictive organizations as the "Henley Forecasting Center," and the "European Planning Federation," that they were spied on continually by the KGB.

Strangely, mediums have an exceptional record in contacting the dead, but not too good in pinpointing future events.

A wise old Greek philosopher once said, "The improbable, but possible, is always preferable to the probable but *im*possible."

This palm print is of a well-known British football personality who was often seen with the Beatles.

Football today generates huge sums of money out of all proportion to the contribution it makes, and football and loutish behavior go together like politics and corruption. Psychologists agree that encouraging one nation over another breeds racism and division. This is not helped by government policy of mixing football in with the national news, even mentioning it before the casualties during the war on Iraq.

Any obsessive behavior is psychologically suspect, and so many are dependent on football for their fix, to the unhealthy degree that it governs their lives and their behavior.

Our subject today is as well known for drunken brawling and traffic offenses as his sport. Nevertheless, he is the idol of many "older schoolboys" countrywide, for his colorful personality, his fancy footwork, and "sporting" prowess.

His popularity remains undiminished, no matter what the newspapers may say. The tabloid press mentioned him again recently at a court appearance for drunken brawling.

Famous Footballer

The palm print shows a very heavy stiff thumb, set low. This feature, with the short fingers, shows—with the strong palm with its broad base—someone with great physical energy; a typical sportsman, in fact, who is able to think and sum up very quickly, but someone not head-centered at all. Alas, footballers are trained from schoolboys to be physical athletes, not intellectuals, and the strain of knowing you will be thrown over by the time you are in your thirties, pushes many to live for today.

Psychologists generally agree that the lure of football is a homo-erotic one, the all boys together with no trousers on, the leather balls, the Freudian symbolism of trying to put your balls in someone's net, the net representing the feminine aspect, and the kissing and groping on the pitch, coupled to the alcohol, laddism, voyeurism and the revolting "roasting rituals," does not inspire confidence, and is far from masculine behavior.

However, the thinning of the life line after the influence line hits it from Venus (the thumb), (1) tells us that, like a river pushing through difficult terrain, the gastric system becomes damaged through drink and drugs at this time, which dates on the life line at 23 years of age, coinciding with his first conviction for anti-social behavior (2.) He is known as a practical joker, but add alcohol to the equation, and fireworks usually ensue. A thick, strong, square palm, with short fingers, can show a performer, or show-off, an ability to gauge the emotional temperature of an audience, and play to it. His extroversion on field is legendary.

His present determination to get back to peak fitness, and to conquer his demons, has been difficult. Often people addicted to exercise have only used it to replace an addiction to alcohol, tobacco and other drugs, along with short, destructive addictive relationships as shown by his ragged and fragmentary heart line (3) and slightly curved little finger. This is not helped by his argumentative and pugnacious disposition. I did warn him of indications of career trouble ahead, as storm clouds were gathering, and the next few months would be crucial, both to watch his step, and not to drop his guard—as a scandal was looming up fast, as depicted by the fragmented Apollo markings (4).

Palmistry sees the spine or backbone represented in the hand by the fate line. That is the longitudinal line that runs from the wrist to the middle finger. This hand only has the first part most visible. It peters out after the age of 34, and retirement from football (5). This could signify an injury of some sort, but after this age, he will find some contentment—the lull after the storm.

Our footballer drives a very fast car and has had several crashes over a three-year period; "bumps" he calls them. The thickness of his thumb shows obstinacy and stubbornness, and these "bumps" in his car usually lead to fisticuffs, and appearances in both court and the Sunday papers.

Incidentally, when footballers retire, they often take to alcohol in unhealthy amounts, and several signs here can show eating problems or alcoholism. Unluckily for a footballer, he shows feet and ankle difficulties also. He claims this is all in the past, as are the drink-related incidents.

His non-appearances last season coincide with his belief that he is being watched by aliens, and that they are responsible for house keys going missing, milk turning sour, that America filmed the Moon landings in Arizona, but away from the drink and drugs he seems quite well.

President Nixon once said, "*He who has not stood at the foot of the valley, cannot appreciate the view from the mountain top,*" and for this once great footballer, his mountain view is still not there.

His body type is Mesomorph, the muscular type with strong arms and legs. In later life, their main weakness is the cardiovascular system, and the stop-start heart line is indicative of nervous heart or tachycardia, which often goes with the anxiety shown in his early fifties. Here big changes are apparent in the markings leading up from the heart line toward the fingers, confirmed by no moons on his fingernails.

The good news is really in his late thirties, using his sports monies in business ventures. There is much fulfillment for him. His hands speak of journalism—perhaps radio, fast foods, and some sort of sales franchise, and in or close to his 35th year, a secure, warm relationship which is far more nourishing than his hit-and-miss, here-today, gone-tomorrow quickies he is used to.

Our football star worries about losing all the money he made as a young star, which will have to carry him into old age. But in the words of Hilaire Beloc, "*Loss and possession, death and life are one, there falls no shadow where there shines no sun.*" So, in essence, while the sun shines he must make "financial" hay.

He feels a certain amount of guilt about the way he has led his life, and concern over meeting his maker. I reminded him, "It's not the certainty of death that frightens people, it's the uncertainty of life."

I told our footballer, a very superstitious man, to look forward to his new life after age 35.

46

Osteopath and Vegan Neil Fennel

"The primal sin is the killing and eating of God's animals."

— Epictetus

Here we have the palm print of society osteopath and vegan healer Neil Fennel.

The Max Planck Institute found that people born in the autumn live longer than spring-born babies, and are less prone to illness. Also, the birth month relates to life expectancy.

In natural childbirth, the child is born at the exact moment when the planetary conditions in the outer world are directly aligned to those of the world within.

Workers at the Medical Research Council say the date on your gravestone was settled in the womb, and what determined this was what your mother ate and drank, and what medication she took—while you were in her womb.

This print shows an exceptionally good start in life, the life line beginning between the thumb and index, or Jupiter, finger (figure 1).

With a series of small lines, like the roots of a tree, they take their nourishment from the Jupiter mount (2), giving pride, ambition and urge to power, resulting in strong religious and political feelings.

Age 2-3 the life line, which encircles the thumb, shows a choking incident, perhaps on a toy, causing much concern; could be a decorative bit of a Christmas tree.

The open life and head line, on a busy or full hand, shows someone sensitive and changeable, yet headstrong, impulsive, impatient, frank, and with an ambitious and serious inner nature, often with quick life expectations inconsistent with reality, leading to low levels of anxiety and early desires for independence.

At approximately 7 years of age, a strong maternal influence is shown, which will give feelings of being at ease in feminine company throughout the life, yet at this time nocturnal bruxism, or night-time teeth

50 Case Studies in Modern Palmistry

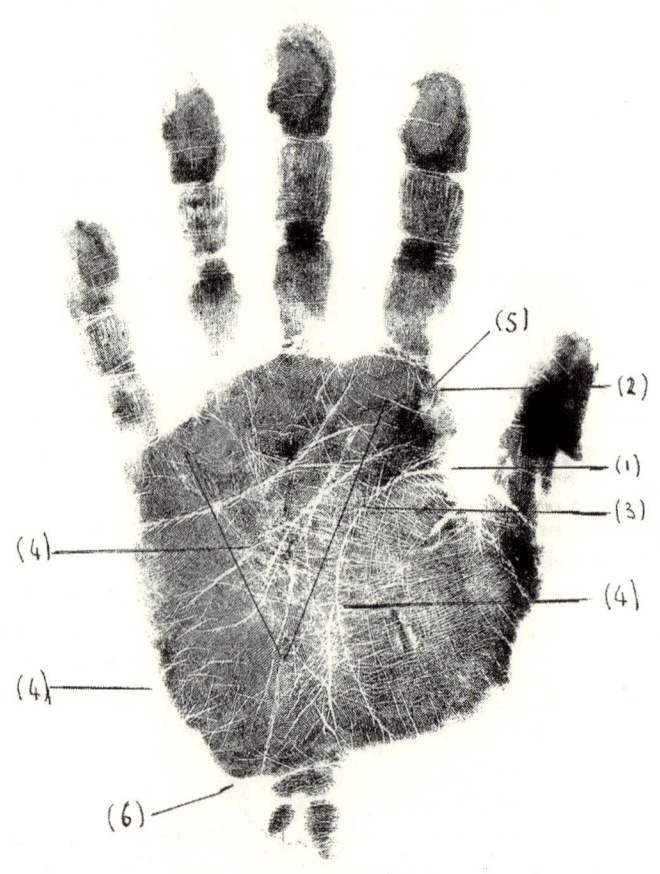

grinding, coupled to a determined willfulness, where he would bang his head on the floor in temper.

At 17 years of age, his hand says he wanted to be an artist or draughtsman, but chaffed at the bit to be out either wind or water surfing.

Emotional change is shown at 25 years—a time of decisions, taking on responsibilities.

In more recent times, Neil has given total commitment to the alternative health agenda, and combines spiritual healing with reflexology and Reiki, with his classical osteopathy and dietary advice. Neil often gives talks on animal welfare and vegetarianism, and links it to spirituality.

Nowadays, when every second person you meet is a healer, someone with real talent is a novelty. Neil, a vegan, runs many marathons. His signing-in book reads like a Who's Who of the entertainment world.

His hand is unusually large for his frame; his body type is Ectomorph, which anatomists say is slim, quite small, with low body fat and good metabolism.

Incidentally, the fingernail should be the same shape and size as the front tooth. His are all excellent.

Look at the palm. The branch of the life line at age 44, coupled with the lines on the Luna mount (heel of the hand), added to the branched head line, and we have the urge to travel, due to inner restlessness, and a need for independence.

Neil will like to move home a lot, to take on too much perhaps, with a feeling that he may not achieve his life goals. This is part of the symptom cluster that can define the andropause, or male menopause, that social anthropologists speak of. It sometimes shows in the fear of aging that men have, resulting in a renewed desire to ride fast motorbikes, climb mountains, seeking football-type camaraderie, or growing a beard. Some severe examples exhibit all these symptoms. Neil, a Scot, has a great love of country, which is evident at his lectures on health and spirit.

So, at age 44, there is a feeling that change is forthcoming and inevitable. The occult saying, *"A coming event casts its shadow before it,"* applies here as a feeling of being in some sort of a shadow. Remember that all change and the causes of change are firstly always internal.

Neil is a Cancer sun sign, which relates to the Luna mount on the hand heel.

The square on Jupiter's mount, with the odd radial fingerprint loop, tells of teaching ability bearing fruit (5).

Where the fate or destiny line starts right from the wrist crease at the hand base (6), coupled with the life line "tree roots," to the first finger base, known as Jupiter's mount, we know of someone here on a mission, a decision before birth to be a healer, actually more than a decision—a *compulsion*—to heal and teach others.

Neil is very conscious of the threat from the European Union to ban or regulate all alternative medicines and practitioners; stage two is to outlaw psychic and spiritual healers. Christian fundamentalists and the drug cartels are a powerful force.

Hindu palmistry, which teaches reincarnation, can be helpful in establishing life's goals, which should lead to an inner fulfillment, a feeling of being in the right place.

His late 40s show some stomach, liver or bowel concerns. Abraham Lincoln said, *"The best thing about the future is that it only comes one day at a time."*

50 Case Studies in Modern Palmistry

This type of hand is known as an Earth hand, giving stability and love of the outdoors and changing seasons, with the rhythms of nature. Neil must try to resist starting the next project before finishing the last. He is someone who has to keep busy, and can jump to conclusions—someone that can jump in with both feet, as it were—so should look before they leap, and with a feeling they are always on duty.

But good news ... the older he gets, the more he is able to slow down and switch off, so he will be able to reflect and rein in his impulsive side and overconfidence. So no more taking the financial risks he took in his youth. The theory of Heraclitus is that *"nothing remains the same, that all things are in a constant state of flux, and their permanence only illusory, nothing is but only becomes."*

Often the things we deem important in our lives are of no lasting value, or long-term importance.

A lot of what palmistry is about is guidance, and taking stock of your life, and defining which rung you stand on the ladder of life.

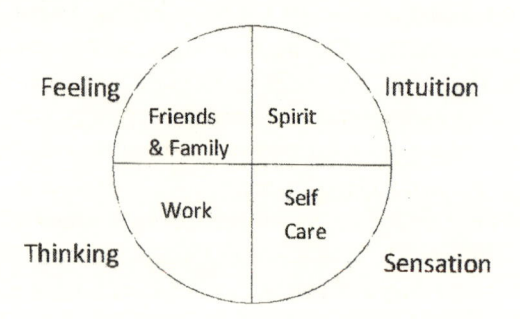

```
           |
  Feeling  |         Intuition
    Friends | Spirit
    & Family|
    --------+--------
            | Self
      Work  | Care
  Thinking  |         Sensation
           |
```

A graph I occasionally use to illustrate this is based on the four divisions laid down by Carl Jung, after his Zodiacal studies, his quarters: "Thinking, feeling, intuition and sensation" is used in an exercise of amplification, which is a good aid in counseling.

The four separations I call the four horsemen of the Apocalypse.

In terms of the graph, balance is everything, and Neil is too much in the work zone, at present neglecting both self-care and spirit. Sometimes we miss chances by being unbalanced in our lives.

Remember ... *"The days come and go like muffled and veiled figures sent from a distant friendly party, but they say nothing and if we do not use the gifts they bring, they carry them as silently away."*

— Ralph Waldo Emerson

47

Strange Death of Ehud Netzer

Ehud Netzer—Strange Facts

"Archeologist who spent a lifetime looking for Herod's tomb and when finding it, dropped dead at the site." — the description in the *Daily Telegraph*

The world has lost an amazingly learned historian, who overturned many of our existing views on the early biblical period, including King Herod, who ruled Judea from about 37 BC. Herod was said to be a complete butcher of his rivals' adversaries—and even his family—but it is the "Massacre of the Innocents" for which he is remembered.

Herod's plan was to murder all the newborns in Bethlehem—to kill the baby Jesus—but the three wise men, who followed the star, are believed to have been astrologers. Ehud was fascinated by the three wise men story.

But the fact that Herod is said to have died in either 4 BC or 5 BC has long muddied the waters. Ehud Netzer excavated a series of sites across the Holy Land and said new information from these sites proclaimed Herod to be a legendary builder king, who was able to steer round political intrigue to finish huge building projects that have left an incredible architectural legacy, which has endured for over 2,000 years. Ehud was a scholar of the Holy Bibles and, in particular, the Old Testament.

Ehud Netzer claimed in the book *Architecture of Herod, The Great Builders*, published in 2008, that Herod was a practical and thorough man, with a very broad world view, outstanding organizational talent and ability to improvise, and able to adapt to changing situations and surroundings. He was a man who could anticipate the future.

Ehud worked on excavations at the Canaanite city of Hatzor and all over Palestine and Israel, and in fact the most important sites in all the Holy Land, including Herod's monumental palace at Massada, overlooking the

50 Case Studies in Modern Palmistry

Dead Sea, where Jewish rebels defied Rome's 10th Legion, and all committed ritual suicide rather than be captured.

This uprising had been after Rome's destruction of Herod's second Jerusalem temple in AD 70.

Ehud became the senior lecturer at the Hebrew University in his pivotal year of 1981. Steven Spielberg was said to have been inspired to base his character, Indiana Jones, on Ehud.

Ehud gave almost 30 years to the Herodian palace complex, built on a manmade mound of 300 feet near Bethlehem, first discovered by an American scholar in 1838. Ehud was to say the 600-seat theatre and landscaped grounds and luxurious settings were to impress the Roman general, Marcus Agrippa, in 15 BC. And although many scholars had searched for Herod's burial place through the centuries, often using the latest technology and scanning devices, the 900 feet long and 80 feet high mausoleum was found by the great Emeritus Professor Ehud Netzer at "The Winter Palace," from which he fell from a height of 19 feet after a wooden rail gave way.

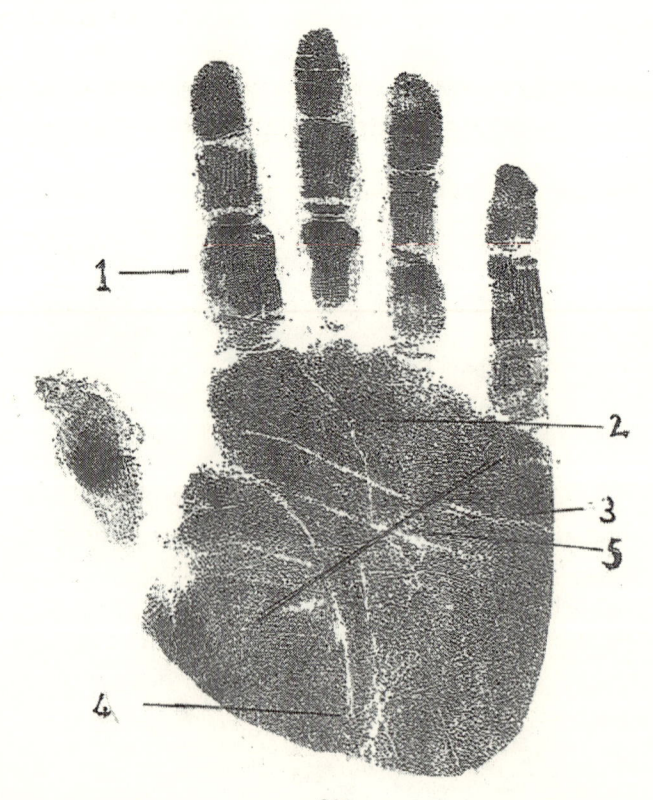

Strange Death of Ehud Netzer

He subsequently died in a hospital on October 28, aged 76. He is survived by his wife, Devora, and is believed to have died of circulatory failure.

CUCKOO LINES—A cuckoo line is a line which does not belong where it is seen.

* This heart line goes all the way across with a thick base to the first, or Jupiter finger, consistent with a meat eater. Both *The Lancet* and the *British Medical Journal* have warned consistently of heavy meat-eating, clogging heart and arteries (1). This formation also tells us he was an emotional and excitable psychological Type A. His blood type looks like B +, which is alcohol intolerant. His fate or destiny line at (2) veers toward Jupiter as seen in those in authority, and his heart line suggests an enlarged heart. Lines like this, which are stop/start, often show a heart which can stop for a few seconds before carrying on (3).

His death is suggested at (4), at approximately the age shown by a bar or impediment line hitting and stopping the life line.

(5) This line, drawn from the exact center to the fingerprint apex on the Mercury mount, should almost always cross at age 35. From this we can deduce Ehud's death in the winter period of his life at age 75-76 years of age.

Let's look at how numbers and destiny can play a role in our lives. This is the standard numerological chart along with the key words in his destiny:

Ehud Netzer's name has 10 letters = 10

1	2	3	4	5	6	7	8	9
A	B	C	D	E	F	G	H	I
J	K	L	M	N	O	P	Q	R
S	T	U	V	W	X	Y	Z	

October is the 10th month
Ehud died on the 28th, added together = 10
He died in the year 2010
Jewish = 28 =10
King Herod = 10

50 Case Studies in Modern Palmistry

Herod's death 5 BC, 5 + B + C = 10
3 wise men = 37 =10
Holy Land = 37 = 10
Holy Bibles = 46 = 10
The Old Testament = 19 =10
The Dead Sea = 28 = 10
Massada Jews defied the 10th Legion = the 10th
3 wise men equals 37 = 10
The pivotal year 2008 = 10
Ehud Netzer's speciality was Judea, which began in 37 BC = 10
Steven Spielberg = 55 = 10
1981 = 10
The "Winter Palace" = 10
The Mausoleum = 46 = 10
Herod Tomb = 46 = 10
He was an "Israeli" = 37 = 10
He became the senior lecturer in 1981 = 10
Wife "Devora" = 10
The word "hospital" = 10
The wooden rail was 19 feet high = 10
October 28, 2010 = 46 = 10
November 6 = 10
Circulatory failure = 10

But could this knowledge have prevented his death on the very day he found the tomb after a 50-year search?

The Creator in his wisdom has given us many signs and omens, and a good fortune teller will see a man's life as an open book.

The Bible has many incidences of what is called "periodicity in numbers," and the Hebrew experts have always been good at this science.

The number 10, which reduces to a figure 1, is the number symbolizing the Sun, and the beginning, the start of events with creativity, and positive influences. In the tarot pack, it is symbolized by the "Wheel of Fortune," and so it was when the wheel turned to October 28, 2010, this great man's time was up.

48

Matt Monro
Portrait of My Love

The famous British singer died aged just 54 in February 1985. The newspapers said cancer had so ravaged his body, he was barely recognizable. Unable to eat or drink, he had become dangerously thin and frail.

Born in poverty in 1930s London, Terry Parsons was the youngest of five children who lost their father Fred, from TB, when Terry was 3. His mother, Alice, struggled to clothe, feed and house the children after her husband's death, and after a mental breakdown she went into a sanatorium. Terry was then taken to a foster home, where he could not settle.

Moved from one school to the next, he hardly ever turned up to lessons, and by the age of 16, he had lived in numerous homes, had no memory of his father, and had little contact with his mother. So he joined the army at age 17. (1) (*See small line crossing life line*)

On leaving the army, he became a London bus driver, and he would sing as he drove the bus. Complaints began pouring in that the bus was too full to take any new passengers, as the passengers refused get off, and when people began coming to the bus garage to ask for "the singing bus driver," the manager regretfully said they had to let him go.

But this was the making of Terry, and under the name Matt Monro, he went from strength to strength, and in poll after poll Monro was voted Britain's best male singer, despite performing easy-listening ballads at a time when the charts were full of Beatles, Rolling Stones and rock and roll.

Even more remarkable was the fact that he reached such heights, despite facing the huge obstacles of hunger and poverty in his early life.

Monro was chosen to sing Britain's entry in the 1964 Eurovision Song Contest, and although he only came in second, it heightened his profile

50 Case Studies in Modern Palmistry

immensely. He went on to become one of the decade's best known performers of hit film theme songs, from *Born Free* to *On Days Like These*, featured in the Michael Caine comedy, *The Italian Job*.

Popular in the US, South America and the Far East, he found himself touring constantly. Among those often seen at the back of his performances was Frank Sinatra, who said Matt was among the three best singers of all time.

His wife Mickie said, "With Matt spending so much time on the road, it is not surprising that he suffered from homesickness. He always said that he lived out of suitcases so much that he forgot what it was like to open a drawer." (2) (*restlessness and travel lines*)

Whenever he was on the road, he calmed his boredom and homesickness with alcohol and, as his drinking became heavier, his doctor

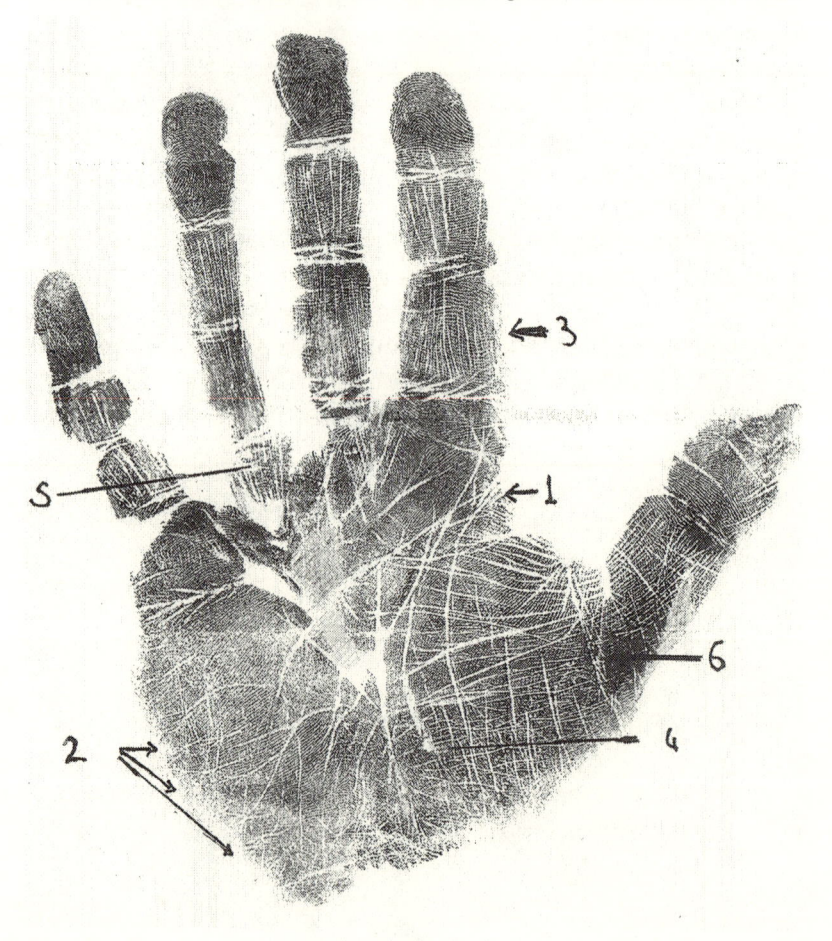

Matt Monro, Portait of My Love

noticed his liver had become dangerously swollen and wrote that, at a conservative estimate, he was drinking at least half a bottle of Scotch a day.

The hand print was taken in the early '70s, when Matt was having difficulty handling his fame. His fingers suggest a shy, quiet man, but a perfectionist.

But less than four years after becoming tee-total, he began feeling ill and doctors diagnosed cancer of the liver. (3) (*base to Jupiter finger swollen as in emotional eaters and drinkers*)

An attempted transplant was abandoned when it was found the cancer had spread too far, and he died on February 7, 1985. (4) (*life line and fate line stopped in fifties and echoed in several other palmar places*)

His last wish was that people would play his music, and indeed the music world mourned the passing of such a great star. But some noted that despite topping the charts in other nations, Matt Monro had never enjoyed a UK No 1.

In 2005, wife Mickie discovered a recording of him performing what had been in a family garage for nearly 40 years. The film was put on DVD and released as "An Evening With Matt Monro." It shot to the top of the DVD music charts. Matt Monro had finally achieved the recognition at home—the UK No. 1 he had always craved. Matt may have gone, but his music lives on in pubs and clubs all over the London that he loved. (5) (*shows Apollo or sun lines show late life success*)

And at (6) we see lack of a family ring round the thumb base, confirming the uncertain early start to the life, and late start to the fate line.

Some of his most loved hits, which are all on YouTube, are *Born Free, From Russia With Love, Softly As I Leave You, Portrait of My Love* and *Be My Love.*

"*He was a man and taken all in all, we shall not look upon his like again.*"

— Hamlet, Act I, Scene 2

49

The Stolen Childhood

Shakespeare's quotation springs to mind: "*All the world's a stage, and all the men and women merely players, they have their exits and their entrances.*" And this young woman's "entrance" to life was very problematic.

The most important part of any reading must be the healing aspect, and we should always emphasize anything positive and uplifting, but this is a difficult hand, and honesty is so important. Just as a meeting with a doctor or priest should be private and confidential, so should a reading, as it partakes of both.

This hand typifies many of the young single mothers seen in the Britain of today. The short and emotionally undernourished little finger (1), allied to the ragged markings of the early joined life and head configuration, suggest the bonding process with her mother was dysfunctional and damaged.

The mother, a psychology lecturer in the 1960s, followed the prevailing belief at that time in letting the baby cry itself out, parental input being kept to a minimum so as to make the child "more independent."

Warmth, comfort and feeding were given, but little nurturing. The proverb, "*Spare the rod, spoil the child,*" was often quoted by psychologists to excuse corporal and other punishment. We know now how destructive the withholding of emotional nourishment can be to the emotional bedrock. This treatment could bring on much separation anxiety in later life, and this shows on the lines of life, heart and head at approximate ages 19 and 34-35 (2).

All relationships are based on the first or primal relationship, the one with our parents, and if this is dysfunctional in any way, then we carry the baggage with us to each and every relationship we ever make, and because of this, some people never learn to build or sustain relationships. We see this primarily in the short, low set, curved little finger, poor heart line (upper transverse line) and the first, or Jupiter finger, being shorter than the third, often a sign of intra-uterine estrogen imbalances, and low self-esteem (3).

The appearance of a small explosion shows on the life line at age 9. This coincides with time spent at a Catholic convent school with physical

The Stolen Childhood

NORFOLK COUNTY COUNCIL Social Services
Director : David Wright

West Norfolk District Sub Office
Child and Family Care Division

Hamilton House,
64 Goodwins Road,
King's Lynn, PE30 5PD.

Tel : (0553) 76696

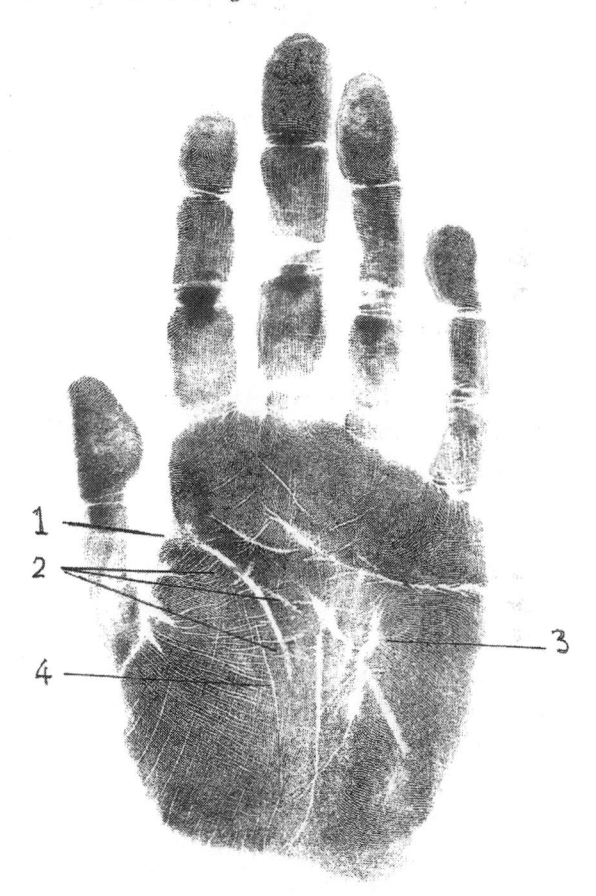

and sexual abuse by two nuns, a not uncommon happening in the Ireland of a few years ago (2). Alas, the precious soil that gives us flowers, may also give weeds.

Of the two lines that run across the hand under the fingers—the upper, or heart, is both ragged and fragmentary—always compare the two lines. An increasing phenomenon for young males is to have a poor lower or head line, and the upper or heart lines to be poor in women.

The July 1999 *Lancet* magazine gave voice to concern on the "cocktail effect" of excessive alcohol consumption, smoking and the contraceptive pill, all exacerbated by a junk food diet. This is the symptom cluster, particularly for impending cardiovascular difficulty, with which we associate the pill.

This lady's heart line shouts at us that a change of lifestyle is very necessary, as does the life line at (4).

Even teen-age women are vulnerable to deep vein thrombosis, and such horrors as breast and cervical cancer, strokes and arterial problems are increasingly common.

Luckily, she had listened to her body's early warning signals of insomnia, depression, weight gain, anxiety, panic attacks, headaches and fading sexual libido, coupled to a negative self-image, and an inability to make and sustain healthy relationships.

The *British Medical Journal* says, "One of the most worrying things today is the amount of alcohol now being consumed by young women."

Truth has many faces. Some may smile and radiate contentment and joy, while others may show that the crop of a bitter harvest is due for reaping.

Look closely at the hand print.

- Each finger leans onto a very strong and large second, or Saturn, finger.
- Fragmentary low heart line forks under Saturn.
- Poor quality head line broken under Saturn, and the central knuckle is prominent, like a knot in wood and eye-shaped.
- The heel of the hand (opposite the thumb) is very prominent and always ruled by the Moon, showing too much imagination.
- Health line (just offset from palm center) leaving a flame effect up the palm.
- Two main dividing bars across the center of thumb, with short life line.
- Steeply curved Apollo or ring finger.

Well, what does it all tell us?

This is the hand of someone emotionally vulnerable, who has never known kindness from a man. Her relationships have all been with social inadequates, controllers, violent alcoholics, criminal sexiopaths, drug users, the emotionally constipated, and infantile football obsessives. She has had them all.

Psychologists tell us women who attract these poor specimens of manhood are subconsciously acting out childhood-relating difficulties (C.R.D.) with their father.

A rule of thumb that I use to emphasize ... this is what I call the four "esses." I sometimes use this rule in counseling. One by one, relate each of

The Stolen Childhood

the four fingers to the rule: He must be *Sober, Solvent, Sane* and *Single*. In other words, no drunkards, no madmen, the money in his pocket must be his (and not yours), and not in 10 other relationships.

Coming back to the bulleted markers:
- Large and strong Saturn finger, shows someone fatalistic, and prone to depression, with possible teeth or skeletal problems later, e.g., osteoporosis.
- Heart line here indicates the subject would be prone to the feeling that individual relationships do not work for her, and would channel her feelings to society as a whole. A lot of careers and philanthropists fall into this category. One of the meanings of this symptom cluster usually is the psychological phenomenon of projection, whereby the blockages in the emotional infrastructure results in a great love for animals and their welfare. In her search for romantic approval, self-worth and contentment, she may have difficulty with monogamy.
- This head line is indicative of migraine and anxious confusion, and she could also suffer from a morbid imagination. We all know someone who, if you are five minutes late, becomes convinced you have been in an accident on the motorway, etc.
- This flame-like shape is often indicative of kidney difficulty, or general digestive malfunction, often through alcohol abuse, which may be connected to her anxious temperament.
- The bent ring finger with its emotional linkage is symbolic of unfulfilling relationships, the subject's needs cannot be met, her low self-esteem and the thumb markings show she cannot galvanize her will or reason to help herself at present.

Her primary difficulty at the bottom of her psychological landscape is her inability to engage with another human being at a deep level, and the use of alcohol is solely an escape mechanism.

Her hands were sore and chapped from constant washing, which the London College of Psychiatry lists as one of the increasing signs of anxiety neurosis, and she also has occasional bouts of self-harming, particularly cutting. "*And the meek shall inherit the earth.*"

The coming trauma shows at age of 35, on both her heart and head line, an "Emotional Armageddon," with confirmation of health difficulty, particularly emphasized on the line of life ending shortly after. Which shows that without major life change, she has big problems ahead in her mid-30s.

Studies show that palms which are quite thin in section often indicate a premature birth. This can also be indicative of both later physical and psychological predispositions; cardiovascular difficulties are on top of this list. She had been badly let down by both her psychologist and counselor, as well as her uncaring General Practitioner, who just kept dishing out anti-depressants and contraceptive pills.

I would quote Job: 13-4: *"But all ye are forgers of lies, ye are all physicians of no value."* A lot of my weekly postbag contains stories of failure of the health care system, and working closely with local complementary therapists, we are only able to help so few.

B.M.A. (British Medical Association) statistics recommend 14.8 mg. of iron per day for women whose ages are between 15 and 50, so anemia is commonplace.

A big problem for single mums is that they cannot socialize. The cost of reliable baby sitters is prohibitive, and so many are meeting men through newspapers, or over the Internet. A questionable pursuit!

PROGNOSIS

A good talking to was in order, and agreement was reached on the drastic cutting down on her consumption of alcohol, crap burgers and cigarettes. She promised to limit recreational drug use and to have a regular bedtime. She also understood about long-term damage of Prozac and the contraceptive pill, and she has made new friends at her local Gingerbread "singles" group, and at the complementary practice, where she now comes for healing.

She is now on a daily dose of Vitamin C and D, echinacea, iron, calcium and selenium, with a small B6 (pyridoxine). Her eyes are bright and her complexion is great, and she said she is even starting to enjoy her daily salad, and—most gratifying for me—her life line is showing signs of new growth after the age of 35.

The poet Browning said:
*"Truth is within, it takes no rise,
from outward things, whatever you may believe,
there is an inmost centre in us all
where truth abides in fullness."*

Sometimes a little help is needed to find that center. Never stop asking for help. *"For thou shalt love thy neighbor as thyself."*

50

Spiritual Counselor Wendy Brindley

A very square palm such as this suggests a practical and determined basic outlook that seeks order, regulation and conformity within the rules, timetables and structures of life.

They love the outdoors and relate to the Earth, and this influences all their thoughts. The thick base to the Jupiter phalange (1) tells of food, and she is well known for her preserves, chutneys and jams—these being her practical honoring of nature.

As a designer, her work is unusual and depicts a natural, free-flowing theme. Incidentally, her whorl fingerprint on Jupiter, as here, means an individualist. Cancer the crab subjects love their home, and hers is a riot of shapes and color.

The strong small, or Mercury, fingers (2), tell of a need to communicate or bring a message. The curving in the top section of the left Mercury tells us this is a spiritually based message, and the short central, or Saturn finger, says she can be irreverent and will have a ready sense of humor, and the ability to laugh at adversity.

A stiff, strong thumb will tell of stubbornness, a power of resistance and persistence in the face of heavy odds. She is not a quitter. The downfall of these thumbs is they tend to hold onto past hurts. Moving forward is not easy for them.

Each hand is a mirror image of the other. This is unusual. As each side to the brain rules the opposing side to the body it reflects, this shows that she is the same person she always was.

The title, "Minister Wendy Brindley," is in numerology 8-8-8. For both hands to be mirror images, and both names to be mirror images, would suggest in the East, *Sanchita Karma,* which is "the sum total of all past actions in balance now with the present."

The three strong primary lines of head, heart and life dominate the hand and are at odds with the plethora of small, secondary lines across the hand. Only the Venus mount (3) is relatively clear. A mass of small lines show long-term stress and the possibility of adrenal burnout. This is confirmed by the fingertip lines, especially on Mercury, showing the thyroid is affected. But when a cobweb of fine lines is seen, particularly on Luna, this would suggest uric acid build-up in the urine, and often the main base for this is long-term emotional unrest and turbulence of overwork. These fingertip lines are often seen around the time of the menopause, but this looks like long-term overwork.

Revd. Wendy Brindley

One Spirit Interfaith Minister & Spiritual Counsellor

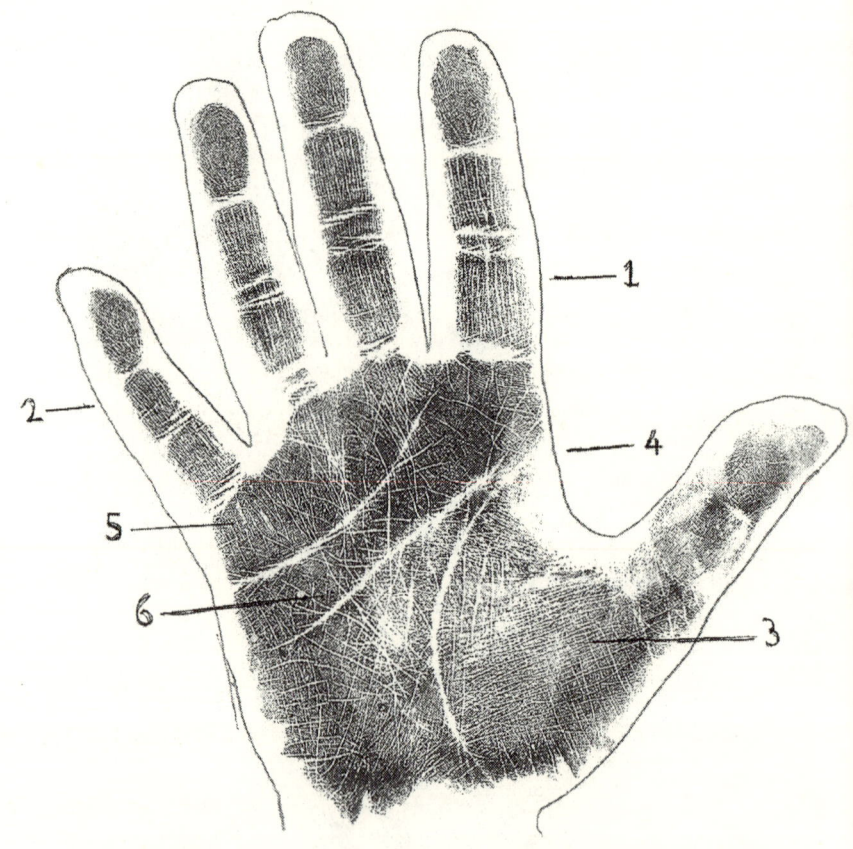

If we see the start to the life line, it is thin and comes from a blot at age 10 (4). Her school years were very difficult for her, due mainly to poor eyesight. The island under the left Apollo finger on the heart line can tell of many eye conditions, from eye strain to age-related macular degeneration.

Spiritual Counselor Wendy Brindley

Revd. Wendy Brindley
One Spirit Interfaith Minister & Spiritual Counsellor

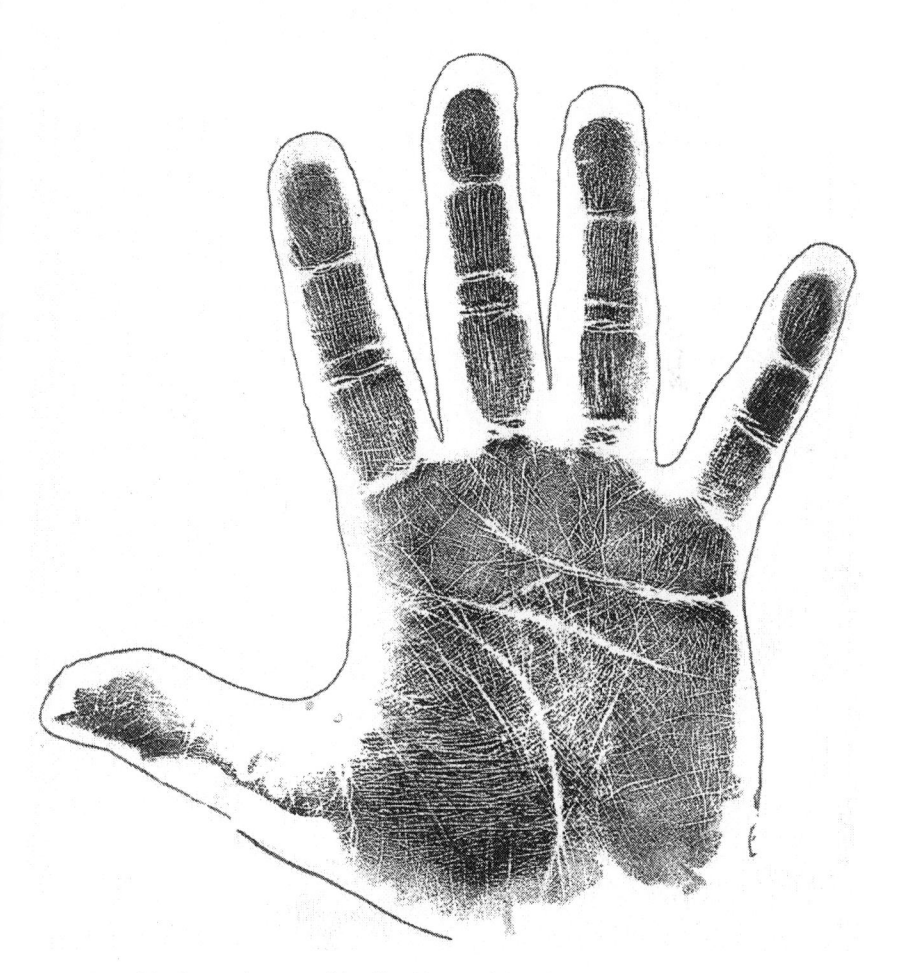

But this formation would tell of long-sightedness. The cross-hatching lines on Saturn's mount are often seen in those with teeth and skeletal difficulties. Any child who is different may be bullied.

The small, vertical lines across the Mercury mount are often called Samaritan lines (5), and always show a healer, and the square on Jupiter's mount is known as a teacher's square. Healers and teaching go together like politics and corruption, and healers and teachers often sing from the same hymn sheet.

Spiritual and artistic people usually have dropping head lines to Luna, which rules the imagination, but hers is not the head line we expect from such a person. This shows a rational, logical, down-to-earth approach with a need to lay down secure, material foundations (6).

This is the correct head line for this shaped hand. It is the hand of an economist, psychologist and business woman, but she is all these things too.

This straight head line is known as a Sydney line, and shows people who can cut out emotional input and run on the mental plane. But evidence of the Sydney suggests some natal problems in the DNA, often from allopathic medication build-up in the pregnant mother, but in a milder way than the Simian formation.

Age 28 on the life line shows a deterioration in general health patterns, and from here we see a thickened life line, like a sluggish river pushing hard through the topography of the landscape with difficulty.

The lack of a fate line shows a ship without a rudder, someone without a life plan, and is sometimes seen with lightworkers always on call for others. Incidentally, a change is indicated at age 55, where the restlessness and insomnia and inner turmoil means timeout for a coming life rethink. The scattered markings on the Apollo mount show someone who spreads themselves too widely and too thin, often seen with those with no fate line.

An interfaith minister is someone who counsels and cares for all people, be they pagans, Hindus, Muslims, etc., or those without any belief without prejudice.

"There shall be no compulsion in religion." — Quran 2-236

Epilogue

The 50 articles shown are taken from over 70 magazines from the past 50 years, from all over the world.

Unfortunately, a lot of the boxes of hand prints of sportsmen, show biz people and minor royalty hand prints had deteriorated in a damp shed, and the quality was now too poor to use.

But as I now approach the end of my life, the pressure to write a book was colossal. I hope these articles shown will spur students to make their own studies of the human hand, and as I signed off on all my articles ...

"Happy Palmistry"
palmist@fsmail.net
www.t-stokes.co.uk

Made in the USA
Columbia, SC
31 December 2017